*Routledge Revivals*

# Mourning Dress

First published in 1983, *Mourning Dress* chronicles the development of European and American mourning dress and etiquette from the Middle Ages to the present day, highlighting similarities and differences in practices between the different social strata. The result is a book which is not only of major importance to students of the history of dress but also to anyone who enjoys social history.

# Mourning Dress

## A Costume and Social History

### Lou Taylor

First published in 1983
by George Allen & Unwin Ltd

This edition first published in 2009 by Routledge
2 Park Square, Milton Park, Abingdon, Oxon, OX14 4RN

Simultaneously published in the USA and Canada
by Routledge
270 Madison Avenue, New York, NY 10016

*Routledge is an imprint of the Taylor & Francis Group, an informa business*

**Publisher's Note**
The publisher has gone to great lengths to ensure the quality of this reprint but points
out that some imperfections in the original copies may be apparent.

**Disclaimer**
The publisher has made every effort to trace copyright holders and welcomes
correspondence from those they have been unable to contact.

ISBN 13: 978-0-415-55286-8 (hbk)
ISBN 13: 978-0-415-55654-5 (pbk)
ISBN 13: 978-0-203-87132-4 (ebk)

ISBN 10: 0-415-55286-9 (hbk)
ISBN 10: 0-415-55654-6 (pbk)
ISBN 10: 0-203-87132-4 (ebk)

# MOURNING DRESS

*My name is Death, cannot you see?*
*Lords, dukes and ladies bow down to me,*
*And you are one of those branches three,*
*And you fair maid, and you fair maid,*
*And you fair maid must come with me.*

From an English ballad, 'Death and the Lady',
dating from the late sixteenth century, which
originated in morality plays of the Middle Ages,
quoted in Lloyd, A. L., *Folk Song In England*,
Lawrence & Wishart, London, 1975.

# MOURNING DRESS

## A

## Costume
## and Social History

## LOU TAYLOR

London
GEORGE ALLEN AND UNWIN
Boston          Sydney

**George Allen & Unwin (Publishers) Ltd,**
**40 Museum Street, London WC1A 1LU, UK**

George Allen & Unwin (Publishers) Ltd,
Park Lane, Hemel Hempstead, Herts HP2 4TE, UK

Allen & Unwin Inc.,
9 Winchester Terrace, Winchester, Mass 01890, USA

George Allen & Unwin Australia Pty Ltd,
8 Napier Street, North Sydney, NSW 2060, Australia


First published in 1983

**British Library Cataloguing in Publication Data**

Taylor, Lou
    Mourning dress.
1. Costume—History        2. Mourning etiquette
I. Title
391'.8        GN418

ISBN 0–04–746016–4

Set in 11 on 13 point Garamond by
Bedford Typesetters Ltd,
and printed in Great Britain by
Butler & Tanner Ltd,
Frome and London

*To Joe*

# CONTENTS

# ILLUSTRATIONS

# ACKNOWLEDGMENTS

I should like to thank the following people for their kind and generous help: Miss Daphne Gifford of the Public Record Office at Chancery Lane; Professor D. C. Coleman; the late Mr Martin Battersby; Miss Natalie Rothstein, Keeper of Textiles at the Victoria and Albert Museum; Edit Fel, of the Ethnographical Museum, Budapest; and Miss Judith Prendergast of the National Portrait Gallery, London.

I want in particular to thank the late Mrs Corina Nicolescu, the eminent Romanian art/textile historian. She was so patient and generous in her help. She was killed in Bucarest in the terrible earthquake of 1977. She is missed by everyone who knew her.

I have also to somehow try to pay adequate tribute to the debt I owe to the late A. L. Lloyd, the folksong historian, who died in September 1982, and from whom I learned so much, but wish I had learned more. He was always enormously kind and vastly knowledgeable. His death leaves a void that will not be filled.

For the use of their illustrations, I would like in particular to thank Mr Ray Watkinson, Mrs Evelyn Antal, Dr Elspeth Clarkson, Professor Helmut Gernsheim, Professor Jack Goody, Mr & Mrs Roger Handley, Mrs C. M. Salmon, Mrs Esme Turner, Pearl Binder, Courtaulds Ltd and Northiam Parish Council.

For help in translation from Italian and Finnish, I thank Mrs Anne Moscatelli and Mrs Joe Townsend. For help from America I thank Mrs Cipie Pineles Burtin. For help in typing this book I thank Mrs Ann Foster and my friends and colleagues at Brighton Polytechnic and Brighton Museum. I am most grateful to Miss Baird at East Sussex County Council Brighton Reference Library, and the staff at Brighton Polytechnic Library.

I am especially grateful to Mr Zul Mukhida for his photography work. I thank my mother, Pearl Binder, in whose footsteps I follow, for her constant encouragement and help. I thank my husband, Joe, for his support and patience.

# PREFACE

Costume history – defined as a study of stylistic change in dress – is a source of unending fascination. The pleasures derived from handling rich eighteenth-century silk velvets and the fine cobwebs of 1930s' georgettes, or admiring the minuscule stitching on early Victorian embroidery are indeed satisfying in themselves. The supreme elegance of really well cut clothes, be they from the House of Worth in 1900, or designed by Balenciaga in the 1950s, provide us with a perpetual source of creative inspiration and unequalled example.

Clothes become an even more interesting topic when examined within the social structures in which they were worn. Who wore them? Who made them? Where were they worn? Where did the style come from? How 'in fashion' are they? Where were they bought? The answers to these questions allow us to penetrate the major preoccupations of society and to follow its changes and interests. Costume history is, therefore, more than a surface study of fleeting, pretty clothes. It is this special combination of art, design and social and economic history which makes the subject of dress so particularly interesting.

Madge Garland, editor of *Vogue* and first Head of the School of Fashion at the Royal College of Art in London, recently defined the whole area in one phrase. 'Fashion,' she said, 'is a visual image of a social condition.' It is this visual image of dress which is explored in this book and related to one specific area, that of fashionable European mourning dress. Mourning is worn at the most traumatic moment in peoples' lives. One might think that grief and the terrible sense of loss of husbands, wives or close relatives would overwhelm any interest in sartorial detail. This was not the case. The extraordinarily complicated sumptuary laws and styles in mourning dress were a reflection not of grief but of the changes that took place in society. It thus provides us today with a study source that transcends all class barriers and reflects clearly the social role of women.

In 1969 Anne Buck's article on nineteenth-century mourning

dress was published in the Proceedings of the Second Annual Conference of the Costume Society. At about the same time my interest in this subject was deepened by an exhibition organised at Brighton Museum by the Director, John Morley, called 'Death, Heaven and the Victorians'. My contribution was to collect together a display of mourning dress.

Since then, there has been a growing interest in this area of research, both here and in the United States of America, shown by the publication in 1972 of Phillis Cunnington's and Catherine Lucas's book, *Costumes for Births, Marriages and Deaths*, and by two exhibitions in America. The first, called 'Mourning Becomes America – Mourning Art in the New Nation', was organised by Anita Schorsch at the William Penn Memorial Museum, Harrisburg, Pennsylvania in the spring of 1976. This covered mourning mementoes up to about 1850 – embroidered pictures, jewellery, ceramics, etc. The second and more comprehensive exhibition was put together by Martha V. Pike and Janice Gray Armstrong at the Stony Brook Museum, Stony Brook, New York. It was called 'A Time to Mourn – Expressions of Grief in Nineteenth Century America', and was shown from May to November 1880 before moving to the Brandywine River Museum at Chadd's Ford, Pennsylvania in 1981. This exhibition included a section on American mourning dress.

Lou Taylor
*Brighton, 1982*

CHAPTER ONE

# *The Function and Ritual of European Funerals*

Clothes mirror every nuance of the society in which they are worn, reflecting not only an individual's aesthetic judgement but also his or her social standing and attitudes to society. Clothes also chronicle political and artistic upheavals. The study of dress, therefore, is a key which opens the door to a deeper understanding of the developments that take place in society and its social ambitions and aspirations.

Taste in dress is controlled by many factors and its functions, in whatever type of society it is worn, are many and varied, but basically clothes have been used from the earliest times as a means of clearly defining and enforcing the class divisions in society. They provide an ideal vehicle for displaying wealth and social status and sometimes for demonstrating political and religious convictions. This still applies today when anti-fashion is high fashion and second-hand clothes are as much a status symbol for the young as haute couture clothes are for the wealthy.

Women have always been used – nearly always with their own enthusiastic agreement and support – as a means of displaying their families' rank. The ideal occasion for such a display was, and indeed still is, at public gatherings where expensive clothes could be seen by all. Ritual functions, such as the public ceremonies to mark birth, coming-of-age, marriage and death, provide a perfect setting for just such an open demonstration. The clothes worn on each of these occasions became and to some extent still are, highly elaborate and extravagant – far beyond the bounds of necessity and frequently in defiance of sumptuary laws. Babies were christened in full-length satin robes, with yards of lace hanging down below their toes, debutantes were presented at Court in Britain with ritualised, white, trained ball dresses, complete with tulle veils and white ostrich plumes. Brides or their parents still save up for months to provide the symbolic robes, full-length veils and orange blossom they will never wear again. For mourning a vast array of special clothing developed over the centuries, to be worn by the bereaved and particularly by widows. The study of fashionable European mourning dress provides us with an extraordinarily revealing insight into the functions of dress and the social position of women.

In order to appreciate the intricacies of mourning dress and to follow its stylistic evolution, it is necessary first to examine the development of European funeral ritual, which provided the public setting in which these clothes were worn. Funerals were an ideal stage for a public display of wealth and rank. Relatives were even able to improve their standing within their community by putting on an impressive and obviously costly funeral ceremony. This aspect of the death ritual grew to overshadow all others, until vast fortunes were being spent on grave offerings, mausoleums, funeral feasts and processions at royal and aristocratic funerals – as it was in ancient China and Egypt, so it became in Renaissance Europe. The rules of funeral etiquette became more and more intricate in a deliberate attempt to outmanoeuvre those further down the social ladder who could not hope to compete with all the expense. In Britain the gradual spread of funeral and mourning rituals from royal circles to the industrial working classes took about two hundred and fifty years, starting in the late sixteenth century and reflecting exactly the changing format of society and the rising aspirations of first the middle and then the working classes.

In Europe grandiose royal funerals only became possible when the heir to the throne was publicly declared and accepted before the death of the king. Before that time disorder and confusion reigned whilst the various hopeful aspirants to the Crown sought to establish their claims. Royal authority prevailed only after the king had been consecrated and crowned. Before that could occur the main concern of the heir apparent was to collect together his supporters and

1   King Edward VII and Queen Alexandra in April 1901, three
months after the death of Queen Victoria, photographed at the
State Opening of Parliament. Queen Alexandra is in deepest
mourning. From *The Sphere*, 6 April 1901.

organise his own coronation. This left little time (and little money) for the arrangement of an elaborate funeral for his predecessor. On the death of William the Conqueror in 1080 the nobles fled the Court to their estates, leaving the servants to steal the dead king's silver. The expenses of the simple royal funeral were paid for by the generosity of Herluin, one of William's knights.[1]

Once immediate succession had been established, the way was paved for grandiose burials which symbolised the power and stability of the Crown – the more extravagant the better. The example was set in France when Philippe III carried his father's body back from the Crusades in 1270–71 for a grand formal burial.[2] Royal burials in France gradually developed into highly elaborate and lavish rituals which laid the foundations of mourning etiquette in Europe.

Ancient practices, including the offering of grave goods, funeral feasts and the wearing of special mourning clothes, were preserved in European Renaissance funeral traditions and survived until the nineteenth century. The offerings of expensive goods and foods, which had previously been placed in the grave, were, by the Renaissance period divided between the church, the king's officers and other important officials who had taken part in the funeral cortège. Spoils from the funeral ceremonies included items such as coffin palls of cloth of gold, expensive wax tapers and royal horses. Protracted and bitter arguments took place between rival claimants. In 1422 the salt-carriers of Paris who carried the coffin of Charles IV claimed the cloth of gold pall, to the annoyance of the church authorities at the Abbey of St Denis, where all royal burials in France took place.[3] After the funeral of Anne of Brittany in 1514 it took six years to settle all the disputed claims.[4]

The ancient custom of burying or burning the dead man's horse, to transport his soul to the spirit world, was modified and the horses were instead led in the procession. In France after a grand funeral the horses were given to the church to help maintain the Crusader States. By the fourteenth century when the Holy Land had been lost horses were classified along with the wax candles and expensive black drapery, as part of the deceased's offering to the church. At the funeral of François I in Paris in 1547 the parade horse or *cheval d'honneur* was covered 'with a black crepe cloth, covering its royal purple trappings, leaving only the eyes visible.'[5] In medieval and Tudor times in England one of the late king's chargers was ridden up the nave of Westminster Abbey at his Requiem Mass, to be given to

2  Riderless horse at the funeral of George II, Landgrave of
Hesse, Germany, 1661. An engraving by Adrien Schoonebeek.

the church at the door of the choir. The church benefice of giving
away the horse had died out in France at the end of the fourteenth
century, but the tradition of the dead man's riderless horse following the coffin has survived, particularly in Britain. The Duke of
Wellington's funeral car was followed, in his great funeral procession of 1852, by his charger, complete with the Duke's empty,
dangling boots. The most recent examples have been seen at the
funerals of the Duke of Norfolk at Arundel, Sussex on 5 February
1975 and at the State funeral of Lord Mountbatten in September
1979. Both the processions were led by riderless horses, which were
hung with their owners' riding boots, reversed in the stirrups.

The procedure for royal funeral processions was laid down in
France by the fifteenth century. It was carefully copied in the
nineteenth century and is still maintained at royal funerals today.
Everyone remotely connected with the power of the Crown took
part in the parade, those nearest the coffin being the most important
or chief mourners. Until the late Middle Ages the successor to the
deceased always took part in royal burials, but at the death of

3  Funeral procession of George II, Landgrave of Hesse,
Germany, July 1661, based on French medieval etiquette.
Engraved by Adrien Schoonebeek.

4  Funeral procession of Queen Victoria, 1901. The streets are
lined with mourners – the women in hats, the men without
them. From the *Ladies Field*, 2 February 1901.

François I in 1547 the new heir was forbidden to attend the ceremony and the future Henri II was obliged to watch the procession from a window on the Rue St Jacques. The Procureur-Général of the French Parliament, Jacques de la Guesle, explained in 1594 that, 'It is not fitting to their [king's] sacred persons to associate themselves with things funereal.'[6] Chief mourners at royal funerals were, therefore, not the king's heir but other royal princes and dukes.

Women played little part in grand funerals for men, although the chief mourner at the interment of an aristocratic woman was, originally, always a woman. Queen Elizabeth I's coffin was followed by a marchioness in 1603, whilst Princess Amelia was the chief mourner at the funeral of Queen Caroline in London in 1737. The tradition broke down gradually and by 1817 the chief mourner for poor Princess Charlotte, who died giving birth to her first baby, was her husband Prince Leopold.[7] By the Victorian period middle and upper-class women were declared too delicate and fragile to stand at the graveside during the burial ceremony. They were advised to follow the practice of the *haute bourgeoisie* and nobility, remaining in the church while the actual burial was taking place outside. *Une femme du monde doit toujours eviter de se donner en spectacle* (a society woman should always avoid being seen at a public spectacle) warned the Parisian mourning warehouse Maison de Noir in the 1880s.[8]

The order of royal and aristocratic funeral processions was strictly laid down. First came the almsfolk and friends of the deceased, with the Household officials and their servants. Next, came representatives of the legal profession and mayors, followed by the clergy. The king's heralds, with hatchments, walked or rode immediately in front of the coffin. A tabard embroidered with the deceased's coat of arms, a helmet, sword, shield, banners and orders of insignia made up the hatchments. The weapons of the dead man and those of his troops were carried reversed – as they still are today at State and military funerals. This was a token of truce for the burial. The hearse with the pall-bearers holding the corners of the pall followed, with the coffin-bearers beneath the pall actually carrying the coffin. The chief and most distinguished mourners – close relatives and ambassadors – walked or rode directly behind the hearse. Mourning coaches carrying female mourners and sometimes even empty coaches sent by their owners as a mark of respect brought up the rear. State funerals were swollen by large numbers of troops who marched at the front and back of the procession and lined the streets through which it passed. The Victorian middle classes copied this format on a modified scale. They added 'feathermen' who walked in front of the hearse carrying huge wire trays of tall black ostrich feathers, and the undertakers replaced the Court of Heralds.

Mourning gowns had to be provided for all who took part in the procession and drapery bought to hang in the church, house and sometimes along the route of the procession. The list of mourners to whom Henri II of France gave mourning habits, after his father's death in 1547, ran into fifty folio pages.[9] The hope of obtaining gowns must have been an inducement to the almsfolk to join in the processions. The poor women, mostly widows, who took part in the funeral of Mary Queen of Scots, at Peterborough in 1587, were no doubt comforted by thought of 'the black cloth gowns, with an ell of white holland over their heads; which they had for their labour and nine shillings a piece in money.'[10]

At the funeral of the Earl of Northumberland in 1489 over 2,200 yards of black fabric was used to equip mourners and provide the necessary draping. The price of this fabric amounted to three-quarters of the cost of the whole funeral.[11] The woollen and silk velvet cloth was very expensive and the costly black dye increased the price even further. The cost of grand burials, in consequence, grew enormous. In late sixteenth and early seventeenth-century England the cost amounted to as much as a year's income.[12] Social prestige required that funerals should be as obviously opulent as possible. Queen Elizabeth I, who understood this perfectly, paid the funeral bills of her friends and relatives herself, in order to be absolutely satisfied that everything was done correctly.[13] Court life was at that time ostentatiously extravagant and sumptuous, with severe sumptuary laws to mark class differences between the fashions of the Court, the middle classes and the country people.

From the late fifteenth century the funerals of all English aristo-cratic arms-bearing families were conducted under the supervision of the Court of Heralds. The Heralds' job was to ensure that no social-climbing upstart families displayed arms or carried out grand funerals to which they were not entitled. The presence of the Heralds at a burial was the mark of royal recognition of the noble standing of the family. Their absence implied either royal displeasure or that the family was simply not grand enough to merit the presence of the Heralds.

By the end of the sixteenth century there was growing unrest over the cost of grand funerals, for two reasons. First, the price was now beyond all reason and secondly the amount of social prestige gained by extravagant burials was declining. They were simply not worth the money. The filtering down process had already started – despite all the efforts of the top ranks of the aristocracy. Many families (whose arms were not recognised by the Court of Heralds) began to perform their own grand burials in imitation of heraldic funerals. The Heralds complained bitterly about the new fashion for burial at night by torchlight: 'Manie in the dark doe presume without warrant to bury the dead either with invented ensignes of gentry or with such as rightly belong to other men.'[14] They even introduced a system of fines in 1618, to punish families usurping the rights of their betters, but all to no avail. Nothing can keep down the aspirations of the socially ambitious.

Exactly the same problem existed in the Low Countries, where edicts issued by the King of Arms covering every aspect of funeral ritual were constantly ignored. Laws were published in 1616 and 1696 forbidding all except the most noble from providing their servants with mourning livery: Egide Boet was summoned before the Conseil Souverain at Brabant in March 1714 for breaking this regulation. He denied the infraction vehemently, stating that his servants wore only 'old, second-hand, dark grey clothes', and he attacked the King of Arms for his incessant vexations which were causing unrest amongst the public. The King of Arms, in his reply, described to the Court the incriminating livery, stating that it rivalled that worn by grand noblemen. 'The excuses of the accused are laughable. How can he, who is a wealthy and vain-glorious man, give worn clothes to his servants?'[15] It seemed unlikely that he would dress his coachmen in rags. The outcome of this particular case is not known but people caught infringing etiquette were fined considerable sums of money.

The Heralds in the Low Countries continued their battle against these usurpations of royal privilege until the French Revolution, but in England they gave up the struggle in the seventeeth century. The fashion for extravagant aristocratic funerals was destroyed by the Commonwealth, when the Puritans' hatred of high living and extravagant sartorial display overcame the waning social prestige that could be exacted from a vastly expensive funeral. The Heralds found themselves rejected by the noble families who no longer

5   An eighteenth-century undertaker's sign and advertisement. William Grinly, coffin maker – 'all things for a Funeral as well as ye meanest as those of greater Ability upon Reasonable Terms more particularly Coffins, Shroud, Palls, Cloaks, Sconces . . . Hangings For Rooms, Heraldry Hearses and Coaches, Gloves, and all other things not mentioned here.' From Bertram Puckle, *Funeral Customs, Their Origin and Development*, 1926.

required them to organise burials, and defied by the non-armorial wealthy families who infringed their rules and regulations with impunity. 'It was my hard hap,' wrote John Gibbon, the Bluemantle Pursuivant in 1671, 'to become a member of the Heralds' Office when the Ceremony of Funerals, (as accompanied with Officers of Arms) began to be in the wane . . . in eleven years' time I have had but five turns.'[16] The rot had set in.

From the late seventeenth century onwards the barriers which had prevented the British middle classes from holding grand funerals crumbled and a whole new section of society threw itself with enthusiasm into the previously forbidden delights of aristocratic mourning etiquette. Only three true heraldic funerals were recorded in the eighteenth century. The presence of the Court of Heralds was finally restricted to royal and State funerals – as it remains today.

The growing popularity of grand funerals was reflected in the increasing number of undertakers' establishments set up in the eighteenth century – becoming an avalanche in the nineteenth century. The aristocratic complexities were maintained, as seen in this bill, sent to the pioneer mill owner Jediediah Strutt, in 1774, after his wife's burial.[17]

£ s d

'For the Funeral of Mrs. Strutt

| | £ s d |
|---|---|
| To a Strong Elm Coffin with a Double lid and Covered with fine Black Cloth, Close Drove with the Best Brass Cased nails & Double Pannelld, a Double Bordered Metall Plate with Inscription, 3 pair of the largest Patent Handles with wrought Gripes & Embelleshed with a Glory & an Urn & 8 Dozen of the Ornamentall Drops all neatly Guilt the Inside Lined & Ruffled with Superfine Crape | 6.6.0. |
| To a Suit of Superfine Crape consisting of a Shroud Sheet Cap & Pillow | 2.2.0. |
| To 2 Men in with the Coffin & putting in the Body | 3.0. |
| To screw Pitch & fixing in the false Lid & making up the Body | 2.0. |
| To the Use of the Best Velvett Pall | 10.0. |
| To 15 Plumes of the Best Black Ostrich Feathers for the Hearse & 4 Horses | 1.16.0. |
| To a rich Armozine Scarf for the Minister | 1.14.0. |
| To 6 Pair of Mens Plain Kid Gloves | 13.0. |
| To 3 Silk Hatbands | 1.4.0. |
| To 3 New Crape Hatbands | 10.6. |
| To 4 Pr of womens Plain Kid | 11.11. |
| To the Use of 3 Cloaks the Mourners | 3.0. |
| To the Use of 4 Hoods & Scarves | 6.0. |
| To a Hearse with 4 Horses to Bunhill fields Burying Ground | 1.2.0. |
| To 2 Coaches with Pairs to Do | 1.2.0. |
| Paid for Fetching Company | 1.0. |
| Paid for Carrying the Minister to Lowlayton | 6.0. |
| To 2 Porters with Staves Covers with Silk Scarves and Cloaks | 10.0. |
| To 2 Hatbands & 2 Pr of Gloves for Do | 7.0. |
| To 3 Cloakes 3 Hatbands 3 Pr of Gloves the Coachmen | 13.6. |
| To 6 Men in Black to Bear the Body & attend as Hearse Pages with Caps and Truncheons | 1.1.0. |
| To Silk Favours & 6 Pr of Gloves for Do | 12.0. |
| To a Hatband & a Pr of Gloves for the Men that attended the Funerall | 3.6. |
| Paid for the Turnpikes | 1.1. |
| Paid for Beer for Men | 2.0. |
| Gve the Grave Digger | 1.0. |
| Attendance at Funerall | 3.6. |
| A Man fetching Company | 1.1. |

6    State funeral of Nelson, London, 1805. The funeral car is
pulled by caparisoned and plumed horses. From Richard Davey,
*A History of Mourning*, 1889.

The whole bill added up to the sum of £22 3s 1d. The use of black
ostrich plumes at Mrs Strutt's funeral was an eighteenth-century
introduction, one which was to flourish during Queen Victoria's
reign. Mrs Strutt's mourners were still provided with mourning
clothes – here cloaks and gloves.

By the 1850s British undertakers and mourning outfitters were
enjoying a booming trade. Women's magazines were full of anxious
inquiries into the minutiae of mourning etiquette. No one cared to
lose status by publicly revealing their ignorance of the finer details of
the ritual. Princess Daisy of Pless wrote in 1907, after the death of
her father-in-law: 'People are talking about my going about with
footmen in red livery. I told Hans [her husband], that I thought the
servants ought to be in black, that I did not think black on the hat
and a black band on the arm was sufficient but he said it was
impossible to put all the servants and the stables in black and that it
was never done in big houses.'[18]

The *Ladies Field*, who well understood their readers' preoccupations and aspirations, published a list of articles of dress not considered suitable for deep mourning three weeks after the death of
Queen Victoria in 1901:

'Among articles of dress definitely not deep mourning may be mentioned the following: sable, chinchilla and ermine, deep collars, cuffs and trimmings of white or cream lace, black net ruffles with touches of gold in their folds, and chiffon and net, hats with white flowers or knots of white tulle, and gold gauds, such as gold muff-chains, purses and chatelaines. Neither velvet, nor panne is strictly mourning material, but for those who are not attached to the Court, they may pass muster, toned down with the dullness of silk or chiffon.'

The constant reference made to Court and aristocratic mourning dress and behaviour was the yardstick by which every ambitious Victorian middle-class woman measured her own social behaviour. Lady Charlotte Schrieber, the widow of a Welsh mine-owner, floored her vicar with aristocratic tradition when quarrelling with him over the length of time that the mourning drapery should remain up in the village church after her husband's funeral. 'I find,' she wrote to him in 1853, 'that although in public i.e. Royal funerals, it remains up but six weeks, yet that it is the custom in private ones to keep it up much longer. In this county Lord Eldon's remained a twelve-month, Lord Shaftesbury's fourteen months, from which may be argued that at all events the rule is such in this part of the country.' Lady Charlotte also agonised eighteen months later over the propriety of attending a performance of 'Fidelio' at Covent Garden. 'I felt some scruples on this matter of first going out again,' she wrote, 'but I muffled up going and coming and sat in the back of the box and so escaped notice.'[19]

The easiest way to cope with all the problems of organising a funeral was simply to hand over everything into the eager hands of the undertaker and his staff. Two 'mutes' were immediately posted outside the front door, dressed in black coats with black sashes and black top hats with weepers. Mutes are believed to be a survival from Roman days, when mime actors were employed at funerals to imitate the actions of the deceased. Ursula Bloom remembers that: 'They had to stand on either side of the front door staring at the passers by with obvious tragedy written on their faces. Etiquette demanded that they should never speak a word and they were therefore known as mutes. They were chosen for their glum faces and it was said that on occasions they squashed out a pretentious tear.'[20]

The mutes walked in the funeral procession carrying draped wands, followed by the undertaker's 'feathermen', from one to four of them according to the price of the burial. The layout of the procession was planned just like a royal funeral, and great status was gained by a large turn-out. The number of mourning coaches was the telling factor. Relatives and friends would often hire a coach and send it empty if they could not, or did not wish to, be there themselves, thus continuing an old practice, for Pepys makes frequent references to the coach numbers at funerals he attended. In 1663 his cousin Edward Pepys was buried at Shoreditch, with 'about twenty coaches and four or five with six and four horses'.[21]

The turn-out of the horses was of great importance. In order to achieve a properly imposing effect they were sometimes dyed black, and given glossy false tails. They wore black velvet caparisons with black harnesses trimmed with silver. The feathers were mounted between their ears with special black rosettes worn on the forehead. They never moved faster than a dignified walking pace. The funeral procession wound slowly on its way, through the main streets of the town, to achieve maximum effect. Sometimes the coffin had to be

7   One of the hearses available for hire from Hannington's department store, Brighton. About 1900. (*By kind permission of Hannington's Ltd, Brighton*)

transported over a considerable distance, necessitating stops en route for refreshments – all of which was charged up to the deceased's family. A bill in the archives of Hannington's of Brighton for a funeral in 1792 includes the sum of £1 10s – 'Paid Turnpikes and other expenses at the Three Crowns, Bushey Heath and at the Anchor, Harrow.' The Albin Brothers, a firm of London undertakers, stopped every twenty minutes at the nearest pub when they were taking part in long distance funerals. The 'Thatched House' in Leightonstone had at times more than forty funeral coaches waiting outside it.[22]

The major factor in all these arrangements was the cost. The Renaissance custom of providing a funeral feast still survived. In 1587 4,000 people were said to have been fed on the left-overs from the funeral feast of Edward, Earl of Rutland.[25] Samuel Pepys, in his less affluent early days, struggled to provide suitably respectable refreshments after the death of his brother, Tom, in 1664. 'But at last one after another they came, many more than I had bid,' he com-

8    The best hearse from Hannington's of Brighton, used at a Brighton funeral in October 1910. (*By kind permission of Hannington's Ltd, Brighton*)

plained, 'I believe there was nearer one hundred and fifty. Their service was six biscuits a-piece and what they pleased of burnt claret.'[24]

By the nineteenth century a suitable funeral meal would include 'chicken and a roast, a nice cold ham and vegetables on the side. This was followed by discreet sweets, junkets, fruit pies trifles and jellies'.[25] Seed and plum cake were particular favourites whilst an assortment of cheeses and alcoholic drinks were provided for the men. The women made do with pots of tea – sometimes served on a special funeral tea-service. The practice of providing a funeral meal survives today, particularly in the north of England and in Scotland and Wales.

Further cost was entailed by the traditional gifts to all the mourners. Specially printed booklets, giving details of the ceremony were kept as souvenirs. They contained the order of the service and were often bound in leather, with the name of the deceased stamped in gold letters on the cover. This practice continues into the present century. One in the archives of Hannington's of Brighton states: 'IN MEMORIAM, James Legg, DIED 15th FEBry, 1890, IN HIS 79TH YEAR, INTERRED IN THE FAMILY VAULT IN THE BRIGHTON CEMETERY'. The giving of rings, gloves and scarves replaced the giving of mourning gowns, which could now be hired from undertakers. By the seventeenth century, plain engraved mourning rings were given away (see Chapter 9) but by the eighteenth century were being replaced by the cheaper items of gloves and scarves. All these gifts were given away strictly according to the social status of the recipient and even the gloves were thus graded.

Sir Ralph Verney wrote in 1685 that 'Sir Richard Pigott was buried very handsomely . . . Wee that bore up the pall had Rings, Scarfs, Hat-Bands, Shamee Gloves of the best fashion . . . the rest of the Gentry had Rings and all the Servants Gloves.'[26] When Parson Woodforde buried his father in 1771, he was most meticulous about the quality of gloves given out to mourners. All his women relatives had the best 'black shamee' gloves. The six women wakers, who had sat up all night with the corpse, were given gloves of black lamb. The pall-bearers, who would have been friends of the family, had shammy gloves, the sextons were given lamb and the clerk had mock shammy gloves.[27] The giving of funeral gloves lasted into the late Victorian period, as did the custom of giving away scarves – white at the funeral of a child or woman and black for men. They were of silk, about three yards long and were worn at the funeral by male mourners diagonally over the left shoulder, replacing mourning cloaks. Vicars received gloves, hatbands and scarves at most funerals and must have been at a loss to know what to do with so many. Parson Woodforde gave his maid Sally Gunton a hatband of two yards of black silk after she had nursed him when he was ill one night.[28] A vicar's wife in the West Riding of Yorkshire saved up the lengths of such fabric until she had enough to make a dress.[29]

By the seventeenth and eighteenth centuries European mourning ritual had been transplanted to Colonial America where it took firm and healthy root, especially along the Atlantic East Coast of the New World. European mourning silks and crapes were imported for those who could afford them, such as the 'Dutch black padisoys for mourning' advertised for sale in Boston in 1728 by Mr Jonathan Barnard.[30] Nineteenth-century evidence suggests that by the 1760s mourning ritual in Boston had become so extravagant that sumptuary laws were passed dictating simpler mourning ceremonies and garments.[31] In the pre-revolutionary period and certainly in the immediate years after the War of Independence, American mourners were encouraged to wear local rather than expensively imported European fabrics.[32] American mourning traditions have recently been clarified in the well documented exhibition, 'A Time To Mourn – Expressions Of Grief In Nineteenth Century America', organised by the Museums of Stony Brook, New York, in 1980.

Mourning feasts and the giving away of quantities of rings, black gloves and scarves, were as typical of eighteenth and nineteenth-century funerals in America as they were in Britain. The Stony Brook exhibition contained a rare bill for the sale of mourning rings, dated 11 July 1705 and now in the collection of Greenfield Village and Henry Ford Museum, Dearborn, Michigan. The bill, for £8 19s 3d, 'currant money of new England', was made out by David Jesse to cover the cost of the gold and the making up of eight mourning rings for the estate of a Mr James Gray of Boston. It seems that Mr Jesse had to wait until 7 October to receive his money.

P. G. Buckley, in his researches into mourning ritual on Long Island, found a splendid description of an early nineteenth-century funeral meal in a country district. The meal was held before the ceremony. Relatives of the deceased prepared 'a large quantity of cold provisions, such as roast turkeys, boiled hams, roast beef . . .

also rum, brandy and gin, with pipes, tobacco and cigars.' The mourners sat 'smoking their long pipes and drinking, hearing and telling the news and laughing and talking together for two or three hours before the funeral would move.' Afterwards there were, not unnaturally, scenes at the funeral 'of much noise and very inappropriate to the purpose for which they had assembled.'[33]

Mr Buckley explains that amongst the new and struggling East Coast communities funeral ritual was a familiar and integral part of community life. As in early nineteenth-century Britain, the local sexton, carpenter and village women were all involved in planning and taking part in a local burial. As the social structures of the villages developed in complexity so did funeral rituals. By the 1830–60 period, along America's East Coast, 'the professionalization of burial preparation and the development of undertaking as a business'[34] occurred, as it had done in European cities a good hundred years before. Funeral etiquette in large American towns from the mid-nineteenth century mirrored developments in Europe, though the old traditions survived into the present century in remote rural districts across the length of America.

In Britain by the middle of the nineteenth century, the overriding worry in the minds of the bereaved, particularly amongst the women, was the terror of being publicly shamed by their failure to carry through the etiquette of death correctly. It was enormously complicated and pitfalls lay at every turn. The worries were exactly the same for the poor as for the rich. The country and urban working classes struggled to provide their own dead with funerals as near to those of the rich as they could afford. They copied middle-class customs. It was naturally no less important to them that their dead should be buried with the same respectable and socially required ceremony as the rest of society. This human aspiration was never understood by the middle classes who were constantly admonishing the poor for their extravagant funerals, all the more important to them because their means were so much less. Many elements of grand funerals were found in poor people's burials. Indeed some of the most ancient customs, such as wailing, lamenting, and the wearing of mourning dress have survived in these communities a long time after they have gone out of fashion in grander circles of society. Amongst country people and the urban poor, once a tradition becomes established it is less subject to fluctuations of fashion and therefore tends to survive longer. The family unit is a much stronger bond in these areas than it is in many middle-class groups. Families often live closer together and their ties are stronger – the pattern of life often passes from one generation to another almost without change.

The value attached to a 'respectable' burial was deep rooted and care was taken to ensure that adequate money was available to pay for the necessities. Burial societies were started to make certain that working-class funerals were carried out with all the correct dignity and ceremony. Such clubs date back to ancient Rome[35] and in England were in existence from the twelfth century onwards, as part of the trade guild system. The guilds controlled the craft within each town, fixing quality, prices and wages and, on payment of their annual subscription, members could count on being given a decent burial by their colleagues. Widows were often provided with some financial assistance, though women were not allowed to join the guilds in their own right.[36] A large turn-out at a guild funeral was guaranteed because members were fined if they failed to attend. The London Weavers Company imposed a fine of 8d, in 1492, on defaulters. Many of the great Companies of the City of London owned magnificent palls or hearse cloths. The Saddlers' pall was of crimson velvet with a centre of yellow silk, whilst in 1575, the London Weavers Company owned a hearse cloth with the company coat of arms in yellow, probably on a blue velvet ground. In 1650 a richer, gold embroidered pall had to be pawned – for the sum of £120, which was a lot of money in those days. The pall 'was hired, presumably by members of the Company or their widows, for fees which ranged from £1 to £3.' In September 1671 the Company were paid £2 by 'Widow Shepeard for the use of the hearse cloth'. This tradition seems to have ended in the London Weavers Company in the eighteenth century.[37]

Guild archives also record the financial assistance sometimes given to members' widows. The Weavers Company provided almshouses and occasionally even pensions and jobs for both widows and their sons. The Court book of the Worshipful Company of Armourers and Braziers reveals that in 1593 they 'paid to Antony our Officer to give to Richard Stalworth a cobbler to relieve his sickness 5s but finding him dead when he came he gave his Wiff 2s 6d.'[38]

Out of the guilds grew the Friendly and Burial Societies, starting in the early seventeenth century. One of the earliest was at the tiny

# PLEASURE TRIP

FOR THE BENEFIT OF THE

## WIDOW & ORPHAN'S FUND

IN CONNECTION WITH THE INDEPENDENT ORDER OF ODD FELLOWS, M. U.,
ST. HILDA'S LODGE, HARTLEPOOL.

THE PUBLIC ARE RESPECTFULLY INFORMED THAT THE

FAST  STEAM

SAILING BOAT,

# GLEANER

WILL LEAVE THE

Corporation Quay, STOCKTON, at : before 6, and MIDDLESBRO' at : past 6,

Returning the same Evening,

## On Thursday Morning, Aug. 29,

FOR

# SHIELDS

Calling at SUNDERLAND, in going and returning.

### FARES THERE & BACK.

STOCKTON & MIDDLESBRO' TO SUNDERLAND & SHIELDS, 1s. 6d.

On this occasion parties wishing to witness the

# QUEEN

Pass over the High Level Bridge, at Newcastle,

On her route into Scotland, will have an opportunity of doing so, as the Boat will start precisely at the time advertised.

The Committee have much pleasure in calling the attention of the Brethren of the Order and the Public generally to the
above Trip, and beg to assure them that this being their first Trip, nothing shall be wanting on their part to secure the comfort
and accommodation of all on board.

## AN EXCELLENT QUADRILLE BAND WILL BE ON BOARD.

AUGUST 22nd, 1850.

From the Office of J. PROCTER, High Street, Hartlepool.

9    Friendly Society poster for a pleasure trip 'for the benefit of
the Widow and Orphan's Fund of the Independent Order of Odd
Fellows, M.U., St. Hilda's Lodge, Hartlepool.' From Robert
Wood, *Victorian Delights*, 1967.

port of Bo'ness in central Scotland, where the United General Sea Box of Borrowstouness Friendly Society existed in 1634. Huguenot refugees who settled in England after the Revocation of the Edict of Nantes in 1685 formed their own clubs – among them the Normandy Society of the Spitalfields silk weavers of London. The society, founded in 1703, aimed at 'promoting social intercourse and providing assistance in sickness and old age and the expenses of the burial'.[39]

By the end of the eighteenth century there were many thousands of such societies, which attests to the great determination of the poor to avoid a pauper burial at all costs. The size of the weekly contribution varied according to the pocket of the contributor. In Blackburn, in 1872, members of the local Philanthropic Burial Society paid 1d or 1½d a week out of their mill wages. The Enginemen and Firemen's Mutual Assurance, Sick and Superannuation Society, founded in the late 1840s at Swindon, the headquarters of the Great Western Railway, confined its membership to footplatemen. They were the highest paid group of workmen in the railway workshops and paid 1s 6d or 1s a week subscription. The usual rate at that time was 2d to 9d a week.[40]

By the end of the nineteenth century the societies had grown into vast organisations with huge funds and extensive membership lists. The ten largest collecting societies were all founded between 1843 and 1862. The largest of all was the Royal Liver Friendly Society of Liverpool with, in 1850, 550,000 members (all Irish) and funds of £264,795. As with the old guilds, members could still be fined for non-attendance at their society funerals.[41] They were issued with advice about mourning wear, although some clubs only asked that their members should appear clean and decent for the occasion. Most working people in the middle of the Victorian period, when industrial conditions and wages were at their worst, could rarely afford new clothes for daily use, and certainly could never have afforded to buy mourning clothes. Some clubs, in order to avoid the hiring charges of the undertakers, bought their own basic funeral paraphernalia. The Museum of Labour History at Limehouse, in London's East End, has a very simple black woollen dress, shawl and bonnet which belonged to the Dockers Union and was loaned out to widows from 1880 to 1914 so that they could appear in mourning at their husbands' funeral.

Even amongst the poor there were grades of funerals. The grandest involved the use of a horse-drawn hearse, but much more common was a 'walking funeral' where the coffin was wheeled on its hearse, not driven. Philpot, a painter and decorator in Robert Tressell's novel, *The Ragged Trousered Philanthropists* written in the early 1900s, was given a proper horse-drawn funeral, because he 'was insured for £10 in a society',[42] but a hand-pushed cart or truck-hearse was much more common. They were constructed with two handles at the back to hold on to as they went downhill and two handles in the front to help pull them upwards. One hearse, now owned by Northiam Parish Council, could be used as either a hand-pulled or horse-drawn vehicle, according to the financial state of the customer (see fig. 11).

The class divisions of Victorian society showed up most starkly in their funerals. In 1843 the *Supplementary Report on the Results of a Special Enquiry into the Practice of Interment in Towns* published their survey of the average cost of funerals. A person of rank or title could not be buried properly for less than £800 rising to £1,500. A middle-class burial cost about £100, while that of an artisan amounted to £5. A pauper funeral added up to the sum of 13 shillings which included a coffin of the cheapest quality, at 3s 6d. 'It had a shroud, but no cloth, nails, name-plate or handles, and often broke into pieces when taken to the grave.'[43] Tressell described the appearance of the vicar at a working-class funeral: 'Perhaps it is not right to criticize this person's appearance so severely, because the poor fellow was paid only seven-and-six for each burial, and as this was only the fourth burial he had officiated at that day, probably he could not afford to wear clean linen – at any rate, not for the funerals of the lower classes.'[44]

Charles Booth reported on funerals of the poor in *The Life and Labour of the People of London*. He, too, was shocked by the bleakness of the proceedings. He attended a double funeral in about 1897, where the graves were dug side by side. 'In two or three minutes all was over. The mourners seemed hardly to realize it and the parson slipped away unobserved . . . the forlorness and the very impersonal character of the whole proceedings was its most marked feature. Death the Comforter seemed far away.'[45]

Burials of the poor were frequently delayed while the relatives struggled to raise the money to provide a respectable burial. Most working-class burials were conducted on Sundays – the only non-working day of the week – to the dismay of the rest of society, which condemned this practice as desecration. If the family could not raise the money by the first Sunday after the death occurred, the corpse had to be kept in the home until the following Sunday came round. This caused very serious health problems, as the corpse usually had to be kept in the same overcrowded room where the family slept. Costers in the East End of London raised money for funerals at pub concerts where raffles were held and also in the home of the widow. 'Every coster entering the shabby room would drop a coin on the plate, as large as he could manage,' reports Pearl Binder. 'The wake was deliberately conducted with jocularity . . . in marked contrast to the cultivated gloom of middle class funerals.'[46] Charles Booth noticed that mourning coaches were inclined to stop outside the nearest public house, while the mourners retired to cheer themselves up,[47] much to the disgust, no doubt, of their better-off neighbours.

A pauper funeral – a funeral paid for by the local parish – was regarded as a mark of deep dishonour not only because of its lack of dignity but also because of the disgrace it brought upon the family of the deceased and the community as a whole. Families would put themselves into penury pawning whatever they could, in order to avoid such a public humiliation. 'Even the poorest will pay £8 to £10 for a burial and then starve for a week,' an omnibus driver told Charles Booth in 1898.[48] Tressell described a pauper funeral:

> It was a very plain-looking closed hearse, with only one horse. There was no undertaker in front and no bearers walked by the sides. Three men (the dead man's sons) dressed in their Sunday clothes, followed behind the hearse. As they reached the church door, four old men who were dressed in ordinary everyday clothes, came forward and, opening the hearse, took out the coffin and carried it into the church, followed by the other three . . . The four old men were paupers, inmates of the workhouse, who were paid sixpence for acting as bearers . . . The roughly made coffin was of white deal, not painted or covered in any way and devoid of any fittings or ornament with the exception of a square piece of zinc tacked on to the lid . . . roughly painted in black letters 'J.L. Aged 67'.[49]

The working-class dream was a funeral to vie with those of the better-off and even the grandest of society. Burial Society funerals often included mutes, feather-trays and black horse with nodding plumes, but funerals by public subscription were sometimes even grander. Death by misadventure or disaster, if spectacular enough to receive big publicity, could ensure the provision of not only a grand funeral but even a large inscribed tombstone, a success story totally beyond the aspirations of the poor. Four youths killed in a mining accident at the village of Little Dean in Gloucestershire in 1819 were given an imposing gravestone with the following inscription:

> These four youths were suddenly called to eternity on Tuesday the 6th day of April 1819 by an awful dispensation of the Almighty. The link of a chain employed to lower them into Bilston Pit breaking, they were precipitated to the bottom of the Pit. Their bones literally dashed to pieces their bodies thus presenting a frightful spectacle to all who beheld them . . . A Funeral Sermon was preached on Sunday April 25th 1819 in the Church of Little Deane before a congregation of 2,500 people . . .[50]

The youths were aged twenty-six, nineteen, sixteen and twelve.

Charles Booth described a public funeral in Plaistow in the East End of London in the 1890s. A mother, together with her eight children, was burned to death in a fire. On the same day, the father of the family died of consumption. Such an extraordinary tragedy could not pass unmarked and a public funeral subscription was raised. A band paraded, playing the 'Dead March', followed by four hearses with plumed horses, the mutes with their flowing crape hat bands and four mourning carriages. There were also four omnibuses prepared to take passengers to the burial ground and back for one shilling. Each was crowded with women mourners. 'There was a respectful crowd looking on, with thirty policemen to keep order . . . Everybody was on their best behaviour, in their Sunday clothes, washed and dressed for the occasion.'[51]

Another method of raising money for bereaved families, especially in coal-mining areas, where serious industrial accidents were not infrequent, was through the composition of special memorial ballads, which were aimed at working on the feelings of the listeners so that they would give money generously to the relief funds for miners' dependants. The words were often angry and bitter. After the Greshford disaster, near Wrexham in 1934, when 265 miners were killed, a ballad was written recounting the explosion which contained the following verse:

> The Lord Mayor of London's collecting,
> To help both the children and wives,
> The owners have sent some white lilies,
> To pay for the poor colliers' lives.

10   Earthenware plate commemorating 72 miners who died in the Swaithe main colliery explosion, 1875. (*City Museums, Stoke-on-Trent*)

Another ballad written in 1901 after a mine explosion at Donibristle in Fife in Scotland exemplifies, writes A. L. Lloyd, 'the double function of charity-appeal and comment that is characteristic of so many latterday disaster songs.'

They lost their lives, God help them. Ah yes, it was a fact.
Someone put in a stopping, and they never did get back.
Was that not another blunder? My god it was a sin.
To put a stopping where they did, it closed our heroes in.

We never shall forget them, though they have lost their lives
So let us pay attention to their children and their wives.
It simply is our duty now, and let us all beware
Their fathers died a noble death and left them in our care.[52]

Servants, too, were sometimes commemorated with grand grave-stones paid for by their employers, though, as Kenneth Lindley points out: 'It was usual for the employer to include his or her own name on the stone, often in larger letters than the name of the servant commemorated.' In the understanding of the social system it was their association with their employers alone which gave them import-ance – a very ancient concept indeed.

An inscription of 1612 on a brass plate, survives in the church at the village of Turvey in Bedfordshire:

I.H.S. Anno Domini 1612
Heare Lyeth John Richardson
A faythfvl trve servannt to Tvrvey Old Hall
Page to the First Lord Mordavnt of fame
Servannt to Lewes Lord Henrey and John
Paynefvll and carefvl and jvst to them all
Till death toke hys lyffe
God have mercie of his sovle    Amen[53]

The middle classes were outraged by the wanton poor who had so little and yet spent so much on funerals. Why could they not be more sensible and be satisfied with a cheap burial? It was a typically unsympathetic comment that,

11 *(opposite above)* Hand or pony-drawn hearse, 1897, from the parish of Northiam, near Rye, Sussex. This was made by Mr R. G. Kemp of Hawkhurst for £27, to commemorate Queen Victoria's Diamond Jubilee in 1897. It was for the use of all parishioners and was pulled by the same pony as pulled the milk cart round the village. A local builder, Mr Alfred Comport, acted as Caretaker to the Hearse, and he was paid 1s 6d for washing and generally maintaining the hearse every time it was used. It was last used in the late 1950s. (*By kind permission of the Northiam Parish Council*)

12 *(opposite below)* Box type, horse-drawn hearse. First used in Marrick in Swaledale, Yorkshire, in 1828. (*Beamish North of England Open Air Museum*)

If the poor were wise their funerals would be as simple as possible; a plain coffin . . . followed by family and friends in decent mourning, but without any of the undertakers' trappings on their persons would be sufficient. The poor like funeral pomp because the rich like it; forgetting that during life the condition of the dead was entirely different, and that there ought to be a consistency in everything belonging to the various ranks of society.[54]

There was no understanding of the tremendous struggle that went on in the homes of most poor families to provide their dead with a respectable burial. To some death itself was looked to as a blessing and relief, from the travail of life. 'The people is a being brought to that state of destitution,' declared an elderly Spitalfields silk weaver, to Henry Mayhew in 1849, 'that many say it's a blessing from the Almighty that takes 'em from the world.'[55]

13   Lamb Bros hearse from the village of Murton near Appleby, 1870–90. They were farmers as well as undertakers and still own this hearse. (*Beamish North of England Open Air Museum*)

14  Plaque on the tombstone of 'Thomas Scaife: late an
Engineer on the Birmingham and Gloucester Railway, who lost
his life at Bromsgrove Station, by the Explosion of an Engine
Boiler on Tuesday the 10 of November 1840.' (*By kind
permission of Kenneth Lindley*)

# CHAPTER TWO

# *The Social Status of Widows*

THE position of widows in many cultures is one of the saddest in society. The simple fact that they were born women ensured their fate. The moment their husbands died, their own function in life was regarded as ended. Often they were destroyed to accompany and serve their dead spouses in the new life beyond death, as they had in his earthly life. In pre-industrial societies, birth, marriage and death are seen as a natural, eternal cycle with death as a happy inevitability, a step on the road to the next life. Life after death is the reward for those who have completed their life cycle. Having married and raised children to continue the family line, the death of the male head of the family is accepted with joy and celebration by his family. The soul needs only to be sent ritually on its way with the necessities for a happy life beyond death, for tranquillity to be ensured. These necessities consisted of food, drink, weapons, vehicles and the animals to draw them, and of course his wife, wives and concubines. It was necessary to kill these women in order to place them in the graves alongside the dead husband. Women accepted this as their natural end and were brought up to believe that if they died with dignity they would bring credit upon their own spirit and upon their families. Women who resisted this fate were killed anyway because there was no social rôle left for a wife after her husband's death. Her sole function in life was to give birth to his children, to rear them and to cater to her husband's physical and material needs. Her sexuality belonged to him and to his family line. Without her husband she became unnecessary and therefore a social outcast.

Widow murder was the natural consequence of these beliefs. The deceased needed the ministrations of his wives and his concubines and servants just as much in his new spiritual life as he had in his old physical life. They were killed with prescribed ritual, the women often accompanied by those children who were too young to survive without them. In ancient Egypt servants and retainers were buried with their masters up to the end of the First Dynasty in 2900 BC. The ancient Chinese practised similar cults. Archaeologists have unearthed the hasty burials of large numbers of servants probably stunned and buried before regaining consciousness.[56] A Celtic king was given six hundred picked men to guard him, who had all vowed to die with him.[57] The purpose of killing off the Court in this way was an attempt to bring political stability to an unsettled country, no less than providing the king with prestige and protection after his death. Flinders Petrie writes that 'not only did it ensure that all those around the King would be faithful to him, but also, that all around the King would defend him from any outsiders, even at the cost of their own lives.'[58] Courtiers counted themselves fortunate in having the opportunity of entering the next world in such distinguished company.

In exactly the same way, and as late as 1858, there was a law in the Yoruba city of Oyo in Western Nigeria ensuring that the heir apparent, three princes, two titled persons not of royal blood, the king's official mother, and various priestesses, as well as the king's favourite wife, all died when he died, and by their own hand. They were given special 'death cloths', beautiful silk wrappers, which they wore on important occasions. They enjoyed special privileges and could commit any crime with impunity.[59] Similar obligatory deaths took place in China. The first Ch'in Emperor, for example, who died in 102 BC, built for himself a splendid mausoleum near his capital city of Ch'in. When he died all the imperial concubines together with the artisans who had worked on the building were all immured alive inside it.[60]

Such widows were destroyed either by their own relatives or by their own hands. Methods varied. Indian widows threw themselves onto their husbands' funeral pyres in the firm belief that if they died

bravely they would bring honour to their families and would themselves eventually be reincarnated (hopefully as men)[61] – a prospect
which no doubt brought them some comfort. In the days of the
British Raj, much outrage was felt at widow sacrifice. In 1822 a
well-intentioned English officer three times prevented a Hindu
widow from leaping onto the flames of her husband's pyre. She
eventually succeeded on the following day.[62] The *Sussex Weekly
Advertiser* reported on 28 May 1827 that after a public meeting in
York the worthy citizens signed a petition urging Parliament to
outlaw widow sacrifice (suttee) and in 1829 it was formally outlawed
by the Governor-General of India, Lord William Cavendish
Bentinck.[63] Inspectors were appointed to see that the law was
obeyed, but with little result. Emily Eden, sister of another
Governor-General, Lord Auckland, watched the funeral of the
ruler of Lahore in the 1830s. 'The two widowed ranees,' she wrote in
her diary, 'were such gay, young creatures and they died with the
most obstinate courage.'[64] A hundred years later, another lady
traveller in India, Grace Thompson Seton, wrote: 'To this day there
are rumours of widows who destroy themselves at the husband's
death.'[65] The practice may well have survived to the present time. It
was noticeable that after the dreadful Indian mining disaster at
Chasnala, when 372 miners were killed, the BBC Television News
reported on 31 December 1975 that the widow of one of the dead
miners had burned herself to death.

Another method of self destruction was the taking of poison. The
day that the King of Oyo died his female relatives, who were obliged
to die by sunset on the same day, took part in a great feast whilst
their graves were being dug. Having eaten the choicest dishes they
swallowed poison and died. If the poison worked too slowly and the
sun began to set they had to be strangled or otherwise killed by their
relatives.[66]

Techniques of widow murder varied from strangling, clubbing
and smothering to burial alive. In the Melanesian New Hebrides a
special conical cap made of spiders' webs was used for smothering
widows – the task being performed by the widow's son.[67] One such
hood was in the collection of Exeter Museum and another in the Pitt
Rivers Museum at Oxford. In the Congo in cases where the Bena
Kanoika wives did not submit willingly to being buried alive, their
arms and legs were broken to prevent them from escaping. Among
the peoples of the Bomu river area the two prettiest wives of an

important man were buried alive, with a few air holes left free so that they could breathe for a while.[68]

There are a few countries where a widower sacrificed himself on the death of his wife. In parts of West Africa when a man's wife was of higher rank than himself, he would acquire prestige by entering the next world in company with his socially superior late wife and he would therefore be willing to be buried with her.[69] Along the coast of Guinea the husband of a princess was treated as her slave and was expected to die with her. These cases were, however, fairly rare.[70]

It was more usual for some token or proof of marriage, other than the actual corpse of the husband, to be placed in the grave instead. This was done to prove to the guardians of the gates of Paradise that the woman had fulfilled her correct rôle in life through marriage and that she was therefore entitled to pass through to the next world. In parts of Australia aborigine women were once buried with a portion of their husband's beard tucked under their armpit to serve this function.[71] Wedding rings, special married women's coifs and dresses serve this same purpose in European communities.

When the widow was permitted to remain alive, the problem of exactly what to do with her had to be resolved by her own and her husband's relatives. She was often regarded with deep suspicion and suspected of witchcraft, both because of her direct contact with death and the additional fear that she might have been the cause of

15 Widow from the Andaman Islands, Bay of Bengal, wearing her husband's skull suspended around her neck. Early twentieth century. From Douglas Thompson, *Peoples of the World in Pictures*, 1934.

16 Aborigine widow, from the Larrakia, with self-inflicted scars, as a proof of genuine sorrow. Early twentieth century. From T. A. Joyce and N. W. Thomas, *Women of all Nations*, 1908.

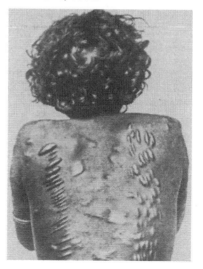

her husband's death. In societies where a widow was allowed to remain alive, she had to be ritually freed from contact with her dead partner before anyone could touch or go near her, as death was believed to be very contagious. After a period of isolation she was permitted to re-enter her family in the unenviable new widow's rôle. The isolation of the widow continues to this day – even in the Western world.

Widow isolation was a reflection of the fears and anxieties associated with death and she had become a hazard. Because of this contact, widows were thought to be a dangerous source of contamination. Relatives of the deceased were also tabooed for specific periods of time, but the longest and most arduous taboos and rituals were reserved for widows. Purification ceremonies were held to cleanse the bereaved, free relations from the risk of bringing harm to their friends and to placate the dangerous spirit of the deceased.

Whilst in mourning taboos were applied to every aspect of normal life – eating, drinking, cooking, sleeping, dressing and dancing were all affected and sexual activities were usually forbidden. Widows were so strongly under taboo that it was believed in some communities that to have sexual union with a widow might cause death. Mourners also were physically isolated until the period of danger had passed. The explorer Richard Burton reported that in the Cameroons in the 1850s: 'The people . . . never shake hands with their dearest friends for a certain time after the death of a near relative.'[72] It was reported in 1920 that Wagawaga widows from British New Guinea were expected to stay isolated inside their huts until most of the funeral rituals had been completed. If they had to leave, then they did so unseen and were required to avoid their neighbours. Tubetube widows from the same area were allowed out only if they were wrapped up in special 'daam' mats which concealed everything except a small part of their faces. They were not allowed to eat any of the same kind of food as their husbands had eaten before death. Seligman writes that, 'in the old days, a widow could be reduced to living on wild roots till often in a.very low state of nutrition.'[73]

In Europe these same taboos were applied to widows in a similar manner, certainly amongst the aristocracy and middle classes. Widows were isolated in their homes for specific lengths of time in rooms hung with yards of black cloth. Their bedchambers were entirely covered with it – the floors, ceilings and walls as well as the

MATRONE VEDOVE MODERNE.

17   A Roman widow, 1596, from Cesare Vecellio's *Habiti Antichie e Moderne*, published in Venice.

furniture.[74] They were not only confined to their homes, but were required to sleep and receive visits of condolence in special black beds of mourning. At the Court of the Burgundian Kings in fifteenth-century France, the widow of a knight was required to remain isolated in bed for six weeks after her husband's death. If she was visited by a princess during that period she was permitted to leave her bed only if she wore her mourning weeds. After her father's death she was confined to bed for just nine days but remained for the rest of the six weeks sitting in front of it on a large black cloth-covered chair.[75] Eight days after the death of William II, Prince of Orange, on 14 November 1650, his widow gave birth to a son – the future William III. A magnificent bed had been especially prepared for the joyous event, but under the changed circumstances the birth took place in a room draped with a royal widow's generous allowance of black cloth.[76]

Aristocratic widows had their own mourning beds to be used during the isolation of deepest mourning. In the seventeenth and eighteenth centuries they were usually four-posters, draped with dull black hangings and valances. These beds were taken out of storage and assembled when the need arose. The Verney family owned such a bed which was kept at Claydon House and was loaned out to members of the family when needed. It was made up from thirteen different pieces, including 'black cloathe hangings three yardes deepe and foure and half yardes longe' and two other pieces, each three yards square. The bed sheets were also black.[77] It is recorded that a young Verney widow, at the end of the seventeenth century, was allowed a white coverlet on her black mourning bed, because she 'is sick and cannot bear black'.[78] Lady Sussex, who was a friend of the Verneys, caused a stir by hurriedly returning the mourning bed which she had borrowed after her first husband's death. She was contemplating marriage to her second husband and thought that the black bed might have had a damping effect on the festivities. Anxious to get it out of her house she wrote, 'the black bed and hanginges your ante never sent for; if you would have me deliver them anywhere I will.'[79]

The beds were very costly and one family, surely one of many, found themselves without the necessary funds to buy one. The Catholic family of the Earl of Traquair, on the Scottish borders, ran into serious financial difficulties from the middle of the seventeenth century because of their religious differences with the Crown. No

18 Mourning bed of the 1680s at Traquair House, Borders, Scotland. (*By kind permission of P. Maxwell Stuart*)

19 Mourning bed of the Countess of Egremont, 1837, Petworth House, Sussex. This painting was one of a series of the interiors of Petworth, painted by J. M. W. Turner in 1837 after the death of his patron and friend the Earl of Egremont. The four-poster bed is hung with black curtains and valances and topped with the family coat of arms in black. (*British Museum*)

alterations were made to Traquair House from the 1680s and when one of the family died in the middle of the eighteenth century, relatives could not afford to buy black bed hangings. The existing ones, which were of a bright yellow colour, were carefully dyed black and rehung. These hangings remained black until the father of the present owner restored them to their original colour.

Black hangings were still in use in Victorian times when widow isolation and taboos against those in mourning remained as strong as ever. Victorian widows became social outcasts for the whole of the first year of widowhood. *Queen* magazine reaffirmed in 1880 that it was 'in the worst taste to be seen in places of public resort' whilst in deepest mourning. All invitations had to be turned down. The only socially permitted visits were to close relatives and to church services.

Even as late as 1907 Daisy, Princess of Pless, while wearing deep mourning for her father-in-law, Hans Heinrich XL, Prince of Pless, upset German high society when she unwisely went to the theatre in London, only two months after the Prince's death. She found it necessary to hide behind the curtains in her box,

> letting no-one see me, although I do think it ridiculous that one can dine out and yet not go to a play when one is in mourning; after all dear Vater was no blood relation of mine; in England, a daughter-in-law would not be prevented from going to the theatre after two months; but then in Germany mourning, like everything else, is taken in extremely large doses.[80]

Daisy was English and found German Court etiquette to be even more restrictive than that of England.

The period of widow isolation varied from one society to another. Amongst the Maoris of New Zealand a widow could not remarry until her husband's body had decomposed. While this process was taking place she wore two special feather cloaks called *kaakahu roimata* or 'cloaks of tears'. The husband's bones were finally exhumed, wrapped in the feather cloaks and reburied.[81] The widow was then free to remarry. The writer John Aubrey (1625–97) also believed that a second marriage should not take place until the first husband's body had rotted. 'It is still accounted undecent,' he wrote, 'for widows to marry within a yeare (I think) because in that time the husband's body maybe presumed to be rotted.'[82]

A middle or upper-class Victorian widow was under the tightest discipline for two and a half years after her husband's death. For the first year, whilst in deepest mourning, she was isolated, allowed out of her house only to attend church services or to see her closest family relatives. She had to wear only dull black silk and crape. For the second year she was confined to ordinary black mourning and her social circle was permitted to widen slightly. For her final six months of half-mourning she was restricted to the half-mourning colours of black, white, grey and mauve. If another close relative died during or just after her mourning period she would be obliged to continue wearing black for many more months. Today, in socially conventional circles, it is still not considered respectable for a widow to remarry within a year of her husband's death.

Even after her period of isolation or decontamination, a widow's problems were far from over. What was to be done with her now? What function in life was left for her without her husband? To resolve these problems arrangements had to be made covering all the remaining aspects of her life. The four most fundamental concerns were the widow's sexual, property and inheritance rights and the future of her children.

The problem of a widow's sexuality was of serious concern. Married women were expected to be absolutely faithful to their husbands and were not permitted the same sexual freedom as that enjoyed by their partners. Where inheritance passed through the eldest male child, fathers had to be quite sure that their son and heir was in fact of their own blood. Women's sexual behaviour was rigorously controlled. Thus in parts of West Africa a man could not even commit adultery[83] for there was no such thing in respect of his wife – his extra-marital affairs carried no penalties. A woman was obliged to be faithful to her husband. This differs very little from sexual attitudes in the male-dominated society of nineteenth-century Britain. A woman caught committing adultery became a social outcast, but it was only to be expected for a 'gentleman' to keep his mistress discreetly settled in a suburban villa in districts such as Chelsea or St John's Wood or in a fine house in East London.

When the distinguished law reformer Lord St Leonard became Lord Chancellor in 1852, his wife was not received at Court though by then she was nearly seventy and he seventy-one – a deliberate public snubbing – because she had eloped with him while he was still at school and they had lived together for a few years before their marriage.[84] Girls were taught to think of sex as a duty and wives were expected to tolerate an erring husband's sexual promiscuity. The truth of the matter was that most women were in neither a legal nor a financial position in those days to do anything about this double standard of morality. There were high society scandals from time to time involving high-placed wives, but the rule was not to be found out.

The right to a widow's breeding potential in some countries

20    Hindu widow from India wearing a plain white sari and with short cropped hair. From a painting by Durgashaukar Bhattacharya about 1925 in *Yes, Lady Saheb*, by G. T. Seton.

remained within the husband's family, even after his death. This was often part of the condition of the marriage contract. In levirate marriages of this type, widely practised in Africa, where a widow is still of child-bearing age, she is expected to marry her husband's next brother and raise more children, who are counted not as the brother's but as the dead man's children.[85] A not dissimilar practice occurred at the Court of Queen Victoria. The Queen's eldest grandchild, the Duke of Clarence, was engaged to marry Princess May of Teck in December 1891. A few months later he died suddenly. After a suitable period of mourning, on 6 July 1893, May was married to the Duke's younger brother, Prince George. In 1910 after the death of Edward VII they become King George V and Queen Mary.

In many countries the widow's sex life ended with her husband's death. Her sexuality belonged to him and was not be shared with another man. Consequently widows, as Queen Victoria wished, were expected to remain sexually chaste for the rest of their lives. This applied particularly to the wealthy upper and middle classes, who could afford to keep a widow conspicuously idle and chaste. Positionless widows had no option but to remarry, even if they did not want to, in order to provide a home and food for their children. In China the Emperor's widows were forbidden to remarry. Marina Warner writes: 'In the sombre recesses of Forbidden City lived generations of imperial concubines, as if they had been confined to the monastic life . . . in 1924, when the Court was finally driven out, three old ladies who had been the secondary wives of emperors were found living in forgotten seclusion.'[86]

In India Brahmin widows were forbidden to remarry. It was believed that widows had, either in their present or previous lives, committed sins grave enough to deserve life-long punishment, which served as a form of penance. If the women bore their difficulties with courage 'the soul could be absolved for past sins and acquire the merit which would entitle it to a more fortunate existence in its next birth.'[87] Brahmin widows were, and to some extent still are, complete social outcasts, used as household drudges, with shaven heads and plain white saris often torn and dirty. Their bodies were emaciated by perpetual hunger. The mere sight of a widow was said to bring bad luck. The situation was made worse by the large number of child-widows. Because of the practice of 'marrying' children at a very young age, coupled with the high infant mortality rate, Brahmin widows could be as young as one or two years of age. They could never remarry, have children or manage a home. In the Madras Presidency in 1901 there were said to be 22,395 widows between the ages of five and fifteen, despite the Act of 1891 prohibiting the consummation of marriage before the age of twelve.[88] Notwithstanding the efforts of Indian and British social reformers there were still reckoned to be 1,515 Brahmin widows under the age of one year in 1931.[89]

In Christian communities, though widows were free by law to remarry, greater respect was given to women who did not do so. Often Catholic widows chose to isolate themselves from society by retiring completely into seclusion in convents. Some entered with their younger daughters and stayed only for a short while, whilst others never returned to the outside world. The records of the order of the English Franciscan Nuns show that in the seventeenth and eighteenth centuries many widows retired to convents in Brussels or Paris. In 1662 Ann Battin of Denshire (*sic*) a widow with twelve children did just this. 'With two of them, she left ye world and took the habit of the 3rd order of our Holy Father, St Francis.'[90] Many convents and orders were established by wealthy widows – St Marcelle, who died in AD 410, set up the first convent in Rome. She had been widowed after seven months of marriage and refusing all offers from prospective husbands, devoted her life to the church.[91] In convents rich widows lived with considerable style. Except for frequent daily prayers and seclusion from the outside world, they enjoyed the service and comfort of a good hotel – preferable no doubt to the exposure to fortune-hunters outside the convent.

From the fourth century the doctrine of the Christian church had been that second marriages were essentially adulterous.[92] This belief was shared by many Victorians, notably the Queen herself. How could a family be decently reunited around the Throne of Light if the wife had two husbands? In 1859 the young Queen of Portugal, Stephanie of Hohenzollern, died, followed in November 1861 by her husband, King Pedro V, after an attack of typhoid fever. Victoria wrote in her diary: 'The only thought which has any comfort in it is that he – dear, pure excellent Pedro – is united to his darling, angelic Stephanie and that he is spared the pang and sacrifice of having to remarry again.'[93] Only one month later Prince Albert, totally unexpectedly, died from the same disease. Victoria was only forty-two. She put on her widow's weeds complete with bombazine and crape dress, and steadfastly remained in mourning for the rest of her life. She died at the age of eighty-two. The last dress she wore before her death (now No. 33.277 in the excellent collection of the Museum of London) was of black satin trimmed with black crape. Victoria made her mourning for Albert into a cult which dominated much of the rest of her life. Her example was admired, respected and copied (though perhaps not in its most extreme manifestations) by many Victorian ladies. Significantly a favourite Victorian mourning ring was inscribed: 'Heaven has in store what thou hast lost.'

Not a few widows did, however, undertake second marriages. For young and independently wealthy widows, their widowed state allowed them a freedom of choice over their second husband which, in the days of arranged marriages, they had not enjoyed over their first. In 1664 Samuel Pepys listened in the coffee house to the scandalous tale of Elizabeth, the daughter of Sir John Gerard of Lamers in Hertfordshire, widow of Sir Nicolas Gold, a merchant 'lately fallen and of great courtiers that already look after her; her husband not dead a week yet. She is reckoned worth £80,000!'[94] The lady finally remarried, only five months after her husband's death, no doubt causing even more of a scandal.

By the Victorian period two years was considered to be the minimum socially correct period before a second marriage. One Victorian widow who remarried on exactly the second anniversary of her first husband's death 'never survived the scandal that her behaviour provoked. Nor did she understand it. In fact when her daughters challenged her later on, she stared at them in a fury and stated; "I don't know what you mean. It was two years and I did wear half mourning." '[95]

Many Victorian widows did remarry, though often with deep qualms over the proprieties of doing so. The problem was debated in magazines and this reply to a reader's letter on the question of remarriage, published in the *English Women's Domestic Magazine* (May 1864) gives typically lukewarm support to the idea: 'Second marriages may, of course be contracted; as to second love, that is debatable. The transfer of the heart's affection is, in our opinion, impossible. Those who have once loved deeply, passionately, earnestly, can never love again with the same fervour, the same intensity.'

For a widower the situation was quite different. He marked his mourning for his late wife with black clothes and a black armband, worn but for a few months and he was encouraged to remarry, especially if he had children.

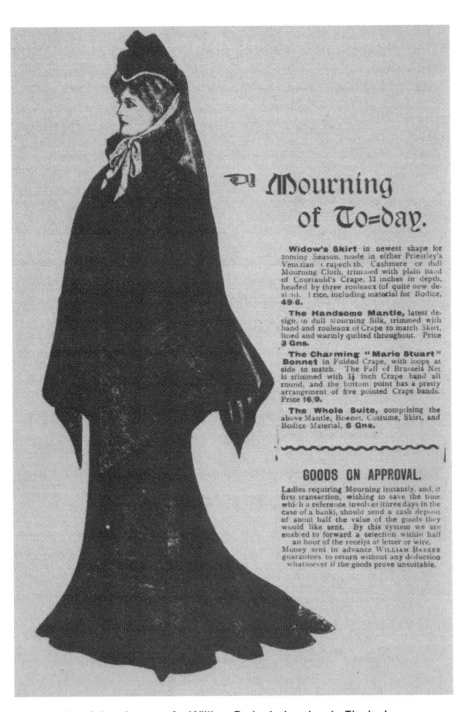

# Mourning of To=day.

**Widow's Skirt** in newest shape for coming Season, made in either Priestley's Venetian Crapecloth, Cashmere or dull Mourning Cloth, trimmed with plain band of Courtauld's Crape, 12 inches in depth, headed by three rouleaux (of quite new design). Price, including material for Bodice, **49 6.**

**The Handsome Mantle,** latest design, in dull Mourning Silk, trimmed with band and rouleaux of Crape to match Skirt, lined and warmly quilted throughout. Price **3 Gns.**

**The Charming "Marie Stuart" Bonnet** in Folded Crape, with loops at side to match. The Fall of Brussels Net is trimmed with 1½ inch Crape band all round, and the bottom point has a pretty arrangement of five pointed Crape bands. Price **16 9.**

**The Whole Suite,** comprising the above Mantle, Bonnet, Costume, Skirt, and Bodice Material, **6 Gns.**

## GOODS ON APPROVAL.

Ladies requiring Mourning instantly, and, if first transaction, wishing to save the time which a reference involves (three days in the case of a bank), should send a cash deposit of about half the value of the goods they would like sent. By this system we are enabled to forward a selection within half an hour of the receipt of letter or wire. Money sent in advance WILLIAM BARKER guarantees to return without any deduction whatsoever if the goods prove unsuitable.

21   Advertisement for William Barker's, London, in *The Lady*, 4 October 1900, showing the correct outdoor wear for a widow in the first stage of mourning.

The question of widow inheritance became a burning cause of those who campaigned for women's suffrage. Until the passing of the Married Women's Property Act in 1882 no married women, except those in the aristocracy and some wealthy trading families who were protected under the Chancery Courts, could own any property or money. Upon her marriage, a woman's possessions and those she inherited later, became her husband's. The children of the marriage were the sole possession of the husband and could be taken away from her if she was judged to be of questionable character. She was not even legally entitled to the money she earned by her own labour. A husband could will all his property and his home away from his wife. 'If he did so, she was entitled to continue to live in their home for forty days after his death, providing she did not remarry within this period.'[96] Amongst the aristocratic families the position of the widow was at least comfortable. She was provided with a dower house, usually set in the grounds of the family estate. Her eldest son, once he had come of age, took over the big house, where he brought his wife and reared his children. Lady Charlotte Schrieber, a mine-owner's widow, handed over the family home, Canford House, to her eldest son, Ivor, four years after her husband's death, on her son's twenty-first birthday. She wrote in her diary in 1856: 'My reign was finished and a thousand thoughts and feelings of the past rushed into my heart . . . This day eleven years Canford was bought. This day four years my late husband left it for the last time. Today I leave it as a home, to be nowhere settled on this earth.'[97]

Middle-class widows, if they were not left home and money in their husband's wills, had to rely on their male relatives for support or try to find work, often for the first time in their lives. Charity organisations for 'Distressed Gentlefolk' were created to try to help them – the key emotive word is 'gentlefolk'. Henry Mayhew, in his researches on living and working conditions for the *Morning Chronicle* in 1849–50, came across not a few middle-class widows and their children, living in conditions of unaccustomed poverty and misery. One widow was trying to keep herself alive by sewing men's nightcaps and cravats. She was paid sixpence a dozen for the cravats and told Mayhew: 'Myself and daughter hemmed the dozen in a day . . . It was really such very hard work that I cried over it. I was so ill and we were wanting food so badly . . . of course now we sleep upon the floor . . . I will tell you that we are still without our clothing both my daughter and myself; and I have chewd camphor and drank water to stay my hunger.'[98]

For working-class widows, especially if left with young children, the situation was desperate. They could find no work that could provide them with a decent income. The only jobs available to women with dependants were the lowest paid types of outwork, such as sewing. The few 'educated' women who became governesses fared little better according to Charlotte Brontë. An East End widow with three children told Mayhew in 1849 that she earned fourpence to ninepence a day making shirts. Unable to earn enough to feed her children she went to the Wapping Workhouse 'with my clothes patched from top to bottom, yet I trust they were clean.' Her children, aged seven, three and a young baby, were sent into a separate 'home' in Limehouse, where one child died of hunger and another of measles. Under these circumstances, it is hardly surprising that many women, both single and widowed, were forced into prostitution. One young needlewoman, with a widowed mother to look after, described her life to Mayhew. 'I struggled hard to keep myself chaste but I found that I could not get food and clothing for myself and mother so I took to live with a young man. It stands to reason that no one can live and pay rent and find clothes upon three shillings a week, which is the most they make clear, even the best hands, at the moleskin trowsers work . . . Young as I am, my life is a curse to me.'[99]

CHAPTER THREE

# The Origins of Fashionable Mourning Dress up to 1600

Widows and mourners were a group cut off from the rest of society, physically isolated by virtue of their bereaved status. Their condition was clearly and publicly marked by the enforced wearing of distinctly different garments. Mourning clothes served several purposes: they indicated the piety and chastity of the wearer; they denoted the wealth and social status of the bereaved family. As royal funeral etiquette filtered slowly down through the class system, widows became a perfect shop window for an impressive display of social expertise. From the Renaissance onwards the sumptuary laws governing mourning dress in general (and widows' weeds in particular) grew into an intricate labyrinth covering choice of fabric, colour, cut and accessories. Widows' clothes became a status symbol – an Yves St Laurent suit or a Zandra Rhodes dress of their day. Today only finance governs our choice of clothes but in Europe, until the end of the sixteenth century, clothes of the different classes were controlled by strict sumptuary laws. These laws were directed at maintaining a definite sartorial distinction between the upper, middle and lower classes, and it was the restless ambition of the middle rank of society which most resented them.

Mourning dress, like funeral ceremonies, was regulated by special rules drawn up by the Courts of Heralds acting under royal instruction. These sumptuary rules set out the correct usage of mourning dress, and fines were imposed enabling the Heralds to punish those who tried to usurp the prerogatives of the nobles. In Europe, from the sixteenth century onwards, as the rising merchant class used their wealth to try to encroach on noble privilege, mourning dress, and in particular that of wealthy widows, reflected this major class upheaval, as did the rest of their funeral rituals. Both mourning dress and funerals grew more elaborate and more widespread – the one a reflection of the other. Both revealed the driving ambition of the merchant class to improve their position in society. Wealth was all important and the merchant class in Europe were determined that their wealth should buy them the power and right to display it as they wanted.

The origins of widows' weeds lie in the establishment of the first Christian convents, in the early years of the Christian church. As previously mentioned, many of these were founded and maintained by wealthy widows who retired into seclusion after the deaths of their husbands. Widows shared many common attitudes with nuns. Both had forsaken normal life, rejecting interest in sexual activity and in variety of sartorial elegance. Nuns wore black, grey and browns, and white to symbolise their chastity, humility and purity. Widows, too, dressed in black, grey and white to symbolise their grief and their rejection of joy. Nuns hid their faces and figures beneath layers of shapeless drapery and some even shaved off their hair to prove their lack of interest in feminine vanity and their dedication to Christ. Widows also disguised their sexuality under veils and draperies and wore deliberately old-fashioned clothes to demonstrate their lack of interest in fashionable society. Both nuns and widows abandoned all attempts at sartorial elegance and because their clothes were designed to be unchanging they were therefore unfashionable. In consequence of this the convent habits survived the passing years – nuns' dress changing only recently after eight hundred years. Widows' weeds, however, succumbed somewhat sooner to the temptations of fashion.

At the first convent in Rome, set up in AD 410 by St Marcelle, the nuns wore black robes. The canonesses of St Jean, established a little later, wore white robes with long black veils. Later orders followed these early examples. The nuns of the order of the Bridgettines founded by a widowed Swedish princess in 1344 wore ash-grey

22 Habit of the order of the Reformed Abbesses of Fontevrault, France, founded by St Brigit in 1344 and reformed in 1463 by the Reverend Abbess Mary of Brittany. They wore ash-grey habits with black veiling. It was an Augustinian order. An engraving by Adrien Schoonebeek in *Histoire des Ordres Religieux de l'un et de l'autre sexe* of 1695.

23 Habit of the noble order of the canonesses of St Marie at the Palace in Cologne. This order was based on a college founded by St Plectrude in 716 for girls and women of noble birth, who found themselves in impecunious circumstances – many of them widows. The canonesses attended prayers in their habits but otherwise wore secular dress. They were allowed to marry. They wore transparent tunics through which their gold trimmed and fashionable secular dress could be seen. This engraving of 1695 shows a long peaked veil (just like a widow's), although by that date ruffs had gone out of fashion and were no longer worn by the canonesses. Engraved by Adrien Schoonebeek in *Histoire des Ordres Religieux de l'un et de l'autre sexe*, 1695.

habits with black veiling. A particularly interesting dress was worn by the sisters of the order of the canonesses of St Marie at the palace in Cologne. This order was founded in AD 716 for noble ladies in difficult financial situations, who were allowed to remarry later. Because of this the nuns were permitted to wear their own secular dress, though it had to be covered with ecclesiastical habits trimmed with gold lace.[100] Many orders for women and girls were first established in Italy and it is not surprising that their clothes closely resembled Italian widows' weeds. It was the powerful influence of the Church of Rome that spread the use of both nuns' and widows' dress across Europe, maintaining it virtually unchanged for hundreds of years. In the early nineteenth century when the widowed Mme de Bonnault d'Houet founded the order of the Faithful Companions of Jesus at Amiens in France, her nuns' habits were copied closely from the weeds worn by French women at that time. The nuns wore caps covered with a veil of black crape, with a short black frill under the

24  Habit of the Faithful Companions of Jesus. The foundress, Madame de Bonnault d'Houet, a widow, in the original habit. Early nineteenth century. (*By kind permission of Poles Convent, Ware*)

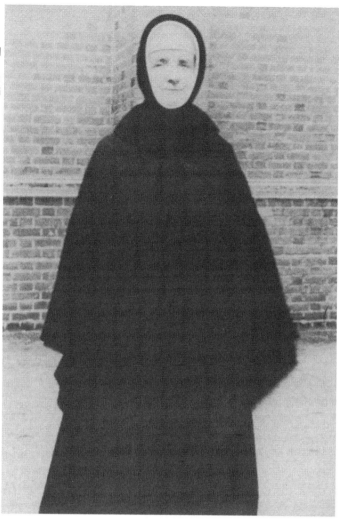

25  Habit of the order of tl
Faithful Companions of
Jesus, as worn in the 1920
at Poles Convent, Ware. (5
*kind permission of Poles*
*Convent, Ware)*

chin. Their black dresses were covered with black shawls. The style remained unchanged from 1820 until 1924.[101]

The link between nuns' and widows' clothes was strong, but there was also a certain similarity between fashionable and mourning dress even in the Middle Ages.

Up to the fourteenth century the clothing of both men and women in Europe was only marginally influenced by fashion. Dress was strictly delineated by class, with the rules laid down by civic and ecclesiastical sumptuary laws. These allowed only the most aristocratic circles to wear the richest fabrics whilst their social inferiors were restricted, according to their precise rank, to simpler materials and styles. Each country issued its own sumptuary regulations. In the state of Venice in 1334, for example, sumptuary laws were proclaimed twice a year from the Rialto and St Mark's Square. They applied to everyone, with the exception of the Doge's family. Women were barred from wearing cloth of gold and no males over the age of ten were permitted to wear silk, velvet, cloth of gold or any ornaments other than fastenings or buttons.[102] These laws were continually challenged and broken.

Styles were slow to change, evolving from draped, rectangular cut garments to more fitting and elaborate clothing. The dress worn by nuns remained unchanged. As to widows' weeds, Strutt wrote that there was no marked difference between the dress of Anglo-Saxon widows and ordinary clothes.[103] No special style of mourning garment appears much before the fourteenth century. It must be stressed, however, that the use of plain black robes by wealthy widows and mourners was a major departure from normal wear. Byzantium, Turkey and Italy were already producing gorgeous brocaded and coloured silks which were traded across Europe. Wools, too, were being manufactured and traded in a wide variety of weights and colours, all favoured by the nobility and the wealthiest strata of society.

Basically both men and women wore black, draped gowns for mourning. The men's garments, cut with deep hoods, had developed from the gowns worn in the sixth century by Benedictine monks. Mourning gowns were worn at funerals only by the nearest relatives to the deceased, with the huge hoods pulled right down covering the face. Women wore kirtles and mantles in black for mourning. Their head-dresses were controlled by sumptuary laws. Late fourteenth-century brasses in English churches show the class differences in widows' 'barbes'. These were gorgets of finely pleated linen, derived from the twelfth-century wimples. Women of high rank were permitted to wear barbes covering their chins.[104] A brass of Eleanor de Bohun, Duchess of Gloucester, dated 1399 in Westminster Abbey shows her wearing just such a barbe over her chin, with a plainly draped veil or coverchief falling onto her shoulders.[105] Less privileged widows were ordered to wear their barbes beneath their chins.

The choice of mourning colours will be discussed in Chapter 10 but it is interesting to note here that black did not yet totally predominate as the colour of mourning in Europe. Chaucer, writing in the late fourteenth century, in the poem 'Troilus and Cresyd' describes Cresyd in 'widewes habit large, of Samite brown' and

26  Brass from the tomb of Eleanor de Bohun, Duchess of Gloucester, in St Edmund's Chapel, Westminster Abbey, 1399. (*By courtesy of the Dean and Chapter of Westminster*)

later in 'widewe's habite blak'. The thirty torch bearers at the funeral of Richard II at St Paul's in 1399 wore white, whilst, in the Hookham Bible of about 1300, the poor widow of Nain at her son's funeral wears a blue hood with a red lining. She is shown with it pulled down right over the face.[106]

Despite these seemingly modest black garments, there were complaints, particularly in Italy, that widows were not maintaining the decorum considered proper for their station in life. Vespasiano da Bisticci wrote in the middle of the fourteenth century that in Italy 'when widows go along the street their faces should be hidden and their eyes should be cast down, but instead they hold their heads high and they wish to see who is passing in the streets.' St Bernadino also complained of widows: 'You do not seem to me to be attired as you were formerly. Today I see the widows go out in a long cloak made with gathers, the forehead is uncovered and the cloak is thrown back, so that the cheek is seen, and how well she arranges it on her forehead, just like a courtesan.'[107]

The truth of the matter was that some widows were beginning to succumb to the temptations of more elegant clothes. As the Renaissance progressed, fashion became a reality. The merchant classes and lesser nobility aped the dress of their social superiors enthusiastically. Sumptuary laws were passed with increasing frequency and severity but decreasing success. In fifteenth-century Italy endless new sumptuary laws were enacted. 'It was like trying to hold back the tide,' writes Philip Longworth. 'Tailors were prepared to risk a month in gaol and their customers glad to pay a heavy fine.'[108] By the end of the sixteenth century in France the threat of fines had no effect at all. 'Despite the prohibitions and penalties laid down in the decree of 1577,' declared Claude Haton in his *Memoirs*, 'the new gentlemen and demoiselles have no intention of reducing their state or discarding their new velvets and habits and I have never heard of them paying the thousand écu fine!'[109]

The nobility in retaliation began to change their style of clothes more frequently, leaving the less aristocratic and wealthy lagging behind. Gradually true fashion cycles developed. One result of this was that the differences between the dress of both nuns and widows and the style of fashionable dress became more exaggerated. Furthermore, the differences between these two types of dress also widened. Nuns' robes still remained basically Byzantine, whereas widows' weeds began to reflect the changing fashions though still lagging behind the accepted style of the day. The basic elements of mourning dress, however, survived the onslaught of fashion. The use of black and white, the veiling of the face, the hair well hidden beneath a draped head-dress, and the effect of simplicity all remained. One reason for this extraordinarily long survival was that sumptuary laws continued to be applied, and to some extent respected, in mourning dress long after they had been abandoned in the sphere of fashionable dress. Mourning sumptuary laws are indeed still in use today, surviving in Court procedures after a royal death or the demise of a figure of national importance. To this very day the Lord Chancellor, for example, has to forsake his frilled and lace trimmed jabot and cuffs when Court mourning is announced, replacing them with ones of plain white lawn. This rule applies to other members of the legal profession as well.

Not surprisingly, the mourning robes of kings and queens were the grandest of all. In France, by the end of the sixteenth century, kings mourned in magnificent robes of purple. It was not considered 'fitting to their sacred persons to associate themselves with things funereal', explained Jacques de la Guesle, Procureur-Général of the Parlement of Paris, in 1594.[110] Consequently kings were not allowed to wear black nor to attend funerals. Purple, the ancient imperial colour of Rome and Byzantium, was chosen instead. In 1547 after the death of François I of France, his heir Henri II attended the lying-in-state ceremony dressed in a purple cloak, which was described as a 'darkening of Royal scarlet but not a blackening of it'.[111] Royal funeral accessories were often purple, including the pall and the wall hangings of the state rooms. After the death of Queen Victoria the streets of London were draped with purple as her hearse was drawn through the city.[112] No other subject would have dared to use the colour. Even the most aristocratic of noble families would not have had the presumption to wear purple. They remained content in the knowledge that their own style of mourning dress was grander than everyone elses with the exception of the Royal Family. The highest in the land wore the longest trains and the most enveloping veils and head-dresses. They wore these uncomfortable and awkward garments with jealous pride because they symbolised the greatness of their rank. Others, including the Court servants and lesser nobility, were allotted shorter trains and different head coverings.

By the fifteenth century the temptations of fashionable dress became too much for aristocratic widows, and from that date onwards, very slowly at first, and then with increasing speed, widows' dresses became more and more fashionable. This was a fundamental change in style and attitude and it brought with it basic changes in mourning dress for both men and women. For widows who wished to remarry, the hope of finding a second husband, as well as the wish to remain fashionable, must have encouraged the use of more elegant clothes. The process was certainly slow, for it took five hundred years for society to permit a widow to be elegant and fashionable whilst in mourning. It was not until the end of the Victorian period that the change took place, when, for example, the *Ladies Field* of 4 October 1900 announced to its lady readers that although 'mourning is unfortunately worn by many – the fashion of the hour is strictly followed.'

27  (*left*) Tomb effigy of Philippa, Duchess of York, in St Nicholas Chapel, Westminster Abbey, 1431. (*By courtesy of the Dean and Chapter of Westminster*)

28  (*below*) Margaret Beaufort, Countess of Richmond and Derby, in widow's weeds with barbe. Artist unknown. About 1509. (*National Portrait Gallery, London*)

During the fifteenth century widows continued to wear the pleated barbe and shoulder-length coverchief with their black robes and surcoats. Fashion crept in slowly in the choice of new head-dresses. The monument in Westminster Abbey to Philippa, Duchess of York, who died in 1431, shows her in a pleated barbe worn as befitted her rank, just covering her lower chin, but she wears it with an inner pleated head-dress which dips over her forehead. [113] This dipped style was later to epitomise the Victorian widow and remained in royal use until 1952. Early influence of fashion can be seen in a portrait of Margaret Beaufort, Countess of Richmond and Derby, painted in about 1509 and now in the National Portrait Gallery, London. Her barbe covers her chin but she wears a fashionable gabled head-dress over a white cap.

Very detailed sumptuary mourning edicts were issued by Margaret Beaufort, mother of Henry VII, in 1495–1510, which decreed that all those above the rank of knights' wives were to wear a black mantle and a surcoat with a plain hooded cape on top. The garments were cut with deep trains both in front and behind. The front train had to be 'trussed up under the girdle or on the left arm' in order to permit walking and riding. Those of 'the greatest estate' had the longest trains to their mantles, which were held up by train bearers. It can be seen from illustrations that the principal mourners must have had considerable difficulty in moving at all. The hoods were cut with long, dangling tippets, a survival from fourteenth and fifteenth-century fashionable liripipes. The queen and queen mother wore tippets 'a nayle and an inch' (3¼ in.) wide and long enough to lie a good length along the train. The tippets shortened by degrees until the baroness's tippet, which was ¼ yard off the ground and 'scarce a nayle' (2 in.) in breadth. Knights' wives and some of the gentle-women of the Royal Household wore their tippets 'pinned upon their arme'. Lesser servants and women commoners were not per-mitted to wear them at all. [114]

In Italy, in the fifteenth century, delicate silk veils were the fashionable form of head covering worn over elaborate coiffures. In the Sforza Inventory (drawn up in Milan after the death of Count Carlos Sforza in 1493), descriptions are given of twenty such veils. One was made of cloth of gold trimmed with enamel hearts, while others were of yellow or gold-fringed silk. [115] In dramatic contrast to these dazzling fabrics, widows wore a black cap low over the fore-head hiding their hair and concealing the neck at the back – tied with

a bow at the back neck and covered with a transparent, crimped, white veil, like a coverchief, falling onto the shoulders. It is possible that these fine crimped fabrics were the forerunners of what was later to become black or white silk mourning crape. Illustrations on medallions[116] and engravings[117] show Catherine Sforza, widowed twice – in 1488 and 1498 – wearing a crimped hood, sometimes covered with another transparent hood worn over the top. A similar head-dress is seen in a painting in the Pinacoteca, Turin, by Gerolamo Giovenone, dated 1514. A detail shows a woman, probably a widow, kneeling in prayer. She wears a black dress with deep sleeves and a low, squared neckline, worn over a white shift. Her hair is pulled back tightly and hidden under a black cap. Over this there is a long, transparent veil in white which falls down her shoulders and is cut squarely across the forehead to leave the face exposed.[118]

Although black was now predominantly worn at funerals, there is evidence that other colours were also still worn for mourning. In 1457 Cosa, the wife of Paolo Niccolini, of the wealthy, Florentine woollen merchant family, died. Paolo gave mourning clothes to relations on his wife's side of the family. Records show that he gave them 'fourteen cubits of dark red cloth, besides a couple of veils and a fine towel' (to wear on their heads). In the same year Paolo remarried. His new wife, Maria, was the widow of Bernado Portinari, and the list of her trousseau still survives in the family records. Her gowns were exceptionally sombre. Instead of the usual bright, silk brocades, woven with gold and silver, she had a purple dress, with silver hooks and purple velvet sleeves, a black gown with tight sleeves, a reddish-brown gown, 'with sleeves like a friar's' and 'one dress of green woollen stuff, without silver or pearls'. She had thirteen large wimples and thirty kerchiefs to wear on her head.[119]

In England there is evidence that a dull shade of brown remained in use as a mourning colour. 'For the poor, drab, often called "sad colour"' was 'a practical alternative to buying black.'[120]

At royal or aristocratic funerals the entire staff were issued with mourning wear regulated by sumptuary laws. After 1400 men's black mourning gowns were worn with deep tubular hoods which completely hid the face from view. Even the tippet lengths were graded according to rank. Hoods were worn over the face only by those most closely related to the deceased and those performing certain ceremonial duties, such as canopy or banner bearers. The principal mourners, entitled to the longest trains, were issued with an extra yardage of fabric, a face cloth in black. Ordinances first issued during the reign of Henry VII and reissued several times during the sixteenth century, give details of allowances for mourning at State funerals. A duke and archbishop were entitled to sixteen yards for a gown, mourning cassock (sloppe) and a mantle, costing ten shillings a yard, with mourning provided for eighteen servants. A marquis received cheaper material at nine shillings a yard, whilst a viscount, who wore only the gown and mantle, had eight to twelve yards, and mourning for only ten servants. Barons were given six to eight yards, knights had five or six yards, while mere 'Esquires and Gentlemen' had to content themselves with up to five yards, for a gown and tippet, of the lowest quality fabric at five shillings a yard and mourning material for two or three servants only.[121]

Copies of the Book of Hours (illuminated devotional manuscripts of the late Middle Ages) provide useful information on male mourning dress. They often include illustrations for the service of the Office of the Dead. Groups of mourners can be seen, either at the grave-side or praying around the coffin in the church. One illuminated manuscript of the Office of the Dead shows the funeral of

Charles VI of France in 1422. The chief mourners, on horseback, wear the longest tippets.[122]

Another Book of Hours, painted in the Netherlands between 1477 and 1490 by the unknown Master of Burgundy for Englebert of Nassau, now in the Bodleian Library, Oxford, shows a churchyard scene. The grave-diggers wear brown and black. Two mourners are in pink and blue. The chief mourners wear the deepest mourning – draped and hooded black gowns with long tippets. A man stands with his hand resting on the shoulders of a young boy, whose tippet hangs from his hood right down to the back of his heels.[123]

The rough tacking or basting of mourning dress for men, which formed part of traditional Jewish mourning etiquette, seems also to have survived in Italy until the end of the fifteenth century. In traditional Jewish funerals the mourners, as a sign of grief, rent apart the tacked-up tears in their mourning dress. Similarly, in the

30    Office of the Dead from the Book of Hours of Englebert of Nassau, by the Unknown Master of Burgundy, 1477–90. The chief mourners, including a young boy, wear their tippeted mourning hoods pulled forward right over their eyes. (*Bodleian Library, Oxford*)

chronicles of the Niccolini family of Florence, it is recorded that at a family funeral in Rome, on 3 October 1470, the deceased's nearest male relatives were dressed in basted garments, *panni imbastiti*, as a sign of deepest mourning. The long black garments 'appeared to have been tacked and sewn hurriedly and badly.' More distant relatives wore unbasted long cloaks and black hoods.[124]

The sixteenth century saw the end of medieval widows' weeds and their replacement by increasingly fashionable styles. Brasses dating from the first half of the century show widows in barbes and cover-chiefs worn with the familiar mantles. During the last thirty years of the century, however, in the Elizabethan period, the fashions changed. Elizabethan aristocratic fashions were lavish, flamboyant and extremely exaggerated. Widows succumbed to the temptations of the wheel farthingale, the elegant ruffs and fashionable padding. During the period 1500–20 a curious mourning accessory was the beck, a black beak of fabric worn over the forehead. The beck was still popular in the seventeenth century and can be seen in many portraits, though worn as a fashionable fancy rather than for mourning.[125]

Mourning dress worn at the funeral itself and for the official mourning periods afterwards was much more exaggerated than the mourning clothes worn after the official ceremonies were completed, when the extra layers of tippeted hoods and trained mantles were put aside. Widows' weeds show a remarkable similarity in style throughout Europe, testifying to their common roots in the early Christian church. A Romanian icon, painted on wood in 1522 from Schitul Ostrov, in Vilcea, shows Princess Despina-Militza dressed in mourning for her young son Theodosie, whom she holds in her arms. This icon is now in the Museum of Art, Bucharest. It shows the princess in a full-length, black velvet cloak, trimmed with fur over a brown robe and a full-sleeved white chemise. Her head is covered by the hood of her cloak, whilst her neck is draped with a dark-coloured fabric, very like a wimple.[126]

A series of engravings by Nicolaus Hogenburg illustrating the death and lying-in-state of Margaret of Austria, in 1531, shows the mourners wearing mourning clothing very similar to that then worn in England. The barbe is extended into a deep frill which falls onto the breast, while the veils worn by the women kneeling in prayer are very finely pleated and fall to the ground covering the back completely.[127] Two portraits, one by Hans Holbein the Younger, of

## Mourning Dress

31  Christina of Denmark, Duchess of Milan, daughter of Frederick I (died 1533) and the wife of Francesco Maria Sforza, Duke of Milan, who died in 1535. She wears a mourning dress in black with a fur-lined black satin coat. Her widow's cap is slightly indented over the forehead. Hans Holbein the Younger. (*National Gallery, London*)

Christina Duchess of Milan (1535) now in the National Portrait Gallery, London, and the other by Titian, of Mary of Hungary (1548), a copy of which is now in the Rijksmuseum, Amsterdam, show aristocratic widow's dress. Both women wear black gowns covered with open mantles in black, with full sleeves and deep fur collars and linings. Mary's is in white ermine, while Christina's is in brown fur. Both wear tightly fitting caps – Mary's white and Christina's black – dipping over the forehead. Mary has, in addition, the vestige of a wimple worn under her chin.

In Britain the sumptuary mourning laws were kept up throughout the sixteenth century. Peeresses were entitled to sixteen yards for a mourning slop or closed gown, a kirtle and a voluminous surcoat with a mantle to cover it all. Also still worn were their white linen barbes lifted over the chin, whereas others down to the rank of knights' wives were obliged 'to wear yt under their throtes; and other gentlewomen beneath the throte goyll.' Such clothes were worn at the funeral of Mary Tudor in 1558. Two years earlier 'the Old Duchess of Norfolk' had been chief mourner at the Westminster Abbey funeral of Anne of Cleves. The Duchess wore a long, black velvet gown 'with a train so long that it stretched between her horse and the bearer's behind.' The Court ladies wore 'Paris heads under their hoods whilst the servants wore the same but without the hoods.'[128]

'Paris heads' were a new style of mourning head-dress, adapted from the French hood and better known now as the Mary Stuart cap, after the paintings of the widowed Mary Queen of Scots. The cap was of closely fitted white linen, dipping over the forehead, with a panel of pleats hanging down the back of the neck. Paris heads were worn by all women in mourning, except the poorest. Only those of the highest rank were allowed to wear them with tippeted hoods.

Portraits of Mary Queen of Scots painted between 1559 and 1561 show her wearing French *deuil blanc* or white mourning, with a white Paris head, a transparent white barbe beneath her chin and a black dress. In the famous portrait by Clouet she is probably wearing mourning either for her father-in-law, Henri II of France, who died in July 1559, or for her own mother, Mary of Guise, who died in Scotland in June 1560. When the courtiers and ambassadors came to pay their condolences to Catherine de Medici, the widow of Henri II,

32  Mary Queen of Scots in white mourning, 1559–61, by François Clouet. (*National Galleries of Scotland*)

they found her in a room with the walls and floors draped in black fabric and lit only by two candles standing on a black altar. Catherine was dressed entirely in black, with a white ermine collar, although her daughter-in-law Mary Stuart was in her white mourning.[129]

Six months after her mother's death Mary's young husband François II, who had been King of France for only three months, died from an abscess of the brain. After a period of forty days in deepest mourning she left for Scotland, landing at the port of Leith on 19 August 1561, as Mary Queen of Scots, dressed in *deuil blanc* for her husband. She found the Scottish Court in full mourning and so it continued to be for a whole year. Mary had brought with her a multitude of dresses, jewellery and furniture, though she had left the crown jewels of France behind in the hands of her mother-in-law. When Queen Mary settled into Holyrood Palace these goods were added to those of her dead mother, Mary of Guise, who as a widow had also worn mourning colours. An *Inventory of the Queen's Movables* was drawn up at the palace in September 1561 by Servay de Conde,[130] the new Queen's valet. It lists tapestries, bed sheets, bed hangings, measured lengths of cloth and clothes which had belonged to Mary of Guise. 'Stickes of silk, great and small peces all mesourit with a Scottis elnwand' included 'twa peces of blak satine containing XVI ellis', 'quhite dames' (white damask) and 'twa restis of gray dames'. Out of fifteen lengths of fabric, nine were in black, three were white, two were of 'tannie' (tan) which was still in use as a mourning colour, and one piece was in grey. Mary of Guise's dresses and cloaks were equally sombre. The inventory lists 'one gown with lang slevis borderit with veluit' (with long sleeves bordered with velvet). Seven black cloaks are listed, one of them being made of 'black veluit richt on baith the sydes' (black velvet rich on both sides). Included in the list is the magnificent cloak of violet velvet described as 'one royal cloik of violett veluit without furring or other thing'.

After one year in full mourning the Scottish Court went into half-mourning, after Mary Queen of Scots had been to 'make an offering of a great wax candle trimmed with black velvet'. It seems, from the inventory of Mary Queen of Scots' clothes, dated February 1562,[131] that the Queen was wearing, and certainly owned, coloured dresses besides black ones sometime before the full mourning period was over. Sixty of Mary Queen of Scots' gowns are listed, many of them made of cloth of gold. One is of green velvet, another in blue

33    An Italian widow, from
Fernando Bertelli's *Omnium Fere
Gentium Nostrae Aetatis
Habitus*, published in Venice in
1563.

silk with silver embroidery. Silver fabric and a dress of orange
damask with silver decoration and orange silk borders are also
included. Many of the dresses listed were black however. There is
one, for example, of *crespe noyer ronde faicte a longues manches
bordee de satin noyer par pistaunc garnye sur les manches et devant
de ladite robbe de petitz sertz de getz noyer* (a round-style dress in
black crepe, with long sleeves bordered with black satin and garnished on the sleeves and front of the said dress with black stones).
This is an especially interesting reference. All the other dresses in
this list are of various types of silk and none of them are in wool or
linen. It seems fair to assume that this particular dress was also in a
type of black silk crepe. Although this dress was almost certainly not
of the transparent type of mourning crape used for widows' weeds
from the seventeenth century, this is nevertheless an interesting
early reference to mourning crape.

In 1563 a fascinating book on costume was published in Venice
giving details of Court, country and mourning clothes. Fernando
Bertelli published *Omnium fere gentium nostrae aetatis habitus*, and
one of the plates shows an Italian widow, *Italica vidua*, dressed in

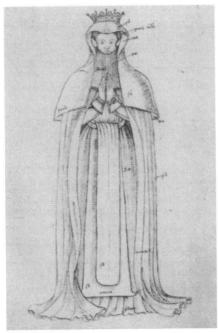

34 'A Countesse in mourninge apparaill', about 1576. The Countess wears a trained mantle, with a Paris head-dress covered by a black mourning hood. The front train of her surcoat, black, is held up by her girdle (sa for sable, ar for argent or white). (*British Library*)

mourning. She wears a plain gown with a gathered skirt and a petticoat with a band along the hem. Her head is covered with a simple veil without a head-dress beneath and reaching almost to the ground at the back.

Phillis Cunnington and Catherine Lucas discovered a fascinating illustration made by one of the Heralds in the College of Arms in London in 1575, which survives today and explains the correct mourning wear for an English countess. She wears a mantle with a train, a surcote with the front of its train looped up over the girdle.

35 The funeral of Lady Lumley, 1578. The chief mourner, the Countess of Surrey, wears an open hood, trained mantle, surcoat folded in front over a girdle and pleated, bib-like, front covering. She is supported by Sir John Selynger and Sir Thomas Browne who wear tippeted hoods and mantles. Her train-bearer, Mrs Coote, wears a black gown with a Paris head-dress. The 'six principall mourners', women, wear open hoods edged with white with their mantles, which do not have trains. (*British Library*)

On her head she has an open mourning hood, in black lined in white, over a 'Paris hedde' with a pleated barbe covering her chin. The Paris head-dress is the only garment which had changed over a period of seventy-five years.[132]

At the funeral of Lady Lumley in 1578, another sartorial change became evident. The chief mourner was the Countess of Surrey. She is shown in a manuscript from the British Museum wearing the usual mantle looped up in the front and with its long train carried by 'Mrs Coote, the Queene's woman'. The Countess has a mourning hood but beneath it she wears a narrow ruff – an innovation. The barbe could not, of course, be worn together with the ruff and its shape alters accordingly. It becomes a pleated, bib-like panel worn under the collar and down the front of the robe. Mrs Coote is shown in a black gown with fashionably padded sleeves, a Paris head-dress and a bib-type barbe. The almswomen at this funeral wore black gowns with wired-out, white veils.[133]

In the same year as Lady Lumley's funeral, a series of portraits of the imprisoned Mary Queen of Scots was painted. Known as the 'Sheffield' portraits because they were made while the Queen was living in Sheffield Castle, they are believed to have been copied from a miniature painted by Nicholas Hilliard in 1578.[134] Mary had by then been widowed three times. The portraits show her wearing a black dress over a white yoke, which replaces the bib-type barbe. She wears a deep ruff and cuffs in white lawn edged with reticella lace and a white lawn Paris head, without the hanging back panel (hereafter known as the Mary Stuart cap). It dips over her forehead and curves over her ears in the front. Edged with lace it is covered on the crown of the head with a transparent white veil (head-rail), threaded with wire, framing the head and shoulders. Veils of this type, wired high up behind the head around the edges of the great fluted ruffs, can be seen in many portraits of aristocratic ladies of the 1575–1620

36   The funeral of Lady Lumley, 1578. 'The Two Yeomen Conductors. The poore woemen mourners in this manner to the number of fortie two According to the age of the deceased.' The men wear black hose and coats whilst the almswomen wear black gowns and head veils stiffened with wire. (*British Library*)

37  Mary Queen of Scots; portrait painted in 1610, after the miniature by Nicholas Hilliard of 1578. (*National Portrait Gallery, London*)

period. They were made of fine, transparent silk, sometimes crimped or woven with delicate self-coloured stripes. The edging was made from white lace or reticella. For mourning use much plainer head-rails were made up in black fabric. These replaced the tippeted mourning hoods by the end of the sixteenth century and were known as arched hoods.

In Cesare Vecellio's book *Habiti Antichie e Moderni*, published in Venice in 1590, there are engravings and descriptions of mourning dress. Plate 29 shows 'A Modern Roman Widow' wearing a dress of black Florentine *rascia*. Noble women are described as wearing a mantle of *buratto* and a cap in white, beneath a veil. 'They appear in this dress with a great show of piety and melancholy for their dead husbands . . . more with the appearance of nuns than in secular dress.' Venetian widows are shown in a veil with scalloped edging and tassels at the front corners. Vecellio writes that they 'forsake all vanity and ornament, cover their hair and must walk on the streets with bowed heads.' When they wish to remarry they uncover their heads as a sign of their future intentions.

In sixteenth-century Venice great popular celebrations were held on feast days. The governor of the city, anxious that mourning should not 'upset the joyous aspect of the town' ordered those in mourning to wear coloured clothes on feast days. A widowed gentlewoman called 'Emo' who attended a feast wearing a golden dress with a black mourning sash became known as the 'Golden Widow'. In the same century Canon Giselli of Bologna disagreed with Vecellio and his description of nun-like widows. He declared:

> 'We are so advanced in freedom, that at the present time we cannot distinguish widows from married women and there are those who do not even wear a band or ribbon as a sign of mourning; gold, pearls, sumptuous dresses of the most vivid colours are the daily loves of widowhood today. If there came into the world today some of those very venerable widows of ancient times, who showed grief at the loss of their husbands, to be compared with the corrupt ones of today, they would say that the widows of today were celebrating because they had been liberated from the slavery of marriage and restored to the freedom they had before!'[135]

Cesare Vecellio's book includes engravings of mourning dress worn in 1590 by French noblewomen and English women. The French widow wears a mantle of black woollen cloth, with split sleeves, showing the black sleeves of the gown. A full-length black or white veil is worn with a pleated, white wimple described as *un velo bianca increspato* – a white crape veil – which was banded with fine braided silk. The English widow is shown in a Paris head-dress, in black, with a black woollen mantle, deeply pleated, with hanging sleeves.

38  An English widow, from Cesare Vecellio's *Habiti Antichie e Moderni*, published in Venice in 1596.

39  A Venetian widow, from Cesare Vecellio's *Habiti Antichie e Moderni*, published in Venice in 1596.

The same sartorial rules covered male mourning dress in the sixteenth century as before. Chief mourners and those with special functions at the ceremony still wore sleeved, floor-length mourning gowns with separate, tippeted hoods. The chief mourner wore a trained gown as a mark of his importance. At funerals in armorial-bearing families, the Heralds of the College of Arms attended wearing brightly coloured silk and velvet tabards on top of their mourning gowns and hoods.[136] Ordinary mourners also wore black gowns, but a curious change developed in the style of their mourning hoods. Instead of simply wearing the hoods down on their shoulders, they wore them slung over the left shoulder and wound around the neck by the long narrow tippets, with the point of the tippet falling down the left front of the gown.[137] By the next century the hood at the back vanished and mourning scarves or sashes developed. These survived well into the Victorian period. Accounts of sixteenth-century funerals include the most careful distinctions between those who wore their hoods up, and those of less importance who wore them on their shoulders. At the funeral of the Earl of Derby, who was buried with magnificent ceremony at Ormskirk on 4 December 1574, over nine hundred men took part in the procession. One hundred 'poor men' walked in twos, in gowns of coarse cloth, eighty of the Earl's Gentlemen rode on 'comely geldings' with their

40   Sir Robert Sydney, chief mourner at the funeral of Sir Philip Sydney in London in 1588, wearing a tippeted mourning hood and a trained gown. Other mourners wear similar hoods but their gowns have no trains. From an engraving by T. de Bry after T. Lant, 'Funeral Procession of Sir Philip Sydney, 1588.' Thomas Lant was then Windsor Herald. (*British Library*)

hoods on their shoulders. The chief mourner, the new Earl of Derby, wore the correct mourning robes for an earl – a black gown, sloppe and mantle, with his head covered.[138]

Elizabethan men fell under the spell of fashionable mourning in the same way as their women. Silks and velvet cloaks were highly fashionable garments in the middle of the sixteenth century, heavily trimmed with braid and embroidery. Towards the end of the century such cloaks began to be worn at funerals by all except the chief participants. 'While more dignified than a coat, the cloak was simpler to make than a gown and could cover all the clothing without having to fit. Mourning cloaks were thus mass produced and usually supplied to the mourners of medium importance.'[139] Another advantage of the cloak was that it was easier to wear with a sword, for by this time, everyone except the poorest, wore dull black mourning swords at funerals and during the deepest period of mourning afterwards. The Lord Mayor of London still has a ceremonial mourning sword with a black velvet sheath and grip, which is carried by his Sword-bearer.[140]

A remarkable document in the British Library shows clearly both the archaic and new styles in male mourning dress worn in the 1580s. It is an engraving of the funeral of Sir Philip Sydney, killed in action in 1587. Engraved by Theodore de Bry from drawings by Thomas

41  Pursuivants from the Court of Heralds at the funeral of Sir Philip Sydney in London in 1588, wearing over their already bombasted clothes not only mourning gowns but also their heraldic tabards. They carry Sir Philip's spurs, gloves and helmet. (*British Library*)

## Mourning Dress

Lant, the Windsor Herald who took part in the procession, it shows the figures of the two hundred mourners who took part in the ceremony. The chief mourner was Sir Robert Sydney, brother of the deceased, wearing a trained mourning gown, with his tippeted hood pulled right over his forehead. Other principal mourners wore untrained gowns. It is noticeable that these garments are cut with very full sleeves, and that they bulge out considerably in the front. The gowns were, of course, worn over the heavily bombasted clothes of that time, with padded sleeves, peascod belly and stuffed doublet. In the dress of the Heralds this effect is enhanced because they were wearing their stiffly embroidered tabards on top of the gowns, giving them a markedly bulky appearance. In the illustration of 'Mr Whyte, Gent', the great banner bearer, described as a gentleman friend mourner, his bombasted peascod belly and doublet can be seen beneath the gown. The conductors at this funeral, carrying their black staves, are wearing the new three-quarter length cloaks, with turn-down collars. The rest of their dress, including their tall crowned and curly brimmed hats, are typical of fashionable dress of

42   Venetian nobleman in deepest mourning, from Petri Bertelli's *Diversari Nationum Habitus*, published in Padua, 1594–6.

43 Man wearing mourning, from Petri Bertelli's *Diversari Nationum Habitus*, published in Padua, 1594–6.

that date.[141]

At the second funeral of Mary Queen of Scots, at Peterborough Cathedral on 1 August 1587, the same year as Sir Philip Sydney's, the hundred poor men wore mourning coats, 'then followed Mourning Cloaks, two by two a great number; whereof the first were the late Queen's Officers.' More distinguished mourners wore gowns and hoods. This funeral was organised by Sir William Dethick, Garter Knight and principal King of Arms, who drew up a list of 'Allowances of servants and blackes'. 'Every Erle had for himself ten yeardes, two Gentlemen in cloakes' (as his attendants) 'and eight yeomen . . . Every Baron had for himself eight yeards, a Gentleman in a cloake and five yeomen.' Esquires were rationed to five yards of fabric and the company of one yeoman only.[142] These regulations had not changed since the reign of Henry VII except for the new use of mourning cloaks. In the rest of Europe, also, mourning cloaks were the main feature of male mourning dress. In Petri Bertelli's book *Diversari Nationum Habitus* published in Padua in 1594–6, a Venetian nobleman is shown in deepest mourning. He wears what seems to be a full-length, trained cloak rather than a gown. It falls in deep folds to the ground and buttons down the centre front. He wears a sash across his left shoulder and a flat, brimless cap.

# CHAPTER FOUR

# *Mourning Dress 1600–1700*

DURING the seventeenth and eighteenth centuries the custom of wearing mourning dress percolated down to the lesser aristocracy and middle classes, though the Courts of Heralds continued to prosecute those who trespassed on aristocratic mourning dress regulations. The Heralds tried in vain to prevent such infringements, but the rising merchant class – with money but no rank – were determined to compete socially with the nobility. Punishment for their presumption was no deterrent. It did not hold them back from trying again. In the Low Countries the Court of Heralds introduced an edict on 14 December 1616 forbidding commoners the use of honours belonging to nobles (including the dress) in private funeral ceremonies.[143] It was to no avail. In 1668 Jean Helmen, Baron de Willebroeck, and his wife were both prosecuted for wearing over-long trains on their mourning gowns at an uncle's funeral. They were fined 240 florins.[144] The infringements continued, despite the heavy fines.

In the seventeenth century the cut of mourning dress became increasingly fashionable. Men's mourning gowns with their hoods and liripipes (almost the last vestiges of medievalism) fell into disuse by the end of the century. The use of deep red as a mourning colour survived but not in elegant circles. A record of the clothes worn by the wife of a Dutch settler in the New Netherlands, in America, in

1641, mentions amongst various black skirts and camlet jacket, 'a reddish mourning gown, not linen'.[145]

During the first twenty years of the century, female mourning dress, especially that of widows, still retained its late Elizabethan forward-tilted wheel farthingales, padded sleeves, long stomachers and ruffs. Surviving illustrations of the funeral of Elizabeth I in 1603 show the principal female mourners wearing these, beneath huge arched hoods combined with trained mantles. The mantles are lined in white and the stomachers covered with white panels. Less important women wore simpler, waist-length black veils, wired out to avoid the ruffs. The ladies clearly show the front of their hair, which was not concealed beneath the caps.[146]

A useful comparison can be made between the clothes of the College of Herald's 'Countesse in mourninge apparaill'[147] of 1576, and the figure on the tomb of Margaret, Countess of Cumberland, widow of George Clifford, Champion of Elizabeth I, who died in 1616. A carved alabaster effigy of the Countess on her marble tomb in Appleby Parish Church, Cumbria, shows her wearing her coronet of gilded metal and her widow's trained mantle, exactly like the countess of 1576. The barbe, however, has been replaced by a small ruff and fashionable elongated stomacher. The trained surcote has given way to a draped skirt, worn over a padded 'bum-roll'.

By the 1620s fashion had abandoned farthingales and ruffs gave way to lace-edged falling collars. Waists began to rise and sleeves puffed and billowed. A similar softer look was fashionable in mourning dress. Marie de Medici was widowed in 1610 on the assassination of her husband, Henri IV. During the next thirty years she was painted by many of the great portrait painters of her day, always in black. Peter Paul Rubens painted her in 1622, wearing black silk. Her huge white collar is wired out behind her head and matches her plain cuffs. She has discarded fancy lace trimmings. The peak of her black arched head-dress falls over her forehead. She wears a pearl necklace and matching drop earrings. This portrait is in the Prado, Madrid.

Arched hoods finally went out of use in the late 1620s and 1630s. Fashions had become less cumbersome and rigid and so too mourning dress. It was fashionable for widows to be painted in their weeds, and there was a vogue for death-bed paintings. These were commissioned after the wife's death (often in childbirth) and include the entire family gathered around the death bed, dressed in mourning

44  Tomb of Margaret,
Countess of Cumberland,
the widow of George
Clifford, Champion of
Elizabeth I, 1616, showing
widow's mantle with the
countess's coronet and a ruff
instead of a wimple. Church
of St Lawrence, Appleby,
Cumbria. (*National
Monuments Record*)

45  Marie de Medici, about 1630, by François Pourbus.
She wears widow's weeds (but not of deepest mourning
here) for her husband, Henry IV of France, who was
assassinated in 1616. Her black beaded gown has a quilted
bodice and a farthingale beneath. Black transparent
veiling falls from her head, behind her sleeves fastening
on the centre front of the skirt. She wears a black wired and
peaked widow's cap and large pearls on necklace and
bracelets. (*The Prado, Madrid*)

clothes, with the cradle frequently covered with black cloth.

Firle Place, in Sussex, has a detailed widow's portrait by an unknown painter showing Lady Penelope d'Arcy, widow of Sir John Gage, of Firle. He died in 1633 and she wears fashionable mourning dress of the 1630s – a black silk dress, with high waist and white silk undersleeves. The front of her bodice is covered with a pleated white panel, and a transparent white collar. This fastens at the throat with a black ribbon bow. Fashion demanded low décolletage but whilst in mourning the front of their dresses were filled with a fine white 'modesty'. Lady d'Arcy wears the new style of widow's head-dress. The Paris head or Mary Stuart cap, reduced to a mere peak, is worn underneath the veil, falling onto the fore-head, and exposing much more of the hair. This peak in a variety of styles persisted till the end of the seventeenth century. Lady d'Arcy wears hers with fashionable pearl drop earrings and necklace, with her ringlets curling onto her shoulder.

Another style of widow's head-dress was simply a veil, shaped to point over the forehead, and worn without a cap beneath. Henrietta Maria, widow of Charles I, was painted in one of these 'shadow' veils in a portrait probably of 1650.[148] Lady Beauchamp, later Duchess of Beaufort, was painted during the Civil War by Robert

46 Lady Hervey, Penelope d'Arcy, widow of Sir John Gage – about 1635. She wears a peak and veil, black silk dress, and white accessories. Painter unknown. (*By kind permission of Viscount Gage and the Courtauld Institute of Art*)

47 Lady Beauchamp, later Duchess of Beaufort, aged 24, in widow's weeds. Sketch in red chalk by Robert Walker, 1654–7. She wears a peak, veil and pearl drop-earrings. (*By courtesy of the Duke of Beaufort*)

Walker in her widow's weeds. A chalk sketch for this painting dated to 1654–7 and now in the Royal Collection shows her veil and peak, worn with pearl drop earrings. The painting itself is now in the collection of the Duke of Beaufort at Badminton House, Sussex.

During the Puritan 1640s and 50s, ostentation in dress was condemned by the Parliamentarians and Nonconformists. The Quakers, from the seventeenth century, wore their usual brown and grey clothes to funerals. In 1682 George Fox wrote: 'And all you that say, that we Bury like Dogs, because that we have not Superfluous and needless things upon our Coffin and a white and black Cloth with Scutcheons and do not go in Black, and hang Scarfs upon our Hats, and white Scarfs upon our Shoulders and give gold Rings . . . How dare you say that we Bury our People like Dogs, because we cannot Bury them after the vain Pomp and Glory of the World?'[149]

During the second half of the seventeenth century mourning mantles finally dropped out of use. Ladies mourned in black gowns, with extra long trains and fine silk black veils. This can be seen in an engraving in the Library of the Victoria and Albert Museum of the 'Funeral Obsequies of George II, Landgrave of Hesse', which took place in Germany in July 1661. Ladies and girls are attired in deepest mourning. The grandest ladies, supported by two gentlemen, boast long trains. Their heads are covered with hoods down to the eye-brows. The rest of their faces are hidden under a panel drawn up over the nose and falling almost to the ground. On top of all this, a transparent black veil is attached to the back of the hood and thrown over the head, reaching to the ground in the front. The less aristo-cratic women are wearing peaked caps, with shorter veils, or just caps, with their weepers or 'falls' hanging down onto their shoulders. Most of the women are carrying muffs. The similarity between these covered-up widows and today's orthodox Moslem women is most marked.

By the end of the century, both in France and England, the mourning mantle was replaced by the fashionable 'mantua' dresses, with their long stomachers and looped-back skirts. These were adapted for mourning use. They were made in dull black silk, with plain, white linen undersleeves and neck-fills. Black and white caps were worn beneath mourning hoods or veils. A portrait of Katherine Elliott, Dresser and Woman-of-the-Bedchamber to the Duchess of York shows her in widow's weeds. It was painted by John Riley and Johann Baptist Clostermann, and is in the Royal Collection at

48  Sophia Eleonor, widow of George II, Landgrave of Hesse, at her husband's funeral in July 1661, in deepest mourning. (*Victoria and Albert Museum*)

49  Women of the household of George II, Landgrave of Hesse, at his funeral in July 1661 wearing short veils. (*Victoria and Albert Museum*)

Kensington Palace. She wears a black robe, her face is framed with a black mourning hood, and she wears no jewellery. The only touches of white are in her undersleeves and in the white handkerchief she holds in her hand. The painting is dated 1681–3. The National Portrait Gallery in London has a striking portrait of the Duchess of Cleveland, aged sixty-four, grown plump and elderly and wearing deepest mourning for her husband, Lord Castlemaine, in 1705. She, like Katherine Elliott, wears no jewellery, but she does have a smart 'fontange'-style head-dress in plain, white linen with a white hood.

In other parts of Europe these more fashionable styles of mourning wear were slower to be adapted. It was not until the end of the seventeenth century that they were worn in Finland, for example. Until then Finnish ladies in mourning wore plain, black woollen jackets and skirts with black fur caps and veils. The fabric had to be non-figured and dull. Even the nobility were forbidden to wear silk for mourning. Margareta Boiji, whose husband Colonel Henrik Horn was killed in battle in 1629, bought: '16½ ells of fine English

50　Katherine Elliott, about 1681–3, by John Riley and J. B. Closterman. Mrs Elliott was dresser and woman-of-the-bedchamber to the Duchess of York. She is shown here in widow's weeds, with a black hood, black robe, and white undersleeves and handkerchief. (*By gracious permission of H.M. the Queen*)

broadcloth, from a tailor in Riga'.[150] By the 1680s, however, 'mantua'-style dresses were being worn in Stockholm and are described in the accounts of Finnish noblewomen soon after that. Middle-class women economised by wearing their black mantuas to festive and church occasions as well as for mourning.

In the seventeenth century, male mourning wear went through the same transformation as that of women. Mourning cloaks and hats, which had come into use during the reign of Elizabeth I, became very popular. By the 1690s the old-fashioned mourning gowns and hoods finally went out of use and 'even the aristocratic funeral was at long last deprived of its mediaeval appearance.'[151] Phillis Cunnington and Catherine Lucas comment on engravings made at the command of Charles II of the funeral procession of General Monk, Duke of Albermarle, who died in 1670. Mourning gowns with tippeted hoods were worn by the chief mourners and their attendants, such as the canopy and pall-bearers. Other gentlemen wore '. . . new fashions, wearing buttoned coats that reach to

51  The Duchess of Cleveland, after Sir Godfrey Kneller, 1705. The Duchess, aged 64, wears deepest mourning, after the death of her husband, Lord Castlemaine, whom she left in 1662. The Duchess died 47 years later in 1709. (*National Portrait Gallery, London*)

mid-thigh, with wide hats and long hair or wigs.'[152] More usual wear for chief mourners was still the full-length mourning cloak, the train still carried by train-bearers. Less important mourners wore three-quarter length cloaks without trains.

John Aubrey described Sir Kenelm Digby, a resident of Covent Garden, with a reputation as a great dresser, whose wife died in 1633. 'After her death, to avoyd envy and scandall, he retired into Gresham College, London, where he diverted himselfe with his Chymistry . . . He wore a long mourning cloake, a high crowned hatt, his head unshorne, Look't like a Hermite, as signes of sorrowe for his beloved wife.'[153]

Hats replaced the old hoods. Curly-brimmed rigid Elizabethan hats gave way to the wide-brimmed softer 'cavalier' hats, and these in turn gave way to the higher crowned hats of the Restoration. An innovation was the introduction of 'weepers'. This was a hatband, made from a length of black or white silk, wound around the crown with the ends falling down the wearer's back. At the funeral of George II, Landgrave of Hesse, in 1661, the gentlemen's weepers were tied in a bow and fell down to the small of their backs.[154] They were to remain in use for a further two hundred and fifty years and are the best remembered image of the Victorian funeral.

The fundamental rule applied to the mourning dress of both sexes was that everything must be matt and dull. Reflective surfaces were not permitted. To this end, broadcloth and other specially woven dull fabrics, such as crape and paramatta (see Chapter 8) were necessary. Shiny leather shoes were replaced by black 'cloth' shoes, dull black gloves, black waistcoat and coat buttons, black stockings and even dull black sword covers and belts. At the funeral of Henry, Duke of Gloucester, brother of Charles II, in 1660, the coachmen were provided with 'black cloath belts and buckles'. The royal 'trumpettors' carried banners trimmed with black 'jeandam', a twilled cotton cloth, and wore 'black Spanish leather belts'.[155] The Earl of Bedford paid Elizabeth Gladwin, of New Exchange, London, the sum of £1 5s 0d for a mourning belt, in 1663.[156]

For those who could afford them, mourning swords were available. After the death of his father, in 1688, Edmund Verney was presented with a mourning sword by his uncle, John Verney, who described it as 'gentile and fashionable', a good buy, perhaps, at 7s 6d.[157]

A new mourning accessory, which became popular during the Restoration, was the mourning sash or scarf. This was made of dull silk, worn draped diagonally across the left shoulder. As mourning gowns went out of fashion chief mourners took to wearing scarves with their cloaks, ordinary mourners wore only the scarves over their black coats. Black scarves were worn at men's funerals and white scarves at funerals of women and children.

Although the enormously extravagant aristocratic funerals of the late Elizabethan period were no longer de rigueur, funeral expenses were still high. The household of the deceased was still expected to provide gowns or cloaks, scarves, hatbands, and gloves for the chief mourners at the funeral and for the family and servants afterwards. For the funeral of Dixy Taylor, personal attendant to the Earl of Bedford at Woburn Abbey, in 1689, all these garments were provided, as well as twenty-five gallons of claret and fourteen bottles of 'canary'.[158]

In the personal diaries and memoirs of impoverished aristocratic and rising middle-class families, from the seventeenth century onwards, there are constant references to the anxiety and financial problems caused by the cost of fashionable mourning. In 1685, when Charles II died, Edmund Verney, a young student at Trinity College, Oxford, wrote anxiously to his father on 16 February:

> I cannot ffully certifie as yet in this matter, But there are two or three ffellow Commoners of our House of wch Mr Palmer is one, that have bought their Black Cloathes, and Plain Muzeline Bands, and Cloath Shooes, and are now in very strict mourning: and others preparing for it, so that within this weeke I suppose the greater Part, if not all of the university will be in mourning.

Edmund's father wrote back three days later to reassure Edmund that '. . . there would be no such thing as to the Generality, Here and There some particular Persons might be gone into mourning, and That would Bee all.' He added '. . . one swallow or two or three makes no Summer.' The matter was resolved when young Edmund discovered with relief that only those with direct Court connections were obliged to wear mourning.[159]

Edmund's grandfather, Sir Ralph Verney, of Claydon Hall, also received a worried letter on the same subject – from a relative called Alexander Denton. He wrote on 9 February: 'Give me leave to aske whether it be my duty for to goe into mourning . . . being in the

Country, and whether it must be black cloth or Crape. I would not be singular.' Sir Ralph advised that a country squire 'may save the cost of blacks by keeping much at home.'[160]

Samuel Pepys wrote frequently in his dairies, in his younger and poorer days, of his struggles to keep up with mourning dress. On 19 August 1661 Pepys's Aunt Fenner died. The funeral arrangements were conducted from the house of Pepys's father. He was a tailor but as he could not afford to provide his relatives with mourning they did so themselves. Pepys wrote that at the church service his father's family were 'all in mourning, doing him the greatest honour, the world believing that he did give us it.' One month later another aunt died, so that Pepys and his wife continued to wear mourning. He wrote, on 17 October: 'To church, my wife with me, whose mourning is now grown so old that I am ashamed to go to church with her.' In 1663 Pepys went to a friend's funeral 'being in as mourning a dress as we could, at present afford, without cost.'[161]

One of the reasons for the great expense of mourning was not only the cost of good quality broadcloth and black silk, but also the cost of the extra mourning clothes, necessitated by the three official degrees of mourning – full or deep mourning, followed by the second and then by the half-mourning stages. The penalty paid by the less well off for their ambitious desire to emulate aristocratic mourning was the heavy cost of buying all these garments, both for private and for General Court mourning. It was considered demeaning to be seen to skimp. This showed both lack of respect for the dead and lack of respect for the ordained social order. It was the combination of these two emotions which gave mourning regulations such a grip on society. 'She only wants me to wash up her old crape,' wrote Pen Stewkeley in dismay when Lady Penelope Osborne declined to buy new mourning clothes after the death of her husband in 1689.[162]

For First, Full mourning, the strictest rules were applied. No jewellery, no shiny surfaces and only dull black broadcloth, dull silk and crape were permitted. After his brother's death in 1686 Edmund Verney, at Oxford, received £5 for 'a black Cloth sute' and a letter from his father: 'And I have a new black Beavor Hatt for you, wch I will send you next Thursday, in a little deale Box, with a black Crape hatband, Black mourning Gloves, and Stockings and shoe buckles and 3 Payres of black Buttons for wrist and neck. And I have also sent you a new ffrench cordebeck Hatt to save yr Beavor.'

A week later, on 23 February, young Edmund wrote back to his father: 'I have made me a new Black cloth suit, and a new black mourning Gown, which with new muzeline [muslin] Bands and Cloth Shooes will stand me in very near ten pounds.' Five months later on 23 July, Edmund wrote again to his father on the subject of mourning dress. He was still in full mourning. 'I have bought me a new sute of mourning and by reason of the excessive heat of the summer, I was forced to Buy a new crape gown, which will stand me in £02.10.00d, but I have not yet payed for my gown.'[163]

For Second mourning, slightly less austere dress was permitted. Pepys wrote in December 1667: 'To White Hall, where I saw the Duchess of York, in a fine dress of second mourning for her mother, being black, edged with ermine . . .' For those who were meticulous about their mourning dress, many of the accessories had also to be changed from full to Second mourning. Pepys fitted himself out in Second mourning in October 1661. 'To the King's alehouse,' he wrote, 'and thither send for a belt-maker, and bought him a hand-some belt for second mourning, which cost me 24/- and is very neat.' This would have been a sword belt. The next day he put on his 'half black stockings and my new coate of the fashion which pleases me very well.'[164]

After the long months in First and Second mourning, the half-mourning stage afforded some relief, for in addition to black, dull mauve and grey were also permitted. Subdued patterns and even silk fabrics were allowed.

In May 1688 Edmund Verney received his new summer clothes from his father. He wrote in some puzzlement from Oxford, asking why they were in half-mourning colours. His father replied:

Child; you wonder why I made it a half-mourning sute, and that you hoped that none of our relations are dead: to which I answer wee Have lately lost one of our neare Relations, my cosen Pegg Danby . . . And I have made my selfe a halfe mourning sute, and I Declare further, My cosen Winwood is also Deade. But, however, halfe mourning sutes are as much worn, and are as modish as any Thing out of mourning.

Edmund's father sent three patterns of striped cloth suitable for a pair of half-mourning breeches, with a gentle reproof of his son's unwillingness to wear half-mourning: 'I see nobody weare Rich sutes but Souldiers, and Mercantile ffellows.' Edmund won the day, however, and finally persuaded his father to let him have a pair of 'damaske Silke Breeches'.[165]

As well as providing all these expensive garments for close relatives, the household servants, too, had to be put into mourning. The Verney papers, once again, give details of the effort involved. On the death of young Edmund Verney's father, also called Edmund, in 1688, Sir Ralph Verney ordered mourning for the servants. This included 'the manservant, the Coachmen, the Groom, the Carter, the Footman and footboy and little Jacob Hughes, about nine years old, taken out of Charity.' Women servants were not forgotten. 'Two chambermaids, Doll the Cooke & Anne the Dayry Mayd' all received mourning wear. As Edmund Verney had died in debt, Ralph Verney had to pay the expenses.[166]

After the death of his mother, in March 1667, Pepys 'resolved to put myself and wife and Barker [his manservant] and Jane, [their maid] and Hewer and Tom [his other servants] in mourning and my two undermaids, to give them hoods and scarfs and gloves.'[167] In the Low Countries the Court of Heralds was, at this time, prosecuting people of Pepys's class for doing this very same thing. They considered that putting servants into mourning was the exclusive right of the nobility.

The only relief possible for families handing out large sums of money for servants' mourning was the cheaper price (and quality) of servants' dress, and the high esteem in which society would hold them for their expenditure. John Verney's 'portly' coachman, Philip Buckley, had to be given 'two specially large dimity waistcoats at 10s and a pair of mild serge breeches at 11s' when mourning his employer's wife in 1685.[168] In the records of the Lennard and Barnet families, dated to 1694, a manservant was given 'a coat of ordinary black cloath', lined with a woollen fabric called 'shaloon', a pair of black worsted stockings and a fashionable mourning hatband. The black cloth cost 12s a yard.[169]

As well as this private family mourning there was, for those entitled, also Court and General mournings. Court mourning was worn only by those with direct Court connections (as Edmund Verney finally discovered) but General mourning involved everyone who could afford it, from the nobility to the middle classes. By the nineteenth century General mourning was even worn by some of the working classes too. These rules of Court etiquette were the same all over Europe.

In Finland, on the death of King Carl Gustav X, in 1660, instructions were issued that 'all his loyal subjects should dress in mourning as long as the mourning period lasts.' A letter from the Council of State was read to the citizens of Turku, instructing the men to wear black broadcloth and weepers in their hats, and the women to forsake silk, wearing instead homespun or black broadcloth with plain white accessories. All splendour and luxury had to be avoided, dancing and acting were forbidden. Brides and their grooms had to wear black wedding clothes and no jewellery or beads were allowed.[170]

Pepys makes several references to Court mourning in his diaries. On 1 April 1666 Pepys went to Hyde Park to watch the King (Charles II) and the Court ladies in their fine carriages. They were all in mourning for the Queen of Portugal, the mother of Charles's Queen, Catherine of Braganza. Pepys wrote: 'I was sorry to see my Lady Castlemaine; for the mourning forcing all the ladies to go into black, with their hair plain, and without spots [beauty spots], I find her to be a much more ordinary woman than I durst have thought she was, and indeed, is not so pretty as Mrs Stewart.' (Lady Castlemaine and Frances Stewart, later Duchess of Richmond, were both mistresses of the King.)[171]

A few weeks earlier Pepys had himself put on Court mourning. On 11 February 1666 he wrote: 'Up and put on my new black cloth suit to an coat, that I make to be in mourning at Court where they all are, for the King Of Spain.' (Philip IV had died on 17 September 1665.)[172]

By the end of the seventeenth century, mourning dress had slipped down the social ladder to include the middle classes who, in their turn, used it as an opportunity to display their own social standing. The Court of Heralds in Britain finally abandoned their efforts to restrict mourning ritual to the upper classes and a general free-for-all began.

# CHAPTER FIVE ·

# *Mourning Dress 1700–1800*

By the end of the seventeenth century mourning dress had become so fashionable that Samuel Pepys, for one, with his fondness for beautiful women, occasionally found it a positive attraction. In 1666 he commented on the appearance of 'my Lady Falmouth . . . now in second or third mourning and pretty pleasant in her looks.'[173] In the eighteenth century this trend towards fashionable mourning wear continued and the differences between mourning and non-mourning dress narrowed even further. They were both cut to the same style, differing only in colour, fabric and accessories. For women, sack dresses, worn over side-hoops or 'paniers' were fashionable for much of the century. They were cut either in the French style (à la française), with loose pleating falling from the shoulders to the floor at the back, or (à l'anglaise) in the English manner, with the back pleats neatly stitched down as far as the waistline. Trimmings, such as lace ruffles at neck and cuff, embroidered stomachers, silver and gilt lace, appliqué work, and tiny silk aprons, were particularly popular during the Rococo period. None of these were permitted for mourning wear. Mourning dresses had to be in plain, dull black or, more rarely, white fabric.

Fashions in elegant dress changed slowly – the fashion being set by the fabric rather than the cut. French silk collections were brought out biannually in Lyon, to be copied by silk designers all over Europe. The fabrics were enormously expensive and only the wealthiest women could afford seasonal changes in their silk dress fabrics. The cost of a silk dress varied between £10 to well over £60. By today's prices, when top couturiers charge thousands of pounds for an evening dress, this may seem reasonable enough, but it must be remembered that in the 1700s a rich merchant could buy himself a whole house for £500,[174] the equivalent of about twenty dresses for his wife. Even ladies who lived within fashionable society retrimmed their silk dresses with new laces and ribbons to make them last over as many seasons as possible. In the journal of Mrs Papendiek, Assistant Keeper of the Royal Wardrobe, written in the last thirty years of the century, accounts are given of alterations she made to one silk dress over a period of twelve years.[175] It seems likely that mourning dresses would also have been kept and refurbished over many years.

The silk industries of both France and England had a direct influence on mourning wear in the eighteenth century. Manufacturers of silk and fancy dress trimmings lobbied their respective Parliaments declaring that repeated months of official Court mourning was causing a decline in their trades. In France, on 23 June 1716, the length of Court mourning was cut by half, and a further announcement was made on 8 October 1730 shortening it still more.[176] In Britain the Lord Chamberlain tried to help the textile industry by choosing differing fabrics and trimmings for official Court mourning and naming only English-made mourning materials.

In 1765 details of Court mourning in France were published in the *Ordre Chronologique des Deuils de la Cour*, giving precise sartorial instructions. Men were permitted to appear in Court from their first days of mourning, except after the death of a parent from whom they had received an inheritance. Widows, however, had to wait six months before they were allowed to mix again in Court circles, and even then they still had to wear black.[177]

Different rules applied on the death of royalty, when shorter mourning periods were ordered by the Lord Chamberlain in France and the Earl Marshal in Britain. In Britain, by the 1880s, twelve weeks mourning were ordered on the death of a king or queen, six weeks after the death of a son or daughter of the sovereign, three weeks for the monarch's brother or sister, two weeks for royal nephews, nieces, uncles or aunts, and ten days for first cousins of the royal family. Foreign sovereigns were mourned for three weeks and their relatives for a shorter time.[178] Each of these periods was divided up into full, or First, and Second Court mourning. For First mourning, everything had still to be black, dull and plain. Black bombazine dresses were trimmed with black crape, black silk hoods, and plain white linen was worn with black shammy leather shoes, gloves and crape fans. No jewellery was permitted.[179] Second mourning consisted of black silk dresses, trimmed with fringed or plain linen, with white gloves, black or white shoes, fans and tippets and white necklaces and earrings.[180] For less formal or 'Undress' occasions 'white or grey lustrings, tabbies and damasks' were considered suitable.[181]

Instructions were no less careful for men. For First Court mourning the rule was black woollen suits, without fashionable buttons on sleeves or pockets. Plain muslin or lawn cravats instead of shirt frills and lace cuffs replaced plain white 'weepers'. Black woollen stockings, shammy shoes, gloves, crape hatbands and special black swords and shoe buckles completed the costume. For Second mourning fringed linen was permitted.[182]

General or public mourning was also ordered after a royal death, as in the seventeenth century, periods varying according to the status of the deceased. Foreign royalty too was publicly mourned. King George II died on 25 October 1760. On 1 November Parson Woodforde 'had a suit of Mourning for the King brought home this very night.' On 25 January 1761 his family 'went into second mourning for his Late majesty.'[183] Ready-to-wear clothes were yet to come and tailors received a rush of orders after the announcement of public mourning. Coats and breeches were excellently cut and sewn, unlike women's dresses, with their rather haphazard sleeve settings. Tailors and their apprentices must have worked long, additional hours to complete their orders on time.

Due to the rising social aspirations of the lower middle classes, public mourning was now displayed by an even wider social range than in the previous century. Mourning dress was creeping one step further down the social ladder – to the disgust of the higher classes. 'Women of inferior Rank, such as Tradesmen's wives behind the Compter should make no Alteration in their Dress since it cannot arise . . . but from a meer Affection of the Mode at St. James's,' declared the *Universal Spectator* in 1731.[184]

Those who could not afford to buy new mourning clothes, but were anxious to keep up appearances, took their ordinary clothes to a professional silk dyer to be dyed black with Indian logwood. The ledgers of Mark Thornhill Wade, a silk dyer of Berwick Street, Soho, show that in 1789 a Mrs Davis of Titchfield Street sent a 'silk handy [neck fichu], 4 bundles of lustg [silk lustring], a small sarsnett cloak, 11 yards ribbon and 1 glove' to be dyed black.[185]

The family of Jedediah Strutt, a well-known nonconformist textile manufacturer, whose business was based on his invention of a ribbed knitting machine, resorted to the use of dyeing ordinary clothes black, after the death of Mrs Elizabeth Strutt in 1774. She died in London on 11 May 1774 whilst on a visit away from her home in Derby. Jedediah Strutt was left with five children, the two youngest boys, George and Joseph, aged thirteen and eight. It was their clothes that caused the problem. Their eldest brother William wrote to Jedediah, who remained in London: 'We stopt George's and Joe's Blue [suits] being cut off when we heard my Mother was so dangerously ill.' The boys were given new black suits instead of the blue ones but this soon proved inadequate. Their sister Elizabeth wrote to her father sometime later in that month: 'As my Brs. George and Joe had but one suit of cloaths each & have wore them every day they begin to look shabby for Sundays & will not last them all the summer. I was thinking that if George's green and Joe's brown ones could be dyed they would do to wear every day & save buying them another suit.'[186] This seems to have resolved the problem.

Guild members, such as master craftsmen and their employees, received payments to help defray the cost of funerals. Some may have been able to afford to buy or at least dye clothes black. In the countryside better-off farmers would have worn plain mourning clothes. Amongst the poorer artisans in town and country, it seems probable that 'best' or Sunday dress would have been worn at funerals. As these were usually in drab or dark colours they would have been considered perfectly respectable. At the poorest levels of society, in both town and country, mourning dress was an impossible luxury. In the churchyards of London, in 1721, paupers were buried in large communal graves, which were left open as long as there was room for one more corpse.[187] In these circumstances the use of mourning dress by their relatives was out of the question. The servant classes, however, did wear mourning on the deaths of members of their employer's family, because it was given to them on the occasion of a family death, though not for their own private bereavements. Servants' mourning was made of cheaper fabrics – upper female servants wearing a type of inexpensive bombazine (twilled silk and worsted), whilst the lower female servants wore 'bombazet' a still cheaper twilled mixture of cotton and wool. [188] On the occasion of his own father's funeral in 1771, Parson James Woodforde fitted William Corpe, a family servant, with 'a black crape Hatband and buckles and a black broad cloth Coat and waistcoat.' [189] After her mother's death in 1774 Elizabeth Strutt gave one of her women servants a crape gown. This particular servant was already owed two gowns as part of her wages. Elizabeth Strutt hoped that the crape garment would be accepted as part of the debt, 'unless we choose to take that one for another servant and then she will expect two.' [190]

One of twelve paintings by Joseph Highmore, painted in 1745, to illustrate Samuel Richardson's novel, *Pamela*, shows the heroine wearing mourning dress for her deceased mistress. Pamela was a country girl, who became a rather superior lady's maid, having been taught to write and cost accounts by her mistress. Young Squire B (whom she finally marries) 'has given mourning and a year's wages to all my lady's servants . . . and he ordered the housekeeper to give me mourning with the rest,' Pamela writes. [191] In the painting 'Mr B Coming Upon Pamela Writing a Letter', Pamela is shown seated 'in my late lady's dressing room', wearing a plain but stylish black robe, tied across the front bodice with black ribbons. She has a white petticoat and a small, frilled white cap, trimmed with black ribbons.

52 'Mr B. finds Pamela writing', Joseph Highmore, 1743–4. Pamela wears fashionable servant's mourning, after the death of her mistress. (*Tate Gallery, London*)

53 Princess Augusta, the widow of the Prince of Wales, wearing a white mourning dress and black veil. Her husband's portrait hangs beside her. The picture by George Knapton is entitled 'The family of Frederick, Prince of Wales', 1751. (*By gracious permission of H.M. the Queen*)

In the Low Countries the acrimonious feuding between the Court of Heralds and rising middle classes continued, particularly over the provision of mourning dress for servants. The King of Arms, André Joseph Jaevens, reprimanded social climbers for putting their servants into brown or 'gris de Moor' (grey) mourning as a means of evading the sumptuary law against giving them black clothes. In 1713 a lawyer called Jacques van Ockerhaut was taken before the Procureur-Général in Bruges for flouting the regulations at the funeral of his brother-in-law. Not only had the cut of his child's coat been too long, but he had also dared to have straw strewn over the streets from the house to the church, and, furthermore, had put his female servants into mourning, causing much public outcry.[192]

The mourning dress of those who were privileged to attend Court was eagerly copied by a widening circle of society. The increasingly complicated rules caused mounting consternation which reached a crisis by the nineteenth century. There were, in the eighteenth century, no women's fashion magazines to give advice. The social magazines and newspapers published details only of Court Mourning Orders, however, and anxious letters were sent to relatives living in London, Paris and the big cities asking for guidance and for mourning fabrics to be purchased and sent to them in the country. After the death of George II in 1760 this reply was sent to relatives of the Williamson family living in Bedfordshire.

My wife hath bought 28 yards of crape for it is equally worn with bombazine. You desire three yards of gauze; it is not the thing. Muslin is the wear and that is 10/- a yard. As the mourning is meant to be as deep as possible, women's hats are plain black silk with crape around the crown, with a bow knot and their silk cloaks of the genteelest should be garnished at the bottom with ditto crape not love ribbon.[193]

The cost of all this was high, but that was the essence of the allure. Mourning dress and etiquette did have royal origins and connections. Loyal citizens were glad to have the opportunity to show off not only their social savoir faire but also their patriotism.

A detailed description of a French noble widow's mourning dress is given in the *Ordre Chronologique des Deuils de la Cour*, of 1765. A widow is instructed to wear mourning for one year and six weeks, with the first six months in black wool, or *ras de Saint-Maur*. Her dress was cut with a train and 'turned back with a braid attached to the side of the skirt, which was pulled òut through the pockets.[194] This style was know as *robe retrousée dans les poches* and can be seen in many eighteenth-century portraits. The overskirt is turned to the back and lifted up, gracefully revealing the petticoat beneath. The centre front 'robings' were joined with hooks or ribbons. The cuffs were cut with one fold and deep hems. A crape belt was tied at the front to hold the pleating at the waist in place, leaving the two ends hanging down to the hem of the skirt. Correct accessories included a crape shawl, gloves, shoes with metallic-bronzed buckles, a black, woollen muff and a black crape fan. Head-dresses of both white batiste and black crape are mentioned.

Court mourning similar to this is shown in a portrait attributed to Pierre Gobert of Louise Françoise, Duchess of Bourbon, daughter of Madame de Montespan and Louis XIV, now in the Tours Museum. She wears white mourning, probably for her husband, Louis III of Condé, who died in 1701, the year that the portrait was painted. Her white veil reaches to the floor and is worn over a white hood, with what appears to be a cap beneath. Her black dress is trimmed with deep fur 'robings' (probably miniver) and matching cuffs. The long train is lined with fur and she wears a black belt with its ends hanging down the front of her skirt. She holds a large white handkerchief in her hand. These are frequently shown in portraits of widows.

The weeds of a middle-class widow are shown in a portrait of Hogarth's mother, Mrs Anne Hogarth, painted by the artist in 1735, the year before she died. This was once in the David Rothschild collection but its whereabouts are now unknown. Mrs Hogarth wears a totally plain black dress with fashionable pleated cuffs. Her white cap has 'falls' which hang down onto her breast and on top of the cap she wears what seems to be another black hood with 'falls'. Two rings on her left hand – possibly a wedding and a mourning ring – are her only pieces of jewellery. The painting is markedly stark and sombre.

The Textile Department of the Victoria and Albert Museum has a rare album of dress fabric patterns dating from 1746–1826 (T 219/1973), which throws light on exactly what type of mourning

54   French court mourning. Louise, Duchess of Bourbon, eldest daughter of Madame de Montespan and Louis XIV, in white mourning for her husband Louis III de Condé, 1701. Painting attributed to Pierre Gobert. (*Musée de la Ville de Tours*)

55 Mrs Anne Hogarth, in deep mourning for her husband, 1735. Painted by her son, William Hogarth. (*By kind permission of Mrs Evelyn Antal*)

fabrics were worn by middle-class women in the second half of the eighteenth century. The album was put together at the time by a Miss Barbara Johnson, using an old accounts ledger. She pinned and glued onto the pages examples of her dress fabrics, with information on prices, fabric names, yardage and dates, filling up the remaining spaces on the pages with cuttings of fashion plates and engravings of country houses, taken from ladies' pocket books and albums of the period. The fabrics include a wide range of block-printed chintzes and linens, wool serges, silk lustrings, sarsnets, taffetas and figured brocades, all still amazingly light, fresh and bright, with the exception of the mourning samples. None of the figure brocades seem to be of the highest quality, heavyweight fabrics fashionable for society women in the middle of the eighteenth century. They were probably beyond the middle-class price range that Miss Johnson could afford. The fabrics she herself used whilst in mourning varied from heavy black wool to delicate white silks and are listed here in date order:

'A grey poplin long sack, mourning for the Prince of Wales,

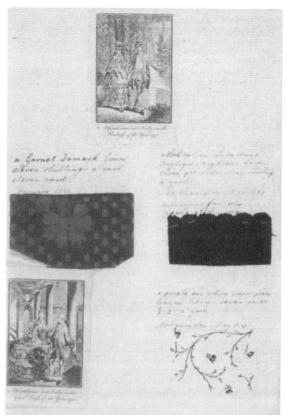

56 & 57 Details from the Barbara Johnson album, 1746–1826. *Above:* The page for January to May, 1771. *Below:* The page for August to January, 1779. (*Victoria and Albert Museum*)

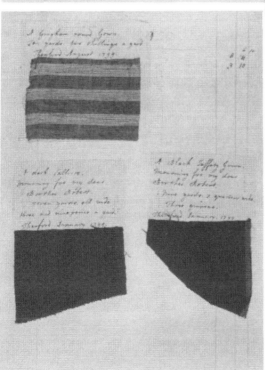

March 1751. 14 yards. 2.6 a yard.' This is a medium weight, mid-grey silk and wool fabric.

'A black stuff gown mourning for the Prince of Wales.' A heavy, scratchy wool fabric in deep black, for deepest mourning.

'A grey figur'd stuff long sack second mourning for my grandmother. 1753. 18 yards.' This is a fine, mid-grey wool fabric with diamond-shaped brocaded motifs. A sack dress was a loose-backed gown.

'A black stuff short sack, mourning for my father. 1756. 14 yds. a shilling a yard.' A heavyweight, scratchy, deep black woollen fabric for deepest mourning.

'A white lutestring night gown, second mourning for my father. 1756. 12 yards. 4.6 a yard, half ell wide.' A silk lustring with a fine crisp finish. A night-gown was a type of informal evening gown.

'A grey stuff negligee, second mourning for my father. 1756. 12 yards. 1.4 a yard.' A fine medium-grey woollen fabric, made up into an informal day gown.

'A bombazeene negligee, mourning for my mother. Feb. 1759. 26 yards. 2s a yard. Given me by my Br. Johnson.' A deep black bombazine in silk and wool, and heavyweight. As Miss Johnson's father had already died, her brother would have undertaken the funeral arrangements, including the provision of mourning fabrics for his relatives.

'A dark grey tabby gown 1759 mourning for my mother.' A mid-weight silk with fine rib. By December of the same year, Miss Johnson had put away her mourning and ordered a 'scarlet Stuff gown', in an astonishingly bright shade of orange-red wool.

'A black Italian Lutestring negligee, May 1771, 18 yards 3 ells wide. 7 shillings a yard. Mourning for my Uncle Johnson. Northampton.' This is a fine, crisp white silk.

'A purple and white copper plate linnen gown, seven yards. 3.2 a yard May 1771.' A fine line printed with a delicate design of meandering sprigs in deep mauve.

'A Stormont Cotten Gown and petticoat, ten yards, two shillings a yard. April 1788, mourning for Aunt Johnson.' A medium weight cotton printed with a tiny repeat speckled design in grey and mauve, the colours of half mourning.

'A dark callicoe, mourning for my dear brother Robert. 7 yds. ell wide. 3 and ninepence a yard. Thenford. Jan. 1799.' This is a medium-weight calico printed with small black rosettes on a mauve

58 Mrs Salusbury, about 1766, by Johann Zoffany. Hester Mary Salusbury had been widowed for four years when this portrait was painted. It passed into the family of the Earl of Shelburne, through Mrs Salusbury's daughter, Mrs Thrale, later Mrs Piozzi. (*By kind permission of Earl of Shelburne*)

ground. The last three fabrics listed here show the growing use of cotton fabric for women's dresses from about 1770.

'A black taffety gown, mourning for my dear brother Robert. Nine yards, three quarters wide. 3 guineas. Thenford. Jan. 1799.' A crisp silk with a fine rib.

'A black Chambery muslin, seven yards, have a crown a yard. Made at Bath. June 1808, mourning for my dear friend Mrs Woodhull.' A delicate almost transparent black silk warp and cotten wefted fabric, which reflects the use of lighter weight fashion fabrics in the early nineteenth century.

'A bombazeene gown. Ten yards, 4.3 a yard, mourning for my dear brother Johnson. Made at Thenford. Feb. 1814.' This is a medium-weight, deep black, silk and wool fabric, noticeably finer than the bombazine Miss Johnson used in 1759.

'A black twill'd Sarsnet gown. Twelve yards. Made at Thenford, mourning for the Duchefs of York. Aug 13. 1820.' A very lightweight, finely ribbed, black silk.

Miss Johnson's choice of fabrics reflects the trends in fashionable fabrics from 1746 onwards. By the 1760s elements of neo-classicism began to creep into women's fashions. Rococo-style flowers and elaboration gave way gradually to simpler striped or smaller motifs, in lighter weight silks and cotton. Plain materials became popular. Side hoops were discarded. After the portrait of Marie Antoinette in a simple wide-sashed muslin dress was exhibited by Mme Vigée le

59 Hogarth engraving for a funeral invitation, 1730–50, showing male mourners. (*By gracious permission of H.M. the Queen*)

*You are desired to Accompany y͠ Corps of*      *from*
*h late Dwelling in*      *to*
*on*      *next at*      *of the Clock in the Evening.*

*Perform'd by Humphrey Drew Undertaker in King-street Westminster.*

Brun at the Paris Salon in 1783, *chemises a la reine* became all the rage. Many of these changes passed into mourning clothes.

About 1799 Johann Zoffany painted Mrs Salusbury standing in front of a portrait of her husband who had died in 1762. Her black silk skirt and bodice reflect the current fashions for ruched silk trimmings and finer fabric. However, she wears unfashionable full-length sleeves, and large buttons instead of an elegant stomacher fasten her bodice. Her hair is hidden from view beneath a white cap, with box-pleated edging framing her face. A transparent black veil reaches to the floor. She holds a large white handkerchief in her hand. This painting is in the collection of the Earl of Shelburne at Bowood House, Wiltshire and was shown in the Zoffany exhibition at the National Gallery annexe in Carlton House Terrace, in 1977.

Men's mourning suits were cut to the same style as their ordinary clothes. By the middle of the century coat skirts had become flared by the addition of pleats in the side and back seams. By the 1770s a slimmer line was once again fashionable. Silks, velvets and coloured woollen cloth, embroidered or trimmed with gold and silver braid and lace for the aristocracy, gave way to black woollen cloth for First mourning. French etiquette was followed, down to the use of black shoe buckles and sword covers. For Second mourning black silk suits and stockings were permitted, though many seemed to prefer wearing grey. Henry Purefoy, who wrote to his tailor in 1751, 'I desire you will come here as soon as maybe to take measure on mee for a suitt of second mourning and to bring patterns of Cloath with you. Pray let the patterns be fine fast cloath. The grey Breetches you made mee are too shallow in the Seatt and must be let out.'[195]

For the funeral itself chief mourners still wore black cloth mourning cloaks, their trains graded according to the rank of the wearer. Black hats were knotted with hatbands, in black or white. These also varied according to the status of the mourner. Parson Woodforde mentions three varieties of bands. At his mother's funeral, in 1766, 'we all had Crepe Hatbands.' At his father's burial in 1771 William Corpe, his chief male servant, had a crape hatband, although the pall-bearers and the clerk had black silk bands. The Parson noted with some disapproval that at the funeral of the local squire, in 1775, 'The Mourners had only sattin Hatbands and gloves, still it was a handsome funeral.'[196] The 'falls' of the hatbands fell down the wearers' backs.

Shoulder scarves or sashes were worn at funerals by the less important mourners. Men, as well as women, wore white accessories at the burial of a woman or child. Mourning armbands are mentioned in eighteenth-century orders for military wear, but were not yet used by civilians. A Gazette issued on 20 May 1775 stated: 'His Majesty does not require that the Officers of the Army should wear any other mourning, on the present melancholy occasion, than a black crape round their left arm with their uniforms.'[197]

Britain during the eighteenth century saw the victory of the middle classes in their struggle to wear mourning dress based on aristocratic lines.

In the Low Countries, however, the Court of Heralds did not give up the fight until the end of the eighteenth century. In 1754 Empress Marie-Therese ordered the strict observance of the edict of 1616 on sumptuary mourning rules, including the order that black swords and scarves were only to be used by the noble or enobled. Prosecutions continued right up to the Revolutionary period in France – till 1781, although they gradually became rarer. Infringements were made by such highly placed families that the government thought it unwise to antagonise them.[198]

# CHAPTER SIX

# *Mourning Dress 1800–1910*

As the nineteenth century opened the passion for fashionable mourning dress flourished undimmed. It continued to slide gently down the social ladder – now permeating the ranks of the middle classes until by the early twentieth century it had finally reached the very poorest levels of society. This process caused no diminution of interest within wealthy families. It seemed, on the contrary, to make them redouble their own efforts in a final attempt to demonstrate their social superiority.

Victorian society was a society under pressure. The middle classes, many of them extremely rich from trading and industrial profits, pushed against the social barriers which kept them out of high society. Long established 'society' families, headed by the Royal Family, were determined to maintain the traditional barriers separating the aristocracy from those 'in trade'. This pressure seemed to reach bursting point during the reign of Queen Victoria, when the richest families of the new industrial middle classes had both the wealth and the will to fight the battle for social recognition and acceptance by the aristocracy.

Presentation at Court and access to Court circles was the dream of every socially ambitious family. It was usually a pipe-dream for the Court kept its distance most carefully from the trading classes' outside. The Court ruling was explicit – to debar anyone with trade connections. Even in Edward VII's more tolerant reign in the early years of the present century, 'Lucile', Lady Duff Gordon, 'lost caste terribly' when she opened her own haute couture business. She wrote in 1932: 'I was told that nobody would know me if I "kept a shop". It would be bad enough for a man but for a woman it meant social ruin . . . I could never be presented at Court, because I was in "Trade".'[199] Her husband Sir Cosmo Duff Gordon was admitted but she was not.

The unattainable Court goal denied them, the middle classes had to make do with more achievable social ambitions. They copied all the minutiae of Court behaviour within their own social circle in the hope that this gave them added social distinction. Every detail of aristocratic etiquette was assiduously copied by families who could afford to do so, and in many cases, by families who could not. The nouveau riche bought and built castles in Scotland and clapped their servants into fancy liveries. The wives organised a social round hopefully based on artistocratic practice. Every nuance of Court etiquette was endlessly probed in the new middle-class women's magazines. Every fad and fashion of the aristocratic world was reproduced as carefully as possible in middle-class homes. The women, in order to be ladies, had to be kept in a state of obvious idleness – they could not possibly be allowed to work. It was bad enough that their fathers and their husbands had connections with trade. The idea that a woman should want to work was, in Lady Duff Gordon's words, 'only one shade better than going in for crime.'[200]

There was, however, a small minority of upper and middle-class women who did wish to work. As for the poor, their women always had worked. Those middle-class women who were forced to take up paid employment, usually through widowhood or unexpected poverty, were often regarded as social outcasts. In the 1860–90 period a few, usually from socially advanced families, entered eagerly into the slowly opening world of medicine, academic life, literature and even politics, but most Victorian women confined themselves to social manoeuvring convinced that, in a man's world, this was their allotted function in life. The aim was to use their energy and personal charms to achieve social success for their families. They tried by every means to gain access to the next step up the social ladder and organised their otherwise idle lives accordingly. Such elevation could be achieved through marriage, business connections or, with a little luck, through social contacts. Charity and church functions were particularly useful in this context, because they permitted a certain relaxation of the rules of etiquette and thus a wider mix of social groupings. They also kept the lower classes firmly in their place – they were there to be provided with charity.

The importance of the royal influence on Victorian mourning etiquette was supreme. In the class conscious, middle-class suburbs, two elements combined to produce such a desirable example that few could resist it. First, all the elaborate etiquette of family funerals derived from satisfactorily ancient royal usage. Secondly, following the sudden death by typhoid of Prince Albert in 1861, the much respected Queen wore mourning dress for the remaining forty years of her life. Her example was copied by many of her middle-class subjects. They might be shut out of high society but they could copy exactly the dress of the Queen herself, for families found themselves frequently going through mourning periods. It was Victoria, the middle-class ideal of Christian widowhood, who fanned the cult of mourning, spreading it to all classes of society during her lifetime. After Albert's death she shrouded herself in crape-covered black clothes, her face behind a black veil. She wore versions of these weeds all the rest of her life, the only difference in her dresses being in her waist measurements. She turned away from the gently fashionable clothes she wore when Albert was alive. Neither the fetching bustles of the 1870s with their tied-back skirts, nor even the imposing leg-of-mutton sleeves of the 1890s, could tempt her out of her plainly cut garments. Later photographs show her as increasingly stout but always in black, white or shades of half-mourning. Her first and last widow's dresses survive in the costume collection of the Museum of the City of London. The first, with the full 'bishop' sleeves and wide skirt of the early 1860s, is entirely covered in black crape. The last, also in black, bears no resemblance at all to the elegant S-bend styles of the early 1900s.

During the 1850–90 period mourning became such a cult that hardly anyone dared defy it. It was like the story of 'The Emperor's New Clothes' – few were bold enough to speak out openly against it. Mourning wear was considered so essential a part of a lady's wardrobe that upper-class women were never without it. Social ostracism – the dread of every Victorian and Edwardian lady – could be caused through the absence of the correct black or half-mourning wear. As late as 1904, Mary Spencer Warren wrote in the *Ladies*

*Realm* of problems that might arise when staying or visiting a country house when royalty was present. She warned that, as well as taking all the correct outfits such as walking, afternoon, dinner and ball gowns,

> they should not, at the same time, omit to take both mourning and half mourning. King Edward and Queen Alexandra are so closely allied to so many foreign courts, rendering occasions for mourning frequent and often sudden, while news is so quickly transmitted that one is never sure when mourning may be demanded and it is etiquette that when visiting where the King and Queen are present every guest must appear in exactly the same degree of mourning or half-mourning. This also applies to those who may be invited to dinner and are not staying in the house.[201]

This image of the unprepared visitor sitting alone in her room unable to go down to dinner with the King and Queen because she did not have the correct clothes to wear was a warning meant to terrify the social backslider.

This tradition still survives today. The late Lady Hilbery, wife of Lord Hilbery, a High Court judge, used to travel on circuit with her husband all over England. She always took with her a complete set of mourning wear, including black shoes, stockings and hat to wear in case there had been a death amongst colleagues at the Bar or amongst municipal dignitaries. She kept this practice up from the 1930s through to her husband's death in the 1960s. It was reported in the *Sunday Times Magazine* on 7 May 1978 that on his State visit to Brazil in 1978, Prince Charles also took a set of mourning clothes amongst his luggage. This should come as no surprise, because as we have seen it is within Court circles that the etiquette of mourning has always been most carefully maintained.

One important new development in the nineteenth century which contributed to the spreading of mourning dress was the publication of fashion magazines. The last thirty years of the eighteenth century saw the increased production of ladies' albums, pocket books and companions, which sometimes featured advice and illustrations of the latest fashions. From the first half of the nineteenth century fashion magazines were printed in increasingly large numbers, with bi-weekly or monthly editions, showing the latest French fashions in their hand-coloured fashion plates. Many magazines included advice and illustrations of mourning dress, particularly if the Royal

60 Court mourning for Queen Victoria, from the *Ladies Field*, 2 February 1901.

*Left:* Day costume 'of faille, trimmed with crêpe: blouse of black chiffon.'

*Centre:* Evening gown 'of soft silk chiffon and crêpe.'

*Right:* Gown of 'fine cashmere and crêpe: flounce of pleated silk.'

Courts were in mourning. By the middle of the century large numbers of magazines were being produced both in Europe and in America at a price that middle-class families could afford and advice on mourning etiquette and mourning fashion plates were featured constantly. These magazines set the standards which dominated the lives of respectable Victorian housewives. The pages are full of information on the latest fabrics and accessories and replies to readers problems, many of which turned around the intricacies of mourning etiquette. The strictures laid down in these magazines fanned the cult of mourning throughout the middle classes, particularly in the second half of the century.

The wealthiest and most fashionable women had their mourning clothes made up by Court or private dressmakers, according to the usual instructions still issued by the Lord Chamberlain on the occasion of a royal death or that of a national leader. Court mourning was still considerably longer than General mourning, which was now worn by a widening circle of the general public. These official periods of mourning applied to countries which observed European mourning traditions. This included all the Royal Courts of Europe,

61  Julia Bock, 1863, by Jozef Simmel, in the Wilanow Palace, Warsaw. She wears General mourning after the defeat of Poland in 1863 by the Russians; black earrings, black coral pendant, bracelet of a cross and chain and an iron wedding ring. (*By courtesy of Bozena Seredyňska, Warsaw*)

from Russia to Scandinavia, as well as the new Republics of France and the United States of America. An unusual use of General mourning took place in Poland in 1863, after the defeat of an insurrection against the rule of the Russian Tsar, Alexander II. Society women wore black mourning clothes for quite a long time afterwards, as a symbol both of private grief for personal loss and also as an expression of nationalism and sorrow for their loss of freedom. Two portraits, both by Josef Simmler, survive in the collection at Wilanow Palace, outside Warsaw, which show Julia Simmlerova and Julia Bock in fashionable black General mourning dresses of the early 1860s with white satin, lace and black mourning jewellery.

Family mourning followed the same lines as Court mourning, though now, with the help of fashion plates, ladies in London, Edinburgh, Berlin, Warsaw, Vienna, New York, Melbourne and elsewhere, were able to satisfy themselves that their mourning clothes were replicas of those worn by the belles of Paris. Less well-off women used the services of cheaper dressmakers and by the middle of the century began to buy most of their mourning at the new mourning warehouses. Some would have made their own outfits or dyed coloured dresses and accessories black. Many women continued to put away their mourning clothes to bring out when they were needed but the crape manufacturers and mourning businesses encouraged the belief that it was unlucky to keep crape in the house when not in mourning and this sensible practice went out of use. When Jane Austen's brother-in-law died in 1808, she wrote to her sister that: 'I am to be in bombazeen and crape . . . My mourning will not impoverish me, for by having my velvet pelisse fresh lined and made up. I am sure I shall have no occasion this winter for anything new of that sort . . . My bonnet is to be silk covered in crape.'[202] The ever-resourceful Becky Sharp is described by Thackeray as she put together a mourning outfit, as 'busy cutting, ripping, stripping and tearing all sorts of black stuffs available for the melancholy occasion.'[203]

The country poor would have done their best to appear as decently

62  Anti-clerical cartoon of about 1815 showing a country funeral. Mourners wear their ordinary clothes, patched and worn in browns, greens, pinks and white. The vicar wears his surplice over his hunting clothes, with his spurs on and his riding crop beneath his arm. The sexton and church officers wear black. (*By kind permission of Raymond Watkinson*)

as possible at funerals in their best Sunday clothes of dark-coloured wool, linen and cotton. They would probably still not have owned special mourning clothes. A print produced in about 1815 shows a country funeral with the parson in his white surplice and the mourners with no signs of mourning on their clothes at all. However, when Princess Charlotte, the only child of George IV, died so suddenly and shockingly in 1817 giving birth to her still-born son, mourning was widespread thoughout the country. Charlotte was the most popular member of the Royal Family and large numbers of commemorative souvenirs were produced and sold after her death, from prints, sermons, poems and tea services to the huge marble sculpture erected by public subscription in St George's Chapel, Windsor. Mourning dress was worn by all who could afford it. Lord Holland who was travelling from Dover to London at the time, noticed that everyone on the road, including the postboys and turnpike men wore 'signs of mourning on their persons.'[204] There would almost certainly have been fewer signs of mourning amongst the urban poor of the new industrial cities. Living conditions were so appalling that mourning dress was a luxury well beyond the pockets – though not the aspirations – of the poor. Dr John Ferriar reported that in Manchester, as early as 1805, he visited sick patients living in 'damp, ill-ventilated cellars . . . where a candle is required even at noon-day to examine a patient. I have seen the sick without bedsteads, lying in rags. They can seldom afford straw.'[205] They could certainly not afford to buy mourning dress either, though with the growth of Burial and Friendly Societies in the nineteenth century they may have been able to borrow dress in order to perform the ritual as dictated by respectable society. Generally the use of mourning dress remained beyond the means of many working class families until the end of the century.

At the other end of the social ladder, however, ladies applied their energies to choosing the most elegant and socially correct styles of mourning, made up at the start of the century in the new neo-classical styles. Every new flicker of fashion detail was now reflected in the smartest mourning dresses – the use of padded hems, the new sleeve puffs or 'jockies' from Paris, and touches of neo-gothick decoration. On the death of Princess Charlotte the fashion magazines issued special mourning plates and the Lord Chamberlain ordered official Court mourning: 'Court mourning for Her Royal Highness Princess Charlotte', on 7 November 1817 announced that 'the Ladies to wear black bombazines, plain muslins or long lawn crape hoods, shammy shoes and gloves and crape fans. The Gentlemen to wear black cloth without buttons on the sleeves or pockets, plain muslin or long lawn cravats and weepers [white cuffs] shammy shoes and gloves, crape hatbands and black swords and buckles.' Dark grey frock coats were considered suitable for undress wear. Two months later instructions were given for the second stage of Court mourning. Ladies were now allowed to wear black silk fabric, with fringed or plain linen, white gloves, black shoes, fans and tippets, white necklaces and earrings, with white or grey lustrings, tabbies or damasks – all types of lightweight silks – for undress wear. Men's wear was unchanged. In the Third and final stage of mourning, women were permitted the use of black silk and velvet, coloured ribbons, fans and tippets and even plain white or white and gold or white and silver stuffs with black ribbons. By that time men too could wear white and gold or silver brocaded waistcoats with their black suits.[206]

Ackerman's *Repository of Arts* featured a whole series of black dresses after Charlotte's death – evening, walking, and carriage clothes – because, of course, a society lady would have altered her whole wardrobe for such an important death. The *Respository* featured a half-mourning dress in the edition of January 1819, all in white, with a matching hat trimmed with ostrich feathers, a black shawl and a black necklace and earrings.

Black, full-mourning bombazine, a mixture of silk and wool which was absolutely de rigueur for deepest mourning, must have been a most unfashionable fabric at this period, when fashion decreed lightweight, floaty muslins, silks and fine wools. Miss Johnson's album of dress fabric samples, in the Victoria and Albert Museum, shows that a lighter weight type of mourning bombazine was available in the early years of the nineteenth century and that lightweight Chambery muslin in silk and cotton and fine silk sarsenets were also used for mourning purposes.

The fundamental rules, however, remained unchanged – nothing about mourning dress, either for men or women, must shine or gleam. Dull bombazine existed for exactly this reason, as did mourning crape. Men removed all their gilt buttons, buckles and Court swords, as in the seventeenth century and replaced them with dull black ones. Men continued to wear mourning cloaks to funerals well into the nineteenth century until they were replaced with diagonal

63 (*left*) Half-mourning evening dress, January 1819, from Ackerman's *Repository of Arts*.

64 (*above*) Mourning bonnet, about 1840–50, trimmed with black crape on black satin (Royal Pavilion, Art Gallery and Museum of Brighton), with black crape veil (Worthing Museum and Art Gallery).

shoulder sashes in black or white crape. An illustration of the funeral of Emperor Alexander I of Russia, at St Petersburg, on 13 May 1826, shows the chief male mourners, including the Duke of Wellington, representing George IV, wearing full-length mourning cloaks with shallow-crowned, wide-brimmed, circular hats. The black weepers fall over the brim on to the shoulders.

Widows continued to wear plain black dresses, though now in the neo-classical style, with black and white accessories. Their hair had still to be completely covered and 'a plain close-fitting white cambric cap, with a very narrow border, crimped each side of the face and plain across the forehead: above it a small black silk hood, with a narrow lace border.'[207] Black cloaks and bonnets, with long, black crape veils thrown over the top and hiding the face were worn outdoors. Brighton Museum had a black satin 'poke' bonnet in its collection, dating from about 1835–40, with two deep tucks of black crape around the edge of the brim, a neat ruched crape trimming on the crown and a large crape bow to secure the hat beneath the chin. It would have been worn on top of a frilled white cap, so that the wearer's face was surrounded with a frill of white edging.

On the death of George IV in 1830 the fashion magazines again reproduced a series of mourning fashion plates. Dorig Langley-Moore believes that most of these were simply the usual season's designs coloured in black and grey by the colourists, though a few magazines like the *Lady's Magazine* did print special plates.[208] By this date, neo-classical fashions were out of style and George was mourned in dresses with huge leg-of-mutton sleeves, stiffened inside with frills of starched cotton duck. The skirts were bell-shaped with waists neatly emphasised by wide belts and sashes, all made up in the usual bombazine and crape. Wide collars, falling onto the huge sleeves, were much admired and these were made up in plain white linen for mourning purposes.

Respectable ladies in even the most far flung corners of the new British Empire made strenuous efforts to keep up with the latest fashions and etiquette. Emily Eden, sister of Lord Auckland, Governor-General of India, was distressed to discover that because of the high rate of mortality, mourning in India was not what it ought to be. In 1837 she wrote in her diary: 'The most intimate friends never stay at home above two days, and they see everybody again directly.' As for mourning dress, it was, in those early days, impossible to obtain it at all. It took a good six months for boxes of clothes ordered from London to arrive by sea before the opening of the Suez Canal, and many never arrived at all. 'My poor box is at the bottom of the sea,' wrote Miss Eden in 1840. 'It is an inconvenient loss . . . I shall have no bonnet to go to church in on Sunday.' Under these trying circumstances the ladies managed as best they could. When on a march to Simla in 1839 one of the British party died and Miss Eden wrote:

We have been setting ourselves up with mourning for poor ——— and collected all the black goods in the place, consisting of four pairs of black gloves, with a finger or so missing, and a pair of black earrings which I thought a great catch; and so they were, in fact, I was quite caught out.

They had evidently been made for the Indian market and had mock hinges and clasps. Nobody could wear them.[209]

Emily Eden's concerns in the late 1830s were a foretaste of what was to come. Another factor which contributed to the huge increase in the sales figures for mourning fabrics was the styles of the fashions themselves in the 1850–85 period. Mourning dress grew closer and closer to fashionable clothes, until by 1897, the *Drapery World* told its readers on 15 May: 'Have you noticed how very smart mourning is nowadays? Crape is adapted to the most fashionable forms of costume such as Zouaves and tight-fitting out-door coats.' Fashionable styles throughout most of the second half of the century required inordinate amounts of yardage of fabric, much to the delight, no

65 'Mrs Howes in deep mourning', about 1860–70. She wears a black dress, with a woven stripe, probably supported by a hooped petticoat, together with kid gloves, a wide 'paletot' jacket with a ruffled hem and she carries her parasol inverted. Her hat is trimmed with a wide silk tie-ribbon and she wears her veil over her face as she would appear in deep mourning when in public or outdoors. (*Museum of the City of New York*)

doubt, of the textile industry. Dresses of the early 1860s could include six to seven hundred yards of ribbon or trimmed edging.

By the 1860s and 1870s, elegant mourning dress was a firmly established fact in the United States of America as well as in Europe. In the older cities such as Boston, Washington, Philadelphia and New York, styles were copied from fashion plates in *Godeys Lady's Book and Magazine*, *Harper's Monthly Magazine*, and *Harper's Bazaar* or *Demorrest's Monthly*. The cut of these clothes, as with fashionable dress, came straight from Paris, sometimes via London. It was, indeed, not only the styling that came from Europe but often the fabric and sometimes even the clothes themselves. Dresses from Paris and London, even in these days before the establishment of the haute couture system, carried great cachet and stylish mourning dress was not neglected.

The Smithsonian Institution in Washington has two interesting examples of European mourning clothes, which were both shown in Stony Brook's 1980 exhibition: 'A Time To Mourn'. The first example is a complete costume; bodice, skirt and bonnet in black silk heavily covered in black crape. It was purchased in 1875 for Mrs Mary Young Barnes (1820–1919) of New York City by her aunt who lived in Paris. Mrs Barnes wore the costume, with its tight cuirasse bodice and bustled skirt, when her father died in 1875 and again in 1878 to mourn for her husband.[210] The Smithsonian's second example is a shoulder cape of deepest mourning with a small collar entirely covered with crape and edged with seven plain tucks around the hem. This cape dating from 1885 was worn in Washington by the widowed Mrs Ulysses S. Grant and still retains its 'Jay's of London' label.[211]

To some Victorian women the smartness of their mourning may have been of some comfort, though to others it must have been a cause of deep concern. It meant that mourning dress could not be put away and kept for a future date because within a few years it would be hopelessly out of date. Impecunious widows often sold their weeds at the end of their period of mourning to other, newly widowed women, who in their turn, sold off the coloured clothes that they could no longer wear. These little transactions can be read in the 'Articles Wanted' columns of newspapers and magazines. In *The Lady* of 4 October 1900 the following advertisements appeared:

'WIDOW'S DRESS: Crape cape, both lined with silk, very hand-some, cost 12 gns – 3 gns, short, slight figure.'

'MOURNING – Two evening dresses, Liberty brocade, blue and pink, yellow and mauve, excellent condition, tall slight figure, 25/- each.'

'MOURNING – cream glacé silk covered in écru lace – 21'' – 39'', 18/6d.'

Costume collectors today have reason to be grateful for the Victorian-Edwardian mourning rules because various examples of dress have survived in trunks, unworn, whilst their owners were in mourning. Brighton Museum, for example, has a collection of dresses dating from 1895 to 1910, which were worn by Katherine Sophia Fare-brother of 'Leehurst', a large house in Salisbury. She was widowed in 1913 and seems then to have packed all her coloured clothes away in a trunk, rather than sell them off. Her son married soon after her widowhood against her wishes and she retired from society. She never felt the need to wear any of her elegant clothes again and they survived intact for over sixty years in the attic of her house.

As well as this vast increase in the use of mourning dress, the etiquette of mourning increased too. The mourning periods grew longer and even the remotest relatives were now mourned, though fortunately only for three to six weeks. The rules became impossibly complicated and the social pitfalls more and more numerous. *Sylvia's Home Journal* advised in 1881 that mothers should wear black without crape for six weeks after the death of the mothers or fathers-in-law of their married children. A second wife, on the death of her husband's first wife's parents, was expected to wear black silk, without crape, for three months.[212] Widowers, unlike widows, were able to remarry as soon as they pleased, even while still in mourning for their first wife. The Grand Maison de Noir declared that such a man should leave off his mourning for the ceremony but take it up the next day. Furthermore 'his new wife should equally associate herself with his mourning', wearing only black or shades of half-mourning in memory of her predecessor.[213] Basically, the more remote the relative the shorter was the mourning period, varying from two and a half years for a husband, eighteen months for a parent, twelve months for a child, six months for a brother or sister, down to six weeks to three months for a first cousin. It was considered correct to wear the same mourning for a husband's relatives as for one's own. The difficulty lay in establishing precisely what was the correct period of mourning because advice differed from one source to another. In about 1902 the firm of Courtaulds compiled a leaflet called *Notes on Fashionable Mourning*, now in their archive collection, with a suitable mauve cover. Finding the etiquette varied, they simply published a list called 'The Leading Authorities of the Correct Periods of Ladies' Mourning' and left their customers to make up their own minds. Their sources were the five top ladies' magazines of the period – *Queen*, *Gentlewoman*, *The Lady*, *Lady's Pictorial*, and *Ladies Year Book*. The differences were small but enough to confuse and worry the anxious reader. *Queen*, for example, recommended that a daughter should mourn her father or mother for a total of twelve months (six in crape, three in black and three in half-mourning), while *The Gentlewoman* advocated a total of fifteen months (six in crape, six in black and three in half-mourning). Similarly, *The Lady* preferred a nine months mourning period by a granddaughter for her grandparents, whereas the *Ladies Year Book* was satisfied with six months. It must frequently have happened that once over mourning one relative, a family would be plunged back into black again on the death of another relative. Families who moved within Court circles would also have the additional complication of observing mourning on the death of foreign royalty. In Britain with Queen Victoria's endless family connections with European royal families, this must have been a quite frequent occurrence.

Mourning dress for men in the nineteenth century, unlike that of their women, lessened, changing from the cloaked figure with trailing hat weepers to that of a normally dressed man distinguished only by a black armband. By the 1860 period mourning cloaks seem to have been worn only by the undertaker's men, the chief mourners wearing black (or sometimes white) sashes, in crape, across their left shoulders. Even these went out of use by the end of the century. The undertakers and their staff continued to wear the crape weepers on their top hats long after ordinary mourners had stopped using them by about 1890. The crape hatband continued to be worn until well into the present century, but, generally by the 1900 period, the only sign of mourning on a man's dress was the crape armband, worn with an ordinary black suit and black tie.

Women were bound by the labyrinth of mourning dress etiquette for a much longer period than their menfolk. They were burdened

66 (*above*) The funeral of Earl Palmerston in Westminster Abbey, 27 October 1865. Gentlemen mourners wear black silk sashes and black hat 'weepers'. From Richard Davey, *A History of Mourning*, 1889.

67 (*right*) Christmas Greetings, showing a man wearing a mourning armband, 1902. (*Lou Taylor Collection*)

with the duty of wearing depressing, and often in their eyes, ugly clothes for many years of their lives, whereas the men, once the funeral was over, needed only to wear an armband. This difference is symbolic of the whole social position of women in the second half of the nineteenth century. Women were used, albeit willingly and even eagerly by most, as a show piece, to display their family's total respectability, sense of conformity and wealth. Amongst the 'respectable' classes, the whole way of life of women was built on these foundations and with these goals in mind. Mourning dress was perhaps still the most perfect vehicle for this purpose as it had been in the past.

The heaviest burden of all fell without doubt on the widows. They mourned their husbands for two and a half years. The first and deepest period lasted for one year and a day. A widow wore a dress, made with a separate bodice and skirt, in dull black bombazine covered almost entirely in black crape. The skirt was covered in one deep, bias-cut flounce of crape sewn onto within an inch or two of the waist. After nine months two flounces or tucks were permitted in the skirt. The bodice was also totally hidden by crape. *The English Woman's Domestic Magazine* of May 1863 advised a reader that 'On a gored silk dress a deep crape trimming, put on plain, would not sit nicely. A fluting of crape would be the most suitable trimming, as this can be held in at the top, where the gores slope off.' The magazine offered further advice. 'In deep mourning, white collars and cuffs should not be worn at all; but when you wish to put on slighter mourning, sleeves of book-muslin, trimmed with black, may be donned.' All other accessories, except for the indoor cap and handkerchief, were black. *Myra's Journal* recommended, on 1 March 1887, 'fast dye black stockings at 2/6d to 13/6d a pair' or 'black spun silk stockings at 2/6d to 5/6d.' Shoes were black, so were gloves, one of the most socially revealing items of Victorian dress. For mourning they had to be in dull black cloth, leather or suede.

Underwear was not neglected either. The usual plain white chemises, drawers and underpetticoats were sometimes slotted with black ribbon. The Gallery of Costume at Castle Howard near York has several sets of mourning underwear in its collection. As well as the usual layers of white petticoats, when in mourning additional top petticoats of black were required. *Myra's Journal* stated that 'black petticoats are of course required both in and out of mourning; they can be had, in nice woven fabrics, at 3/11d–10/6d.'

Widows continued to wear white crape indoor caps, with falls that fell down their backs. Following the example set by Victoria's daughter, the Empress of Germany, black caps were also popular. Outside they wore black, crape trimmed bonnets, with long crape veils. The crape was put on very plainly in deepest mourning. By the 1890s, however, even the most respectable widows were appearing in public with their veils worn at the back of the head only and a fair amount of hair showing beneath the bonnets at the front – a fundamental change. On 4 October 1900 *The Lady* issued a page of advice on widows' First mourning, showing bonnets for outdoor wear, all with the falls worn at the back. The average length of the crape falls was forty-five inches, but they could be longer if desired. The styles are by this date more elaborate than would have been considered proper in the mid-nineteenth century. An elaborate widow's bonnet, for example, has a 'crown of crape and coronet front embroidered fancifully in black silk; height is added to the whole by ears of crape

68   The Empress Frederick of Germany, Princess Royal (eldest daughter of Queen Victoria), in First mourning for her husband who died in 1888. She wears a black crape Mary Stuart widow's cap with a veil. In Richard Davey, *A History of Mourning*, 1889.

69   Widow's weeds of 1897–8. First stage of mourning; bodice, skirt and cape, in twilled wool. The bodice is trimmed with vertical tucks on front and sleeves; the skirt and cape are completely covered in crape. (*Gallery of English Costume, Platt Hall, Manchester*)

at the side; handsome fall of Brussels net with leaf-like appliqué border and embroidered spots complete this smart bonnet.' The price was 39s 6d. The indoor caps had shorter falls, usually 30–36 inches, and were made up in pleated white crape or lisse. One, in *The Lady* of 4 October 1900, was described as 'in lisse, closely pleated and finished off in front with a rosette.' Both indoor and outdoor caps shared one common feature and that was a V-point shaped down over the centre forehead and described always as Marie Stuart style. This point was reintroduced by Queen Victoria on Albert's death in 1861, taken from the portraits of the widowed Mary Queen of Scots. The Queen wore it for the rest of her life and it was taken up by most of her widowed subjects. A further type of cap was worn inside the outdoor hats to cover the hair. *The English Woman's Domestic Magazine* advised its readers in 1863 that

70  Woman, probably a widow, in the first stage of mourning, about 1865, from the Hall family album. (*By kind permission of Susannah and Rodger Handley*)

white tulle caps puffed, are usually put in crape bonnets. These may be made at home in the following manner:— Cut some strips of tulle, double them, and run together. Insert a round stick, arranging the tulle on it to the desired fullness, then hold it over some boiling water for two or three minutes. Dry it and the tulle will have a regular appearance and will not soon get out of condition. It is then mounted on wire and bound with black ribbon to conceal the rough edges.

These seem to have gone out of use by the end of the nineteenth century.

Outdoor garments for First mourning consisted of capes and variously styled mantles, according to the fashion of the day. As with the dresses, the depth of mourning was indicated by the plainness and profusion of black crape. Barkers were selling, at three guineas, in 1900, a 'handsome mantle; latest design, in dull mourning silk, trimmed with a band and rouleaux of crape to match skirt, lined and warmly quilted throughout.' In France, long shawls in black *cachemire d'Ecosse* were regarded as de rigueur but by the end of the century they were being worn only for the funeral ceremony itself and for the first few weeks afterwards. They were then replaced with 'clothes following the fashion of the day . . . trimmed with English Crape.'[214]

Few complete examples of widows' First mourning have survived intact, though the Museum of Costume at Platt Hall, Manchester, owns a very good example dating from about 1900. The style is moderately fashionable but completely covered from shoulder to floor in crape. It consists of the usual bodice, skirt and shoulder cape. It must have been a most uncomfortable costume to wear because crape was stiffened so much that it was coarse and even scratchy to the touch yet fine enough to snag on unnoticed corners.

In the Hall family photographic album (about 1855–1910) in the collection of Mrs and Mrs Roger Handley of Brighton, there is an excellent photograph of a widow of the 1860s in the first stage of mourning. The Halls, from Derby and Newcastle, were evidently quite well-to-do. At the same time the French society photographer, Camille Silvy, photographed a few widows amongst his sitters. The National Portrait Gallery, London, has a large collection of his work, including a portrait of 'Mrs Campbell' in her widow's weeds.

In 1881, *Sylvia's Home Journal* published a complete list of clothes needed by a widow for correct and respectable First mourning:[215]

## Mourning Dress

One best dress of Paramatta covered entirely with crape.

One dress, either a costume of Cyprus crape, or an old black dress covered with Rainproof crape.

One Paramatta mantle lined with silk, and deeply trimmed with crape.

One warmer jacket of cloth lined and trimmed with crape.

One bonnet of best silk crape, with long veil.

One bonnet of Rainproof crape, with crape veil.

Twelve collars and cuffs of muslin or lawn, with deep hems, several sets must be provided, say six of each kind.

One black stuff petticoat.

Four pairs of black hose, either silk, cashmere or spun silk.

Twelve handkerchiefs with black borders, for ordinary use, cambric.

Twelve of finer cambric for better occasions.

Caps either of lisse, tulle, or tarlatan, shape depending much upon age; young widows wear chiefly the Marie Stuart shape but all widows' caps have long streamers. A good plan to buy extra streamers and bow.

Summer parasol of silk, deeply trimmed with crape, almost covered with it but no lace or fringe for the first year. Afterwards mourning fringe might be put on.

71 (*left*) Widow's weeds of about 1898–1910, second stage of mourning; dress with long jacket in black face-cloth, trimmed with black crape edging in zig-zags and chevrons. (*Whitby Literary and Philosophical Society*)

72 (*right*) Detail of a mourning cape, second stage; heavy corded silk edged with crape and appliquéd with black silk braid in a floral design. About 1890. Made by Cole Brothers, Sheffield. (*Worthing Museum and Art Gallery*)

Muff of Paramatta and trimmed with crape.
No ornaments except jet, for the first year.
Furs are not admissable in widow's First mourning, though very dark
  sealskin and astrachan can be worn when the dress is changed.

The jet ornaments mentioned in the list were special mourning jet jewellery, which together with other types of memorial brooches, pendants, lockets etc. were the only types of jewels permitted during mourning (see Chapter 9). The width of the black borders on the handkerchiefs lessened with the crape.

After one year and a day, a widow could move on to the second stage of mourning. She was advised, however, not to do so on the very day she was entitled to, but, for the sake of good taste, to prolong the change for some time. Second mourning differed from First in that less crape was worn and that it was applied to dresses, capes and bonnets in a more elaborate way. This period lasted for a further nine months. Dullish-black silk fabrics were permitted. For

73 (*above*) Black silk cape for Second mourning with shoulder flounce and deep edging of black crape. It is trimmed with black bobble fringing, a silk frill to the neck, in black, and labelled 'Peter Robinson, Ltd, Mantles, 256–262 Regent Street, London'. About 1890–1900. (*Worthing Museum and Art Gallery*)

those who followed every intricacy of etiquette, after the first six months of Second mourning, widows were allowed to lessen their crape still further and add jet trimmings to their toilettes. The milliners and dressmakers worked miracles with crape, creating flowers, buds and leaves, with the help of wire, to trim hats. They sewed all sorts of clever tucks, pleats, rouleaux and chevrons onto the clothes.

Worthing Museum has two excellent examples of Second mourning shoulder capes, both dating from about 1900. One, made by Cole Brothers of Sheffield (No. 2435), is in heavy corded silk, edged with a deep band of bias-cut crape around the hem and front edges. It is brightened up with finely worked appliqué embroidery, in narrow black braid, worked in a floral design. The second cloak (No. 59/170) was made by Peter Robinson in the 1890–1900 period, in black silk, cut in two layers, each one trimmed with a deep crape border, with the added attraction of a trimming of black silk bobbles around the hem of the top layer. The collar is made up in a stylish ruffle of fine crimped, black chiffon.

Whitby Museum and Philosophical Society owns another and more complete example of Second mourning. They have a dress and three-quarter length coat, dating from 1898. Tailored in style, the outfit is lightly trimmed with crape on the bodice, cuffs, and the coat hem, mostly with fine zigzags and tucks. The top of the pleats on the skirt are finished with small crape chevrons. *The Lady* featured some examples of Second mourning headwear on 4 October 1900, including, at 39s 6d, a 'very effective Bonnet in dull silk, fully trimmed with loops of drawn chiffon and fans of accordion pleated chiffon, intermixed with clusters of black silk flowers and ribbon. The falls of silk Brussels net with silk scalloped edge.' This hat was made by Barkers of Islington, who also advertised ordinary indoor widows' dress caps, selling at 2s 11¾d or 8s 6d per quarter dozen, made up in 'tulle with tiny tucked flounce at the back and rosette in the front dotted with elongated jet beads.' They also sold fifteen different varieties of 'crepe-rouleaux or ruched' trimmings from ¾ in. to 2 in. deep costing from 4¼d to 1s 0¾d a yard. A more superior type of indoor cap, cost 3s 11½d, and was described as 'dainty . . . in frilled white lisse, trimmed with black and white fancy embroidery which has a charming effect.' The Museum of Costume at Bath has a very pretty and fragile indoor mourning cap, which may well have been worn for Second mourning. It is made in white

74  Unknown Scottish widow, in the second stage of mourning, about 1878–1880. Photograph by G. W. Wilson, 'Photographers to Her Majesty', 25 Crown Street, Aberdeen. Crape trimming on bodice, skirt, around slashes in upper sleeves and on cuffs; cap of white frilling and black satin. (*Lou Taylor Collection*)

75  Unknown widow, from the East End of London, in deepest mourning, about 1895–1900. Her dress has crape cuffs, collar, bodice front and deep hem. Photographed by 'R. Johnstone, 367 Mile End Road, London'. (*Lou Taylor Collection*)

net, with matching falls and is trimmed on the front with delicate sprays of black flowers and leaves in shiny black lacquered fabric and wire. It dates from the 1870s.

Widows in various stages of mourning can be seen in Victorian family albums. G. W. Wilson, 'Photographers to Her Majesty, of 25, Crown Street, Aberdeen,' photographed a widow in the 1875–80 period, in a cap of white trimmed with black satin, with crape on collar, front panel and cuffs. A later photograph, taken by R. Johnstone of Mile End Road, London, in the 1890s shows a woman with a similarly trimmed dress, possibly second stage of mourning, with leg-of-mutton sleeves. The Hall album includes portraits of two widows of the 1870–80 period, in Second mourning, each with a crape collar trimming.

76 Elderly woman in mourning, second stage, with slight crape bands on bodice and cuffs; note the black undersleeves. About 1875–80. From the Hall family photographic album. (*By kind permission of Susannah and Rodger Handley*)

77 Woman, probably in the second stage of mourning, from the Hall family photographic album. About 1878–82. She wears only a slight vestige of crape in a small collarette around her shoulders. (*By kind permission of Susannah and Rodger Handley*)

After the period of approximately twenty-one months of Second mourning, widows entered the Third or Ordinary period of mourning, in which crape was finally omitted altogether and black silk trimmed with jet, black ribbon, embroidery or lace was allowed. This period lasted for a minimum of three months though *The English Woman's Domestic Magazine* declared in 1876, that 'many widows never put on colours again.'[216] Without the crape trimming it now becomes much harder to identify mourning clothes. Black dresses and mantles were considered correct for evening and visiting clothes, especially for older women, both in and out of mourning.

The Smithsonian Institution in Washington owns one particularly interesting example of Ordinary mourning – an evening dress worn in 1853 by Mrs Pierce the wife of President Pierce. Mrs Pierce's two sons died in 1842 and before her husband's inauguration in 1853 her only surviving son, a boy of twelve, was killed in a railway accident. Her evening dress, with a fashionable V-shaped waistline and fully gathered skirt, is made of black silk taffeta with an overskirt of black tulle embroidered with silver dots. Mrs Pierce wore with it a black lace, net and velvet head-dress trimmed with dull jet and gold.[217]

The Museum of Costume at Bath has a heavily bustled dress, dating from the late 1880s, donated by the Snell family, which is typical of the type that would have been worn in Ordinary mourning. It is made up in very heavy black, corded silk, with beaded jet net and dangling jet ornaments down the front of both the bodice and skirt. The bodice, which is cut with a fish-tail basque at the centre back to cover the bustle, has white cuffs and collar and black lace panels on the front. The skirt, which is extraordinarily heavy, has five deep pleats down the centre front, trimmed with five rows of jet and is mounted on a stiff underskirt of white cotton, with a pad and half a steel hoop sewn inside to support the bustle. Black

78   Ordinary mourning evening dress worn by Mrs Jane Appleton Pierce, the wife of President Pierce, in 1853, in Washington, after the death of her 12-year-old son; black silk taffeta and black tulle, embroidered with silver dots. (*Smithsonian Institute, Washington*)

furs, feathers, passementerie and various types of embroidery were all permitted in Ordinary mourning. After the death of Edward VII the *Illustrated London News* featured several examples of Ordinary mourning fashions, for the benefit of their male readers. On 4 June 1910 they showed an example of black and white evening wear: 'A gown of black silk Ninon laid over white silk: it is trimmed with lines of jet embroidery and tassels: the vest is of fine black net.' This is a very basic description of a highly fashionable hobble-skirted concoction, reflecting the Oriental influence of the French couturier Paul Poiret. 'Black', the magazine suggested,

> is . . . becoming to a great many women who have, perhaps, seldom allowed themselves the opportunity of seeing themselves attired exclusively in black until national feeling required the change . . . Black and white spotted muslin is also pretty on fair women. Grey linen is being much run upon for morning wear and in medium shades is extremely cool and clean-looking and pleasing; revers and cuffs of black satin or moire are optional additions. For evening wear, gorgeous jet embroideries have appeared and give brightness very effectively.

All these clothes would have been made up in the fashions of 1910, with slightly raised waists, long, narrow skirts and toque or cartwheel hats.

After a minimum period of two years, widows went into half-mourning. This lasted anything from six months to a lifetime. Many widows never came out of half-mourning, though the Grand Maison de Noir in Paris advised its customers that 'everyone is free to prolong the period of wearing mourning but it is in good taste to effect any exaggeration in this as over other circumstances.'[218] Half-mourning consisted of the fashions of the day but made up in special half-mourning colours. These included a range of soft mauves, variously called violet, pansy, lilac, scabious and heliotrope – none of them to be confused with the bright Parma violet, which was introduced in the late 1860s on the discovery of aniline dyes.

It is never easy to pin-point a precise colour from a description and it is fortunate that actual examples of half-mourning fabric have survived to help us over this difficulty. The *Journal of Design and Manufactures* (Volume 11, dating from September 1849 to February 1850) includes on page 171 examples of calicoes, printed by Devas, Minchenev and Routledge, in January 1850:

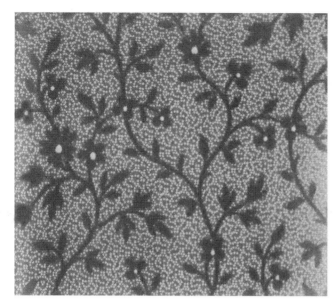

79  Sample of
half-mourning dress fabric,
described as 'a cheerful
variety', from the *Journal of
Design and Manufactures*,
Sept. 1849–Feb. 1850.

The shops are crowded with sombreness in this season of mourning for the lamented Queen Dowager [Adelaide, the widow of William IV] and manufacturers of all fabrics are striving to give some variety to the inherent monotony which must necessarily attach to mourning attire. Messrs. Devas, Minchenev and Routledge have forwarded us two patterns which though modest in pretension to design, we think are commendable, and likely to be effective when 'made up'. The narrow stripe of purple is enlivening and novel.

This particular stripe ran down the right side of a sample of deep grey calico printed with a design of meandering black buds and stems. The second design shows a simple vertical stripe of small flowers and berries printed in deep red on an undulating black stem set on another deep grey ground. The magazine describes it as 'a cheerful variety' and concludes that 'both patterns would be very durable in wear.' It seems that the manufacturers did not have the high fashion market in mind for this product.

Henry Mayhew described in 1865 some of the half-mourning delights that he had admired in Jay's as a child: 'Delicate shades of slate-colour, grey mauve and purple, and a certain delicate robe of the palest violet tint fairly frosted with crystal spots.'[219] These colours were widely worn in the early 1860s after the death of Prince Albert in 1861. Sarah A. Tooley, writing in *Woman at Home* in December 1895, remembered that 'during the first year or two of the Queen's widowhood mourning colours, such as grey, violet and mauve were all the fashion and with charming good taste the young

80   Half-mourning millinery for Queen Victoria, from the *Ladies Field*, 23 March 1901, available at Hancock and James, London.

Princess [Alexandra, Princess of Wales] dressed herself for her entry into London [in March 1863, before her marriage to the Prince of Wales] in a pale mauve poplin, with a purple mantle over her graceful shoulders, and a pale bonnet with rose-buds.'

Every item of dress – from morning and walking dress to ball and dinner gowns – had to be adapted for half-mourning wear, as it had for the previous stages of mourning. All the accompanying accessories changed too – hats, shawls, mantles, gloves, shoes, fans and so on. *Godey's Lady's Book*, published in Philadelphia, featured in June 1861, a stylish set of matching half-mourning chemisette and undersleeves.[220] The chemisette was a false front and collar worn beneath a bodice. The undersleeves, worn particularly in the 1850–70 period when flared 'pagoda' sleeves were fashionable, were designed to be tied or stitched inside the oversleeve and were worn to cover modestly the lower arm and wrist.

In June 1910 the *Illustrated London News* featured examples of half-mourning dresses, during the period of General mourning after the death of Edward VII.

It will be proper to relieve the black dresses with white in the form of yokes, collarettes, frillings, and even white glace or satin linings under transparent fabrics: and grey heliotrope and patterned or striped fabrics showing any one of these colours with white or black will all be in keeping. Meantime all the novelty that there is to note is concentrated in details. Tight and short skirts have naturally been ordered by women who follow fashion's changes, but there has been a very proper feeling that extremes should be avoided.

On 17 June a half-mourning walking dress was illustrated, 'in black-and-grey striped delaine, with vest of black net over white. The hat [a neat toque] is of black chiffon bound with satin and trimmed with plumes.' This particular half-mourning period lasted for precisely two weeks. Only the wealthiest members of society would have ordered new clothes. The *Illustrated London News* remarked indeed that 'there was scarcely any change in the wearing of mourning for the period ordered as half-mourning.' The magazine did, however, continue to show half-mourning fashion plates, including, on 2 July, 'A pretty summer frock in mauve chiffon with band of satin round the feet, and lace trimmings; hat of white lace, crown covered with mauve sweet peas.'

The importance of the fashion influence on mourning dress from the early nineteenth century onwards cannot be emphasised enough. Mourning clothes were made up in every nuance of style, from the great wide skirts of the 1850–70 period, to the narrow

81 (*above*) Half-mourning dress for Queen Victoria. 'Demi-Deuil Evening Bodices,' from the *Ladies Field*, 23 March 1901.

82 (*right*) General mourning for King Edward VII, from the *Lady's Pictorial*, 14 May 1910 – 'in soft black silk, with a dull surface, which is veiled with a tunic of transparent spotted net, ornamented with a fine design in narrow braiding, while the Peter Pan collar is in black silk guipure lace.'

tie-back fashions of the late 1870s and the curvaceous S-bend look of the early 1900s. All these changes can clearly be seen in the illustrations of mourning garments in the magazines and advertisements. It is, however, true that First mourning was generally made up in somewhat modified forms, as can be seen in Charles Dana Gibson's series of drawings called 'The Widow and Her Friends', published in *Life* magazine, between October 1900 and July 1901, showing the adventures of a beautiful young widow. She wears at first very simple widow's weeds, covered from head to foot in crape in a very simple but stylish shape. Nonetheless, particularly from the late 1880s onwards, as the grip of mourning etiquette began to loose its hold, advertisements continually stressed the elegance, smartness and style of mourning clothes. The fashion writer on the *Ladies Field* went so far as to say, on 17 December 1898: 'Almost, I think, under these conditions, mourning is a phase to be courted.'

It must be realised, though, that it can only have been a minority of women who could afford or even wished to dress in the elegant and vastly expensive mourning wear of the fashion plates. Many women, particularly in the middle classes, would have worn modified interpretations of these ideas. Some would have rejected fashionable mourning altogether. A perfect example of this can be found in a photograh of Mrs Turner of Ilminster and Taunton in Somerset. She is shown seated, wearing a typical widow's dress, with crape on the front, skirt and cuffs. She wears a heavy black jet chain necklace and a fancy black widow's bonnet. Without prior knowledge of when it was taken even the most expert costume historian would probably date the picture to the 1890–1900 period or even earlier. It was, in fact, taken as late as 1909. It seems a realistic counter-balance to the transparent, jet-spangled chiffons shown in the mourning fashion plates published after the death of Edward VII one year later, in 1910.

Conventional women accepted mourning as a proper duty even if the clothes depressed them – but how did more unconventional women, the aesthetic dressers, react to the laying aside of their sage green dresses and amber beads?

The diaries of Miss Jeannette Marshall, a surgeon's daughter who mixed in aesthetic circles in London in the 1870s and 1880s, provide the beginnings of an answer. Miss Marshall knew Rossetti, the Ford Madox Browns, the Holman Hunts and attended lectures by William Morris. She frequently described the clothes she saw at

83 'The widow and her friends', drawn by Charles Dana Gibson, from *Life* magazine. A series of twelve drawings published between October 1900 and July 1901. No. 3, 'She finds that exercise does not improve her spirits.' The widow walks in the cemetery in deepest mourning, wearing a crape veil with a deep border.

84 'The widow and her friends', by Charles Dana Gibson, from *Life* magazine October 1900–July 1901. No. 6, 'She is the subject of some hostile criticism.' The widow wears an ordinary mourning evening dress.

85 Mrs Turner, of Ilminster and Taunton in Somerset, in 1909, wearing the first or possibly second stage of mourning – crape-trimmed dress, jet necklace and crape, ribbon and lace cap. (*By kind permission of Mrs Esmé Turner*)

functions and parties, amongst them the clothes of Marie Stillman, the wife of W. J. Stillman, the American art critic and war correspondent of *The Times*. In the diaries Mrs Stillman's clothes are defined as 'artistic', and it is fascinating to note that Marie Stillman wore 'an artistic black silk garment and a wonderful hat trimmed round with feathers . . .' when in mourning in July 1875 for her stepson, Russie, who had died five months earlier. In 1882 when her own infant son, James, died, Mrs Stillman visited the Marshall family six weeks into mourning wearing 'A crepe veil down to the ground'.

Jeannette Marshall was herself a moderate aesthetic dresser and described her own wardrobe in her diaries. In October 1876 her maternal grandmother died. In the summer of 1877, Miss Marshall attended the Royal Academy soirée in a 'most artistic' half-mourning, mauve muslin dress with black trim. Her preferred colours were sage, olive and grey-greens but it seems that, probably in common with other aesthetic dressers, she gave them up for the duration of mourning – wearing black and half-mourning tones

86 'The Crawler' of St Giles, in the City of London, 1877–8. She was the destitute widow of a tailor who had died some years earlier. She received, but not always, a cup of tea and a little bread in return for nursing her friend's baby for eight hours a day. Photographed by J. Thomson and Adolphe Smith in *Street Life in London*, 1877–8.

instead but still retaining the aesthetic cut of her clothes.[221] This view would seem to be confirmed in the April 1889 edition of the Rational Dress Society's Gazette, published in London. Amongst the advertisements and advice for 'Rational Shaped Boots and Shoes', and 'Stabilis serge-dyed by the most durable process', is a paragraph of advice to the aesthetic and rational dresser on mourning:

> Though not in any way connected with the Rational Dress Society, the Society called the National Funeral and Mourning Reform Association has many points of interest to us. One of its objects is to diminish as far as possible the expense of mourning, and in this I think it will find a great many sympathisers. It does not deny that outward and visible signs of grief are natural and right, but it protests against the use of an expensive material like crepe, which, after all, cannot express greater mourning than all black does, and it emphatically protests against the donning of deep trappings of woe in honour of the dead who are not mourned.

As to working-class families, the struggle to provide even the most basic elements of mourning dress still went on and the same sense of shame still remained when this could not be done. Luke Fildes's painting 'Applicants For Admission To A Casual Ward', now in the collection at Royal Holloway College, painted in 1864, shows a young widow holding a baby, waiting in a line of destitute people for entry to the workhouse. She is dressed in full weeds, including the black hat and veil, implying that though she had the correct clothes of mourning she could not survive outside the workhouse.

Bertram Puckle wrote in about 1900 of a

> superior servant, a mere girl, married to a house-painter. Within a year of the event the husband fell from a ladder and was killed. The poor little widow bought a cheap black dress and a very simple black straw hat to wear at the funeral. Her former employee met the girl a few days later swathed in crape, her poor little face only half visible under the hideous widow's bonnet, complete with streamers and a veil . . . She explained that her neighbours and relations had made her life unbearable because she did not want to wear widow's weeds. "They said that if I would not wear a bonnet, it proved we were never married."[222]

The social prestige gained from wearing mourning clothes remained much more important amongst working-class families in the first half of the present century than it was with the rest of society – perhaps because of the difficulty involved in providing it at

*Mourning Dress*

all. A. S. Jasper, writing of his childhood in Hoxton, in the East End of London, remembered the efforts his sisters made to put the family into black clothes after his little niece Flossie died of diphtheria in 1922. His father was a drunkard and they had little money to buy special clothes.

> We got as much money together as we could and started to make arrangements for the funeral. Gerry [his brother-in-law] and Mary [his sister] were staying with us at the time. They bought what black they could and Mary suggested dyeing several articles black so she and Jo got a bath of water and started dyeing. When they were nearly through it was discovered that the old man never had any black trousers, so I gave him a pair of khaki slacks, which Mary and Jo promptly started to dye black. As they had already used up most of the powder of the dye, the trousers became only dark green. To make them black, Mary suggested putting soot in the water, which she did. They had to let it go at that and they were duly dried and pressed. It was a sad day when we buried little Flossie; we just could not believe we would never have her with us again. After the service, we were coming home in the coach when a watery sun started to shine through the window. It settled on the old man's trousers. Sad as the occasion was, we somehow had to laugh. The sun brought out the colour in his trousers and black and green patches appeared.[223]

As in the previous century servants of rich families were the only working-class people who could be guaranteed to wear mourning, though of course, not for their own private grief but for that of their employers. They were put into cheap mourning clothes immediately and wore them for the same time as the rest of the family, though they wore black and white for half-mourning instead of the usual shades. Female servants were given very simple black dresses, with bonnets, collars and cuffs of crape. For half-mourning the trimmings were in white. The manservants were given black suits with no shiny buttons, and suitable ties and armbands, with white weeper cuffs. They were all given two sets of mourning clothes, one set for working use, in especially strong fabrics, whilst the other, worn on Sundays and reception days, was of slightly better quality.[224] For at least eight years after the death of the Prince Consort, the royal servants wore crape armbands on instructions from Queen Victoria.[225]

There is no doubt that the influence of the widowed Queen was one of the prime reasons for the widespread use of mourning etiquette and dress in the second half of the nineteenth century. She was widowed dramatically at the age of forty-two and was left with nine children. Beatrice, the youngest, was only five years old. For the first months of mourning the Queen remained isolated from society at Osborne House, on the Isle of Wight, submerged in her intense and almost demented grief. Victoria, and under her guidance, her children, spent their time making their own memorial tributes to Albert's memory. The Queen and the girls embroidered mourning handkerchiefs, in fine white lawn. Victoria's was decorated with black and white tears and the initials 'V.R.' It is now in the collection of the Museum of London. At Windsor Castle she ordered that Albert's dressing room was to be kept exactly as he had left it. His clothes were laid out every night and hot water prepared. The Queen slept with a photograph of the head and shoulders of Albert, taken as he lay dead, fixed above her head.[226] For years afterwards all the family photographs included a life-size marble bust of Albert in the centre of the group, where he would have stood. The Queen wrote to Earl Canning from Osborne on 10 January 1862:

87 Queen Victoria, from a painting by A. Graffle, published in the *Ladies Field*, 2 February 1901. In 1864 Victoria had been a widow for three years and had not yet made a public appearance. She sits here next to a marble bust of Albert, in deepest mourning.

88 Queen Victoria, in about 1885, photograph by Downey. She wears a white crape Mary Stuart widow's cap, black lace shawl, with tucks of crape in her dress. (*By kind permission of Susannah and Rodger Handley*)

89   General mourning for Prince Albert, *Illustrated London News*, 28 December 1861.
   *Left:* the 'Corinne' in glacé silk, with crape and jet.
   *Centre:* the 'Monta Rosa', a mantle with crape fluting and silk cording.
   *Right:* dress of black tulle, the skirt 'bouillonné', fastened in the form of diamonds.

To the Queen it is like death in life! . . . Her misery, – her utter despair – she cannot describe! Her only support – the only ray of comfort she gets for a moment, is in the firm conviction and certainty of his nearness, his undying love, and of their eternal reunion! Only she prays always, and pines for the latter with an anxiety she cannot describe.[227]

The Queen's grief was shared by her subjects. On the publication of the Order for Court and General mourning by the Earl Marshal, those who could afford the expense, rushed to the mourning warehouses to fit themselves out in mourning dress. The *Illustrated London News* on 28 December 1861 described the scene, which undoubtedly brought in huge profits for the mourning stores:

The late melancholy event which has plunged the nation into so deep and lasting regret, has, as may be imagined, created an almost incalculable demand for mourning. Never was respect paid to the memory of the great and the good more general than at the present time . . . As soon as it was light on the Monday morning after the intelligence had been received, crowds of buyers flocked to Morison's, Leaf's, Boyd's, Cooke's, Ellis's and other city firms. In which-ever direction one moved, East, West, South or North, the shops, particularly in the West End, were crowded to inconvenience.

The fashion column issued detailed advice in the same issue, covering every aspect of dress throughout the day, from day to evening wear.

> The materials usually employed for outdoor dress in deep mourning are cashmere, paramatta and merion . . . For ball costumes, dresses of black tulle, or crape over black silk, or white Chambery gauze figured with black are suitable. Dresses of white tarletane with black trimmings are extremely pretty, and suitable for very young ladies. In a dress of black velvet, for dinner costume, which we have seen, the corsage is high behind and slightly opening in a point in front; it has revers covered with black crape . . . Many elegant undersleeves, collars, and other articles of lingerie, suitable for mourning costume have been introduced. Some of the collars and undersleeves are beautifully embroidered with a pattern in black. Others, without embroidery, consist of organdie hemmed and ruched, or of tarlatane merely hemmed. Mourning pocket handkerchiefs are frequently embroidered in black or violet, and have no trimming of lace.

The accompanying fashion plate shows four high fashion dresses in the wide skirted fashions of the period – a dinner dress in black silk, trimmed with pinked frills and a *corsage à la Raphael*, an indoor dress, in black poult de soie, trimmed with black velvet, passementerie with white undersleeves, and a walking dress, with a black mantle which has a double pelerine 'edged with bands of black taffaty . . . surmounted by an arabesque design worked in soutache of two different widths.' The walking dress itself is of grey cashmere, trimmed with rows of black velvet. The final garment shown is a carriage costume, with a black velvet cloak and a dress of 'dark grey moiré antique. Bonnet of white silk trimmed with black lace and velvet. Under trimming, ruches of black tulle and white roses [sewn on to cover the underside of the brim] strings of broad black ribbon with a narrow edge of white.'

*The English Woman's Domestic Magazine* must already have obtained copies of its fashion plates for January 1862 before the sudden death of Prince Albert the month before. The plates were published even though the two dresses shown were quite unsuitable for mourning wear. One was a pink and white silk evening dress trimmed with wreaths of pink chrysanthemums and a gold spotted net overdress. The other model shown was a black coat worn with a bonnet trimmed with bright green ribbons. Instead of recolouring the plates the magazine simply advised its readers that the style of these dresses was suitable but they they should be made up only in black or white fabrics.

Victoria herself never came out of mourning. Even for her Diamond Jubilee in 1897 she wore her usual black bonnet and black dress in the triumphant procession through the streets of London, holding a white trimmed parasol above her head. A dress she wore in 1892, after the death of the Duke of Clarence, the eldest son of Edward and Alexandra, is in the study collection of the Museum of London. It is in black silk, trimmed, as usual, on the hem, bodice front and cuffs, with bands of black crape. The Queen was by that date stout with a waist measurement of forty-eight inches, as well as extremely short, and the dress is almost square in proportion. In her black dresses and white widow's caps, Victoria became the epitome of virtuous widowhood, though even at the time there was criticism of her failure to appear at public functions over such a long period of time. [228] In the first years of her widowhood she never appeared in public at all, remaining wrapped in the memory of her husband and her plans to preserve his name for posterity. Two family weddings occurred which forced her to come before the Court, if not the general public. In 1862 her second daughter, Princess Alice, married

90   Queen Victoria with Prince Edward of York, 1896. Photo by Hughes and Mullins. The Queen wears a white crape widow's bonnet, a black lace shawl, and a black silk dress trimmed with black mourning crape. (*National Portrait Gallery, London*)

Prince Louis of Hesse. The wedding took place at Osborne House, privately. The Queen appeared at the ceremony in deep mourning, wearing a white cap, streamers and lots of black crape, contrary to all rules of etiquette which permitted and even encouraged widows to set aside mourning at weddings, so as not to cast a gloom over the proceedings.

The second wedding was that of Edward, Prince of Wales, to Princess Alexandra, held in more public circumstances, presumably because he was heir to the throne. The ceremony took place in the Royal Chapel at Windsor Castle on 10 March 1863 in front of a huge gathering of the Royal Family, the Court and foreign dignitaries. The Queen was present – just – standing in total isolation from the throng in her Royal Closet, set high above the altar. W. P. Frith painted one of his huge and detailed paintings of the occasion. It is now in the Royal Collection, but another water-colour sketch of Victoria alone painted by George Houseman Thomas, for his version of the wedding, is more revealing. This sketch is on loan to the British Embassy in Paris, from the National Portrait Gallery. It shows the Queen in her deep mourning again, with white cap and heavily crape-trimmed dress.

91   Queen Victoria, in the Royal Closet, at the Royal Chapel, Windsor Castle, for the marriage of Edward, Prince of Wales to Princess Alexandra, on 10 March 1863. Watercolour by George Houseman Thomas, 1863. (*National Portrait Gallery, London*)

92 Queen Victoria and the Prince and Princess of Wales on their wedding day, 10 March 1863. Victoria is still in first stage of mourning. (*BBC Hulton Picture Library*)

All the official wedding photographs taken afterwards show the marble bust of Albert in the midst of the proceedings. In one the Queen is seated with her little daughter Beatrice examining a framed photograph of Albert. The Queen, Beatrice and Arthur are in black. The bridal couple, Princess Alice and Prince Louis, the Princess Royal and Princess Helena, in shades of half-mourning, stand next to the life-size bust of Albert. The half-mourning colours were worn on the insistence of Victoria. She wrote to her daughter, the Crown Princess of Prussia, advising on suitable dress for the wedding. 'I think decidedly none of you ought to be in colours at the wedding but in grey and silver or lilac and gold and so on but not merely gold and white: it is the first occasion of any of you children appearing in public and as all when in England, will not wear colours next year [1863] I think it ought not to be.'[229]

The unease over the Queen's years of isolation reached such a pitch that she was finally obliged to take part in a public function and did so in February 1866, when she attended the State Opening of

93 General mourning for Queen Victoria – first stage 1901, from the *Ladies Field*, 2 February 1901. Two standing figures in 'outdoor dresses', in fine-stitched woollen cloth, trimmed with crape. *Back:* 'Dinner gown of black satin merveilleux; chemisette, fichu and scarf, of plain and embroidered chiffon.'

94 General mourning millinery for Queen Victoria, 1901, from the *Ladies Field*, 9 February 1901, available from Henry Heath's in London.

Parliament. It was over four years since the death of Albert. She wore a robe of deep violet velvet, the traditional colour of royal mourning, with her white widow's cap and gauze veil. Her daughters were in shades of half-mourning.[230] Thereafter, the Queen always wore a long white lace or net veil with her crown, which still gave the impression of widow's falls.

When Victoria died in 1901 there was widespread grief and mourning. Mourning dress was generally worn and two very disparate groups of the population never came out of mourning for the Queen at all. The wives of bargees on the canals of England put on black mutches, or bonnets, instead of their usual white ones. They never reverted to white ones again, and were still in the black ones in the 1930s.[231] Similarly, the General Manager of the Glasgow District Subway Company, James G. Brown, issued an order in

## Mourning Dress

95 Deepest mourning for King Edward VII, from the *Ladies Field*, 21 May 1910. The bodice and cuffs are trimmed with crape and the skirt is also heavily banded with crape.

1901, changing the gold and silver braid on the brown uniforms of the smokeboys, conductors, drivers, inspectors and chief inspectors of the Glasgow underground to mourning black. The order has never been rescinded and throughout all the various changes that have taken place in the company, including the takeover by Glasgow Corporation, the use of black braid survived. It is still worn by a very few conductors and inspectors, though it is at last being phased out as an economy measure.[232]

The last really widespread and grand display of General mourning took place in 1910 after the death of Edward VII. Once again the *Illustrated London News* on 14 May described the rush to the mourning wear stores, only this time the article was illustrated with a drawing by Max Cowper of the scene at Harrods, with society ladies trying on mourning hats in the millinery department. The shops 'were literally besieged from morning to night.' The period of Court mourning lasted one year and 'the members of the Royal Family have received the King's Orders to take no part in any public event for six months from the demise of the late King and so all their

96 General mourning millinery for Edward VII, from the *Ladies Field*, 21 May 1910.
 *Top:* 'Turban of black straw, with osprey mount and black brocade crown.'
 *Left:* 'Toque of black panne velvet, with jet brim and black goura feather mount.'
 *Right:* 'Plumed picture hat of black Tagel.'

engagements are cancelled until November.' The *Illustrated London News* then went on to explain that the General mourning period was shorter, changing to half-mourning on 18 June 1911. Even before that date, however, at the specific request of the new King, George V, 'at the smart weddings that have recently taken place . . . white, grey, heliotrope and black-and-white were adopted sufficiently to prevent the gloom of unrelieved blacks making the brides feel depressed.'

After the first few weeks of deep General mourning, society once again resumed its usual round of activities, though without the presence of members of the Royal Family. Ascot took place just before the beginning of the official period of half-mourning and most of those present, at least in the expensive enclosures, wore the usual high fashion dresses and cart-wheel hats but all in black and white. The occasion was thereafter always remembered as Black Ascot.

# CHAPTER SEVEN

# *Children and Mourning*

UNTIL the recent twentieth-century advances in obstetrics, child care and immunisation, the death of babies and young children in Europe was a common occurrence. In the mid-nineteenth century when the rapid growth of industrialisation led to the creation of insanitary slums in the big cities, large numbers of children were killed by diseases such as measles, influenza, chicken pox, cholera and typhoid. In 1911 the bad living conditions, poor food and lack of medical care led to an infant mortality rate amongst manual workers in Britain of 152 per thousand, whilst even in the upper and middle classes it was 76.4 per thousand.[233] Almost every family had to face up to the death of at least one child, and often it was more.

Mothers, both rich and poor, were comforted by the teaching of the Christian church that life continued after death. The firm belief that they would eventually be reunited with their dead children aided many bereaved parents. Women's magazines were full of sentimental poems and stories which reinforced this conviction – in monthly instalments. *The Ladies' Treasury* of February 1877 published 'Our Darling's Grave' in which a mother mourns for her dead child. The last three verses read:

> Would I were by thy side, my love,
> My soul with thine in Heav'n above,

These bitter tears I shed in vain,
    I must not call thee back again.

I must not ask thee back, my life,
    Back to this world of woe and strife,
And all the pain that wearied thee,
    Thank God from all thou art now free.

No pain, no grief, no care for thee,
    From all life's weariness thou art free,
Thou'rt 'gone to God', where all is bright,
    And pure around His throne of light.

Another poem, written in 1862,[234] was intended to comfort mothers after the death of a baby:

It was a very solemn day,
    When little baby died,
And dear papa and dear mama
    Were very sad and cried.

And she was in that lovely land
    The white-winged angels' home,
Where all the little lambs of Christ,
    One day shall surely come.

'On the Death of a Little Child', written in 1863 and published in the *English Woman's Domestic Magazine*,[235] repeats the theme of innocence and purity:

Immortal bud of mortal birth,
    To thee brief date was given,
The flower that was too fair for earth,
    Is called to bloom in Heaven.

The theme of flowers and buds occurs frequently on children's gravestones. Kenneth Lindley writes that he has found it, 'with slight variations, in counties as far apart as Shropshire, Leicestershire, Essex and Wiltshire, especially on early nineteenth century stones.' The following epitaph is typical:

This lovely bud so young, so fair,
    Called home by early doom,
Just came to show how sweet a flower
    In Paradise would bloom.

This acceptance of the fragility of life is clearly expressed on another epitaph, from the tomb of two children, who died in their teens, in 1834 and 1836 and are buried at Tockenham in Wiltshire:

> Children are happy that depart so soon
> The morn of life is sweeter than the noon
> We soon spring up, we soon are gone
> So frail's the life of everyone.[236]

The women's magazines catering for middle-class readers reveal clearly middle-class attitudes to the poorest in society – namely that their wretched lot in life was ordained and that they must rely on the belief that their sufferings would be rewarded in the life after death. A poem called 'Mother's Last Words'[237] by Mrs Sewell, typifies the middle-class attitude to the poor. The poem unfolds in thirty-five verses the tragic tale of a London widow who dies in total poverty, leaving behind two young sons, Christopher and John. Christopher dies soon after:

> He left behind his wasted form,
> He rose above the toiling folk,
> Above the cross upon St. Paul's
> Above the fog above the smoke.
>
> And he went in and he saw the King,
> The Saviour who for him had died,
> And found once more his mother dear,
> And little Chris was satisfied.

Even then the tragedy is not ended. The poem concludes by forecasting the death of the last surviving child, John, pointing out that he would be happier and better off dead, reunited with his mother and brother who:

> . . . both together wait,
> Till John shall reach that happy home,
> And often from the golden gate,
> They watch, in hope, to see him come.

This middle-class acceptance of the squalor and horror of the poorest levels of industrial society was not shared by everyone. The early social reformers, Socialists, Christian Socialists and others, raised their voices in protest. There is no doubt, however, that Mrs Sewell's sentiments comforted and sustained many grieving parents, and that such attitudes have changed very little today. The In Memoriam columns of local newspapers are filled daily with verses and messages which have scarcely changed at all from those of the Victorian era. 'Rex, died 5th March 1971. Beautiful memories of my son, happily now reunited with his Dad,' is a typical example – taken from the Brighton *Evening Argus* on 5 March 1979.

This belief in the after-life dominated Victorian attitudes to the death of their children. It was, therefore, vital that babies and children should be christened as soon as possible. They could thus be sure of being received into the Kingdom of Heaven, should the worst befall. Great attention was, in consequence, paid to early baptisms and it is even rumoured that during a difficult birth a priest would stand by ready to splash holy water over the baby as it emerged from the womb.

Mothers were comforted too by the Christian teachings that young children were specially called to the side of the Almighty, where they were received with special favour. When death did take its toll, babies were carefully buried in their chrisoms, or baptismal robes, as proof that the child had been baptised.[238] In Slovakia Catholic babies were carried to church for christening by their godmothers, as early as three days after birth.[239] Amongst the Catholic peasant Matyos in the uplands of Hungary, it is believed that the soul of a dead child, who has not been baptised, will wander about miserably in the countryside, appearing each seventh year in the same bush or hedge until some good soul takes pity on it. 'Such a person should throw a white cloth at it, saying: "I christen you in the name of the Father, the Son and the Holy Spirit; if you are a boy your name shall be Adam, if you are a girl it shall be Eve." After this the soul is immediately freed and turns itself into an Angel and the Gates of Heaven open before it.'[240]

It is interesting here to note the differences between attitudes towards the death of the very young in Christian and pre-literate societies. While the nineteenth-century European mother rushed to have her baby baptised as soon as possible, in pre-literate societies the very opposite was the case. Here the lives of babies were even more precarious and their death was even expected. Young children were in consequence often not recognised as having a real social personality of their own for the first few years of life. They were not seen as established members of the community. They were non-persons, with an uncertain, fragile hold on life. Their death, half-expected, could thus be more easily accepted.

It has been recorded that up till the 1920s the Yorubas of Western Nigeria cast their dead babies outside the villages into the bush, where they were left prey to the night jackals. Nowadays they are buried in the forest or back yard, but still without the ritual bathing, head shaving or dressing that would normally accompany a funeral.[24]

Dead babies and young children were cast aside in a manner which, even to our post-Hiroshima eyes, seems callous and cruel, but because the children had not been ritually baptised, they could not be buried with the usual honours.

These unfortunate children, bringing in death, are regarded as highly dangerous and contaminating. In parts of western Africa no baby can be buried below the earth for fear of offending the Earth shrines, which bring fertility to humans and animals and ward off death from each compound. Amongst the Lodagaa in Ghana un-

97  The grave of an unweaned child, staked to the ground to prevent the child's spirit from wandering. Lodagaa, Ghana, West Africa, about 1960. (*By kind permission of Professor Jack Goody*)

weaned babies are buried at crossroads, by the roadside, beneath a pile of earth with their cradles above, held with stakes. The stakes are driven through the cradles to prevent the children coming back and plaguing their parents again.[242]

The Yorubas of Nigeria call these children *abiku*, or 'those born to die' and believe that abiku demons roam around in gangs at night, leaving their homes in the great iroko trees in the forests. Abiku children can be born again and again – 'each on coming into the world, would have arranged before hand the precise time he will return to his company.' It is believed that, where a woman has lost several babies, if certain rituals are adopted, her abiku infant can somehow be persuaded to stay beyond the prearranged date and thus forget its demon companions. Babies considered particularly vulnerable in this way are protected with charms and given significant names in order to show that their object has been anticipated. Such names include 'Malomo' or 'Do Not Go Again', 'Apara' or 'One Who Comes and Goes', 'Abiku' or 'Dead and Awake' and 'Duro-ori-ike' or 'Wait and See How You Will Be Petted'. Periodical feasts are held especially for these children at which the abiku spirits are believed to be present and thus appeased.[243]

In nineteenth-century Britain children were mourned and buried with exactly the same rituals as for adults. The funeral etiquette was the same, except that the accessories of dress and the coffin and carrying straps were all white – for families who could afford the outlay – symbolising the innocence and purity of the child. The undertakers' mutes, feathermen and coachmen wore white shoulder sashes, carried white wands and had white crape hat weepers. The black horses had white ostrich plumes and white saddle fittings. Male mourners wore white gloves with white crape weepers. They were often given white mourning neck scarves – silk for friends and crape for relatives.[244] The coffins of children were white as they still are today. Parents went into one year's mourning on the death of a child, whereas a child mourned one year for its parents.

The rich and poor buried their children as circumstances permitted. For the poor the problem of providing their dead children with a decent burial remained a constant anxiety. Parson Woodforde noted in his diary on 7 June 1771 that he buried 'a child of Giles Francis's by name J. Francis aged five years.' The child died at Bath and the family could not afford to hire a hearse to carry his body back to be buried at Ansford. Parson Woodforde recorded that the boy's father and eldest brother 'brought the child in a coffin upon their heads from Bath', arriving in the morning after setting out on their walk 'last night at twelve'.[245]

The widowed needlewoman who told her life story to Henry Mayhew in 1849 was even less able to provide for her dead children. Two of them died in a Limehouse workhouse and must have been buried by the Parish.[246] In Manchester a survey taken in 1833 showed that '40% of babies born to married spinners died in very early infancy.'[247] This high rate of infant mortality was not restricted to the industrial slums. In the churchyard of Easby Abbey, in the Yorkshire dales, there is a tombstone which was: 'Erected in the Memory of Joseph Barras of Brampton-on-Swale, who died on Sept. 1st. 1864, aged 57. – Also his children', whose deaths are carefully recorded:

> Joseph May 23rd 1843 aged 8 yrs.
> Eleonor July 20 1843 aged 2 yrs.
> William April 20 1845 aged 12 yrs.
> George Dec. 13th 1848 aged 12 yrs.
> William Feby. 22nd 1849 aged 10 mnths.
> Eleonor July 11th 1852 aged 5 yrs.
> Ann Oct 15th 1855 aged 1 yr.
> Timothy Jan. 1st 1859 aged 16 yrs.
> Robert Feb. 15th 1867 aged 17 yrs.
> Marmaduke Procter Sept. 26th 1868 aged 16 yrs.

The struggle to bury poor children decently continued well into the present century. Between 1909 and 1913 the Fabian Women's Group recorded the family budgets of working-class families in Lambeth, London, where a family 'are likely to loose' one or more of their young children. The familiar problem remained: 'Shall they run the risk of burial by the Parish, or shall they take Time by the forelock and insure each child as it is born at the rate of a penny a week?' Borrowing was an alternative to Parish burial.

> Up and down the street sums are collected in pence and sixpences . . . Funerals are not run on credit; but the neighbours, who may be absolute strangers, will contribute rather than suffer the degradation to pauperism of one of themselves. [Paying the money back was not easy.] For months afterwards the mother and remaining children will eat less in order to pay back the money borrowed. The father of the family cannot eat less. He is already eating as little as will enable him to earn the family wage.[248]

In August 1911 a baby of six months died in Lambeth of infantile cholera. She had been insured with a Society for 2d a week, the bill for her burial was:

|  | £ | s | d |
|---|---|---|---|
| Funeral | 1 | 12 | 0 |
| Death Certificate | 0 | 1 | 3 |
| Gravediggers | 0 | 2 | 0 |
| Hearse Attendants | 0 | 2 | 0 |
| Woman to lay her out | 0 | 2 | 0 |
| Insurance Agent | 0 | 1 | 0 |
| Flowers | 0 | 0 | 6 |
| Black tie for father | 0 | 1 | 0 |
| Total | 2 | 1 | 9 |

This was a respectable burial, but even so, the baby was buried in a common grave with three others. Afterwards 'the survivors lived on reduced rations for two weeks in order to get square again.'[249] The funeral would have been more costly had the child been older, for 'When a child's body is too long to go under the box-seat of the driver [of the hearse], the price of the funeral goes up.'

Another source of money, when the neighbours could not help and the child was uninsured, was the money-lender. 'The terms are a penny a week on every shilling borrowed, with, it may be, a kind of tip of half a crown at the end when all the principle and interest has been paid off. A woman borrowing 6s pays 6d a week in sheer interest – that is, £1/6s a year – without reducing her debt a penny.' As the Fabian group pointed out she was paying 433 per cent on her loan. The money-lenders were a last resort; even loans at that extortionate rate were preferable to pauper burial. One woman declared to the Fabian women that she 'would as soon have the dust-cart call for the body of her child as that there Black Mariar' [the parish pauper's hearse].[250]

Young children are nowadays often shielded from the facts of death but in the nineteenth century, when the realities of death were so much part of family life, even quite young children took part in the funerals of their relatives and friends. An engraved illustration for a hymn called 'The Tolling Bell' published by the S.P.C.K. in the late 1840s shows six little girls carrying the coffin of an infant to the grave-side. 'They wear white dresses in token of the dead child's

98 (*above left*) 'Home from sea' by Arthur Hughes, about 1856.
The young girl is shown in deepest mourning with a crape
covered cloak, skirt and bonnet. (*Ashmolean Museum, Oxford*)

99 (*above right*) Half-mourning dress, Paris, 1812. French
fashion plate, showing woman in grey, black and white and the
baby in white trimmed with black. (*Pearl Binder Collection*)

innocence and black ribbons for their grief.'[251] Ellen Buxton, the
second of thirteen children from a middle-class, evangelical family
who lived at Leytonstone near London, recorded in her diary in
1864 when she was twelve years old, the death of three infants in her
own family. She describes her little brother Leo's burial a year later.
'We went to the little corner in which the grave was dug by the side
of the little twins and Aunt Buxton's little boy.'[252]

Children not only attended funerals but were put into mourning
dress and observed the correct periods of mourning in the same way
as adults. Children mourned the death of a parent for twelve months
– the first six in the dull black and heavy crape of deepest mourning.
For the next three months of Ordinary mourning they wore black
silk without crape. The final three months were spent in half-
mourning colours.[253] Children wore mourning for all relatives and
for periods of General Court mourning.

Until the 1760s children in fashionable society wore clothes that
were exact replicas of adult fashions. Their mourning clothes too
would have been cut following the style of adult garments. In 1529
Sir David Owen left instruction in his will that his children be

100   (*above left*) Maria Elizabeth, one of the daughters of
George II, Landgrave of Hesse, at her father's funeral, July 1661,
engraved by Adrien Schoonebeek.

101   (*above right*) Young male relatives of George II, Landgrave
of Hesse, at his funeral in 1661, engraved by Adrien
Schoonebeek.

provided with mourning wear. 'To make them gownes and hodes
after the maner and facon of morners . . . I wille that everyone of my
children have gownes and hodes of blake clothe.'[254] After the funeral
of the Earl of Rutland in 1587, his three young sons were given 'each
one a cloak of a yard and half' and a matching hose and doublet of
black bombazine.[255]

A folio published in 1662 to mark the funeral obsequies of George
II, Landgrave of Hesse, in Germany, who was buried in July 1661,
shows Fraulein Maria Elisabeth, the Landgrafin of Hesse, shrouded
from head to foot in black draperies, like a tiny black ghost. The
young boys in the procession wear tall crowned hats with long falls
and full length mourning cloaks, exactly like their male relatives.[256]

When Elizabeth Verney died, in 1685, her four children were all
under the age of six. They were put into the best quality crape
mourning at 17d a yard. The cloth crape of their uncle, Sir Ralph
Verney of Claydon House, 'cost but 14d'.[257] Three years later Sir
Ralph's son, Edmund, died, leaving a daughter, Molly, aged thirteen.
A friend wrote to Sir Ralph in some anxiety over the unsuitability of
Molly's mourning dress.

She is forst to ware her blak coat under her whit fustion, & tis a ridiculos sit to see her whit coat next her cloth crape coat for a father, she must have stoft to make her a petycoat to her night gownd, her old callowco petycoat I shall leve as far as it will go & she must have 5 or 7 of the narrow lases . . and blk silke to make it up; she must have 3 yds of any blk cloth crape to peas out her crape coat wch is too short to ware for shee is much growne. Bell must bespeak a pare of blak leather shus for her & charge the woman to make them strong, the very sols of her shus is worn off . . . she wants 2 blk. top knots of tafety, a pare of blk leather gloves & some blk pins.[258]

In the last forty years of the eighteenth century a significant change took place in the dress of young children. Both girls and boys, for the first time, began to wear different clothes from their parents – clothes that allowed for more comfort and freedom of movement. Girls wore plain silk or muslin dresses with wide sashes, and young boys were put into 'skeleton' suits with soft falling frilled collars. An interesting parallel change is seen in mourning dress for children. Although black was still de rigueur for deepest mourning, white dresses trimmed with black became acceptable for boys and girls under the age of about six. This change marked a definite breakdown in the traditional Royal Renaissance etiquette of mourning. Changes in children's dress very often precede a similar relaxation in women's dress. The freer clothes of the 1770's girls were copied some ten years later by their mothers. The less lugubrious mourning dress of the eighteenth-century children, however, did not have an immediate impact on the mourning dress of their mothers but it did introduce a new liberalising attitude to the rigours of mourning etiquette followed later by adults.

A few examples of mourning dress worn by children survive in museum collections. The Museum of Costume in Bath owns a white cotton piqué dress, worn by a young boy, appliquéd with black silk braid, and the Museum of the City of London has an elegant little white, muslin dress for a girl, of the 1860–70 period. The black waist sash is tied at the back to resemble a fashionable bustle. This dress may have been worn as half-mourning. A photograph of Edith Amelia, the daughter of the Countess of Dudley, taken in about 1882, shows her mourning for her grandmother. Edith, aged ten, wears a low-waisted white dress, with black stockings, black button boots and a black hat trimmed with black ostrich feathers.[259]

Many young children continued to be put into black throughout

102  (*above*) Young boy's mourning dress of white cotton duck, with black braid trimming and sash, 1860–70. (*Museum of Costume, Bath*)

103  (*right*) Georgina Elizabeth, Countess of Dudley and her daughter Edith Amelia, aged 10, in about 1882, wearing mourning after the death of the Countess's husband's mother, Amelia, wife of the 10th Baron Ward, on 23 May 1882. Edith Amelia wears a white dress, black stockings and boots and a black hat. Photograph by W. and D. Downey, London. (*By kind permission of Professor Helmut Gernsheim*)

their periods of mourning, and for the older girls black mourning was usual. One girl, in mourning for her grandfather, in about 1878, 'was at once clothed in black cashmere, so lavishly trimmed about with crape that I must have looked like a miniature widow of that period, without the cap.'[260] A photograph taken in 1868 of Miss Emily Wells, aged thirteen, standing next to her father, after her mother's death, shows her probably in Second mourning. Emily's black silk dress is hemmed and edged with crape, and she wears a

long black, chain, jet necklace, with earrings to match. Frances Hodgson Burnett, in *The Secret Garden*, published in 1911, describes Mary in mourning wear for her parents. She 'folded her thin little black-gloved hands in her lap. Her black dress made her look yellower than ever, and her limp light hair straggled under her black crape hat.'[261]

Many of the little Victorian white dresses trimmed with black would have been worn by young boys in mourning. Once past the age of breeching – about four to six years old – they would have abandoned their white dresses in favour of black cloth suits worn with black crape armbands, black buttons and black boots.

Unlike adults, who could keep a set of suitably sombre clothes in the wardrobe from year to year, children would soon outgrow theirs and have to be frequently refitted. It was consequently an expensive business and had always been so. In 1690 Sir Ralph Verney had issued orders that his granddaughter, Molly Verney, aged fifteen, and mourning for her brother Edmund, be given mourning 'as little and as cheap as possible, seeing she grows apace.' Molly objected and demanded a more expensive cloth gown. 'I know my mourning will cost a good deall of mony, but I believe you wod have me morn hansomely for so deare a brother, and since ther is none left but myself to morn for him, and I beg that I may have a tipit bought me, since every gentlewoman has one as makes any show in the world, it will cost £5 at best.' Molly had her way and received both the gown and the tippet, with advice from her grandfather: 'I hope you will ware it with the more care & make it last the handsomer & the longer.'[262]

The familiar standby of dyeing ordinary clothes black was the cheapest way of providing children's mourning clothes, as we have seen with the Arkwright family (Chapter 4). In September 1904 the widow of William Joseph Mason, a butcher, living in Holloway, North London, was unexpectedly faced with the problem of putting her five daughters into mourning, after her husband's sudden death at the age of forty-seven. Meat trading was considered a well-to-do profession but even so Mrs Mason could not afford to buy any mourning clothes for her children. Her daughter, Mrs C. M. Salmon, now in her eighties and living in King's Norton, Birmingham, was then about five. She remembers that the five girls of the family had

104   Miss Emily Wells, aged 13, with her father, wearing mourning for her mother who died in 1868. Miss Wells's black jet earrings are still in the collection of her granddaughter, Miss W. E. Patchin of Brighton. Miss Wells is probably in Second mourning. (*By kind permission of Miss W. E. Patchin*)

105  Mrs Mason of Holloway, London in 1904, possibly in Second mourning, with slight crape trimming on collar and cuffs. Mrs Mason dyed her daughters' apple-green cashmere dresses black, in mourning for their father who died in September 1904. (*By kind permission of Mrs Christine Salmon*)

just been given their new summer dresses – of fine apple-green cashmere. These were immediately sent to the local dyers to be dyed black. Mrs Salmon remembers that afterwards her mother always regretted having chosen green for those summer dresses – since it is traditionally held to be such an unlucky colour.

Even babies were not exempt from the strictures of etiquette. Their white robes were trimmed with black embroidery or ribbon. In a traditional English folk song, believed to have been written on the death of Jane Seymour, third wife of Henry VIII, who died in 1537 after giving birth to the future Edward VI, we read that:[263]

> 'King Henry went mourning, and so did his men,
> And so did the dear baby, for Queen Jane did die then.'

In 1808 Mrs Sherwood, in mourning for her own 2-year-old

child, trimmed her 3-month-old daughter Lucy's cap, with 'bows of narrow, black love-ribbon', and tied a black love-sash around her waist.[264] A French fashion plate published in 1812 shows a widow with a baby at her feet, both dressed in highly fashionable half-mourning. The baby wears a white muslin, high-waisted dress and a frilled white cap. The robe and cap are both embroidered with black thread, in delicate neo-classical style and trimmed with narrow, black ribbon.

The Saltire Society, in Edinburgh, own a similar cap, dating from the middle of the nineteenth century. It is of fine muslin, heavily frilled, embroidered with a floral design in white cotton thread and openwork. It was worn by a baby girl, after her mother had died giving birth to her, and the bereaved relatives added lavish loops and a rosette of the same narrow, black, silk love-ribbon.

Even the cot sheets of a baby in mourning could be embroidered with black thread. This was certainly the practice in eighteenth-century Switzerland, where, according to the *Studio* magazine of 1924, cradle linen was embroidered in black silk floral motifs for mourning. The illustrations to the article 'Peasant Art in Switzerland' by Daniel Baud-Bovy, show cot sheets and pillow cases and even a small infant's 'binder' or undervest, embroidered in mourning black.

Queen Victoria, who saw to it that the minutiae of mourning etiquette was strictly observed by all branches of the Royal Family, wrote a reproving letter to her eldest daughter, 'Vicky', who was married to the Crown Prince of Prussia. Victoria complained that, after the death of her husband's grandmother, 'Vicky' had not put her 5-month-old baby into mourning. The Queen advised that the baby should be put into 'white and lilac, but not colours'. She added: 'You must promise me that if I should die your child or children and those around you should mourn; this really must be, for I have such strong feelings on this subject.'[265] In 1860 Victoria put her own youngest child, Princess Beatrice, aged three, into mourning for the child's mother's half-sister's husband and was very pleased with the result. 'Darling Beatrice looks lovely in her black silk and crape dress.'[266]

When Prince Albert died Victoria plunged all her nine children into the very deepest of deep mourning clothes. Some of these survive today in the collection of the Museum of London, including a suit worn by Prince Arthur and a dress and cape belonging to

106 (*above left*) Princess Beatrice's mourning dress for her father Prince Albert, 1862. Black bombazine dress, the bodice trimmed with black silk crape; dress lightly boned. It was worn with a deeply hooded black woollen cloak (not shown). The Princess was Victoria's youngest child, then aged 5. (*Museum of London*)

107 (*above right*) Prince Arthur's mourning suit for his father, Prince Albert, 1862. A black tailored, woollen Highland suit; jacket trimmed with black braid with black crape armband on left arm; kilt trimmed with a black leather tab, and black buckle. Prince Arthur was the Queen's third son, then aged 11. (*Museum of London*)

Princess Beatrice. Prince Arthur's suit is a Highland outfit – with a black frogged jacket trimmed with dull black braid and a crape armband. A black cloth kilt fastens with a black buckle. Beatrice's dress is in bombazine, with a wide shoulder line, covered by a deeply hooded black cloak. There is a little dress very similar to Beatrice's in the collection of the Costume Institute of the Metropolitan Museum of Art. This one is in dull black silk, with a wide skirt of the 1844 period. It has detachable sleeves, and was given to the museum in 1939 by Miss S. B. Bradley (no. 39, 89, a, b, c).

Attempts were made to free children from the burden of wearing mourning dress when the etiquette of adult mourning was at its height. Ellen Buxton wrote in her diary in 1863 that: 'This evening we got the sad news of poor Mrs Fitch's death, she died between 3 and 4 o'clock, and was quite conscious all the time, when she knew she was dying she fixed that her girls should not go into very deep mourning.'[267]

108 Young girl's mourning dress, 1844, in black bombazine, with detachable sleeves. Ordinary or half-mourning dress, about 1876–7, in black silk faille. (*By kind permission of Joshua Greene, The Costume Institute, Metropolitan Museum of Art, New York*)

Anne Buck quotes from a book called *How to Dress Well on a Shilling a Day*, by Sylvia, published in 1875: 'It is desirable that children should be put into mourning dress as seldom as possible; only in fact for the nearest relatives. The little children do not understand it and it is absurd to invest them with the signs of grief they cannot feel. Absence of a positive colour' (the wearing of white) 'is quite sufficient mourning for children.'[268] Not only, therefore, did children pioneer the breakdown of the use of deep black for mourning but they also pioneered the breakdown of the use of mourning dress altogether. It took another fifty years for their mothers to follow suit.

There is one more category of funeral which falls outside that of the normal adult funeral ritual and that is the burial of young, single adults, especially single girls. In pre-literate, peasant and urban cultures such a death is seen as the most shocking of all. The funeral etiquettes for the young and unmarried of these three cultures are basically similar. Young girls are judged to die totally unfulfilled and their death is attributed to unnatural, magical influences. Such a death is a disruption of the normal process of life and is mourned with bitter regret and anxiety. It is feared that the spirit of someone who has died so young will be refused entry into paradise and, in revenge, will try to take the place of a living person, or in vengeance for its premature death, will wreak havoc on the relatives and community. Special ceremonies are performed to try and remedy this terrible prospect.

Attempts are made to deceive not only the spirits of the next world, but the dead themselves into believing that the unwed had in reality been married before death, by the holding of death-weddings. In these ceremonies the dead are ritually married, often to a living partner. Special services were held in ancient Greece on the death of young, single people, though no evidence has survived to show that these were death-weddings.[269] In England, however, in 1603, the streets were described as being 'strawed with flowers when maids of any sort are buried . . . and for batchelors they wear rosemary, as if it were a marriage.'[270] Bridal wreaths of flowers were put on the corpse of an unmarried girl and also worn by her attendants, or carried at the funeral. By the seventeenth century it was customary for the bridal garland to be hung over the dead girl's pew or in the chancel of the church, where it was left until it disintegrated. Wreaths were also made of dyed horn, gold and silver filigree work gilded birds' eggs and shells and silk and paper flowers.[271] These 'maidens' garlands' are still in use at the church of Abbotts Ann in Hampshire, where the garlands date from 1716 to the present day.[272] Charles Booth recorded in London in 1898 that as a young girl lay dying her fellow members of the local Burial Club brought the girl's funeral wreath to her before her death. 'They were exceedingly anxious she should live long enough to see it, which happily she did, and . . . they went with it in a body to her room. She was immensely pleased and touched.'[273] Phillis Cunnington and Catherine Lucas report the description of the burial of 'a much loved maiden lady who lay in her coffin with a chaplet of eucharis and lilies of the valley.' This was at Teignmouth in Devon in 1892.[274]

Miss Emily Davidson, the suffragette, who died after throwing herself beneath the hooves of the King's horse at the Derby in July 1913, was given a traditional single maiden's burial, though her

109  Bridal wreaths and maidens' garlands, 1860, in the church
at Ashton-in-the-Water, Derbyshire, from Margaret Baker,
*Folklore and Customs of Rural England*, 1974 (*By kind
permission of the author*)

funeral cortège was swelled by ranks of her sister suffragettes. They
dressed in white to mourn their unmarried colleague. Some carried
white madonna lilies, others laurel wreaths, though the front rank of
the procession in a distinctly untraditional manner carried a banner
which read 'FIGHT ON AND GOD WILL GIVE THE
VICTORY'.[275]

The folk song historian the late A. L. Lloyd believed that evidence
survives to show that death-weddings were still occasionally taking
place in Britain in the late nineteenth century. A local newspaper in

the Portsmouth area published in 1881 an account of the funeral of the 20-year-old daughter of a naval officer, who fell ill and died on the eve of her wedding. She was dressed in her wedding dress, the bridesmaids put on their special clothes, the hearse was decorated with orange blossom and the coffin was taken to the church. In front of the congregation the groom, nearly out of his mind with grief, stood by the upended coffin and the parson read the wedding service. This was followed immediately by the funeral service and the corpse with its attendant bridesmaids was taken to the cemetery.[276]

Complex death-wedding ceremonies still survive in peasant communities. Miguel Covarrubias witnessed a death-wake in 1947, in Tehuantepec, Mexico, where there was no mourning because it was considered that the deceased's spirit, uncontaminated by sin, must go straight to heaven. The death-wake, held nine days after the burial, was arranged to 'marry the virgin soul to a young bride or groom – a former friend or sweetheart of the deceased, who sits throughout the night at the macabre party'.[277]

In Catholic Hungary, especially on the death of young unmarried men or women, the funeral feast 'changes almost into a wedding feast' for 'the bridegrooms or brides of Heaven'. Coloman Mikes, a nobleman of Transylvania, who died in 1686, feasted the death of his only daughter who died unmarried. He declared that he had married her to 'Our Saviour Christ' and that 'All who love me are to be gay at my house today.' From the seventeenth century a special death-dance, in which the deceased was represented, was performed at the grave-side during a death-wedding. The dead girl-bride sang the following song:

> My priest is my father,
> And my good minister,
> The choirmaster who sings
> Is my best man and my witness,
> My bridesmaids are
> The spades and hoes here used.
> Such is my wedding.[278]

The fiancé, lover or occasionally a relative acted the part of the bride or groom and was given presents by the family. A dead boy was accompanied by bridesmaids and a girl by best man. The mourners used to walk in procession to the grave, in their festival dress, carrying wedding banners. These ceremonies are still taking place in the north of Hungary.[279]

Records show that death-weddings were still taking place in many other parts of Europe in the present century. The Norsk Museet, Stockholm, has in its archives reports of at least thirty-five funerals between 1912–31, in which unmarried girls were dressed as brides, with wedding wreaths, metal crowns and bridal veils, sometimes with a wedding bouquet in the hand. The Finnish folklorist Prof. E. A. Virtauen reported a death-wedding in West Finland in 1957, where the dead bride wore a wedding ring of shiny paper.

In France girls were buried in bridal white with orange blossom wreaths. Until the early years of the present century wedding dances were performed at funerals by youngsters of approximately the same age as the dead person. They would sing in the procession to the cemetery and afterwards hold a wedding feast with special wedding dishes and dancing until nightfall.

In Germany this ceremony, called *Totenhochzeit*, was practised into this century. In the South the most important feature was the bridal crown, sometimes as much as half a metre high, built up on a wooden frame with branches of myrtle, sprigs of rosemary, coloured paper, ribbons, artificial flowers, beads and tinsel. Some crowns would show the girl's name, whilst others featured a large letter 'J', for *Jungfrau*, virgin. The crown was either buried with the body, left in the church or kept by the family. Death-weddings were taking place in Italy and Austria in the 1950s.

These ceremonies have survived longest in the Balkans and are still taking place in Romania. A. L. Lloyd watched such weddings in the 1960s and described how the dead girl or boy is dressed in wedding clothes by the bridesmaids or best men. In a normal wedding a fir tree is cut down, decorated with ornaments and set up at the gate of the courtyards where the wedding party is taking place. At a death-wedding a group of young men, dressed as if for a normal wedding, choose a tree from the forest singing that it is needed for the wedding of a fine young man or woman. The tree is instead set up at the head of the grave, and the song continues with the tree replying: 'Oh, if I'd known it was for this purpose, I'd never have agreed to come.'[280] (Trees are a life symbol. In many cultures they are believed to provide a dwelling place for the souls of the dead and are consequently planted over graves.)[281] While watching a death-wedding, a peasant woman remarked to the Romanian folklorist Constantin

Brailoiu: 'You know, it's necessary to deceive the dead a little.'

It is not only the unmarried who are buried in wedding clothes. In many parts of the world the dead are buried in their best festival or wedding garments as a proof of their married state. This poses a difficult problem for museum ethnographers, who tour the villages seeking examples of fine old embroideries and clothing that are no longer made. The old women are loathe to part with their clothes, feeling that they would not then be properly dressed at death, and thus many rare examples are lost to museum collections. It was believed in old Russia that if a corpse was buried in secondhand clothes, the dead might become vampires and destroy the original owner of the garment. Fear of the malevolence of the dead features prominently in all these customs. In Sandomierz, in Poland, the contrary belief is held. The dead are never buried in new clothes, in case evil spirits bent on plunder should be attracted to the grave.[282]

The death of prostitutes falls into the category of deaths of the young and unmarried, though not, of course, in the eyes of respectable society. Prostitutes in the Victorian era were buried by their friends and colleagues with all the etiquette accorded to virgins. They were given the respectability in death that was denied them in life. A prostitute's hearse was decorated with the white plumes and ribands of the virginal, to the fury of conventional society. In the 1850s Frederick Rogers witnessed the funeral of a prostitute who had been stabbed to death on Ratcliffe Highway by a sailor, near the London docks. He wrote that, 'some two hundred of the sisterhood, all dressed in deep black', joined the procession making a deep impression on all who watched the parade on its way to Bow Cemetery. At such a funeral, Rogers explained, the hearse was mounted with white feathers and 'as many of her sisters as cared followed it in couples to the grave . . . Usually, also, a guard of men of the kind who were called "bullies" [i.e. pimps] walked on either side of the women, to prevent – so it was said – any hooting or stone-throwing on the part of the virtuous matrons of the neighbourhood through which the procession passed.'[283]

For many centuries prostitutes and actresses, who were classed together, were usually refused church burial. In 1729 the great French tragic actress, Adrienne Lecouvreur, the leading lady in Voltaire's dramas, was not only declined the rites of the church but was refused a church burial, to the great distress of her friend Voltaire. Her body was wrapped in clothes and carted away at night to be buried secretly in an unknown grave.[284] In 1954 Colette, the French novelist and recipient of the Grand Cross of the Legion of Honour, died at the age of eighty-one. She was accused of anti-clericalism and denied a church burial, despite being given a state funeral. Her husband, Maurice Goudeket, wrote later: 'I should have liked to have a cross on the pink and black granite tomb I made for her at the Père-Lachaise.' Instead the tomb carries the inscription: 'Here Lies Colette'.

# CHAPTER EIGHT

# *The Mourning Dress and Textile Industries*

$\text{T}$RADESMEN and industrialists with business interests
in death made a good living in the Victorian period. Some made their
fortunes. The undertakers, mourning warehouses, stationers,
florists, stone masons and textile manufacturers ran thriving enter-
prises. They were careful to maintain the upper-class image attached
to the rituals of death, which appealed so much to the social pretensions of their middle-class customers. They stressed the royal origins
of their trade and exploited their royal and aristocratic patrons in
advertising campaigns. Rushton's, manufacturers of hair mourning
jewellery, of Clerkenwell Road, London, for example, named 'the
nobility, gentry and clergy' as their customers in an advertisement of
1860.[286] Priestly's went one better in the 1890s using the name of
Queen Victoria's eldest daughter, Victoria, the widowed Empress
of Germany, to promote their mourning textiles in America. 'The
Empress and her daughters wear gowns, Marie Stuart caps and long
veils all of black crape . . . Following her example the black crape cap
has at last replaced the white one at the English Court – only the
Queen retaining the white cap.'[287] Using the familiar technique still
used by today's commercial advertisers, they hoped to attract the
lower ranks of society by naming the rich and influential as their
customers. Even the meanest undertakers' establishments in the
slums of the industrial cities were impressively decorated in black

and gold paint. Every attempt was made to make mourning ware-houses and undertakers' shops as grandiose as possible.

The mourning warehouses or 'Maisons de Deuil' (as the grander English establishments preferred to be called) undertook to supply everything that was required for a socially correct funeral, including the undertaker and his staff, the hearse, horses and all the mourning clothing and accessories. They made it as easy as possible for their customers to part with their money. Assistants would be dispatched to the house to take the measurements of the family and servants for their black clothes and to advise discreetly on the social correctness of the proceedings. Many warehouses issued booklets setting out in detail all the etiquette of bereavement. The ritual was so complicated that this advice was welcomed by families frightened of losing face by slipping up on the rules. No details were forgotton by the warehouses. The telegraphic address of the Mourning Department of Harrods in 1895 was 'Everything, London', and they did indeed supply everything for a 'funeral in town or country', including open and closed funeral cars (which must have been very new indeed) or the traditional mourning carriages. They issued photographs of tombs, memorials and headstones, as did Hannington's of Brighton, listing the varied stone types and prices. They undertook cremations and embalmings and offered a choice of lead, oak or elm coffins. Their mourning wear department offered a wide range of everything necessary for elegant mourning wear, sending materials and patterns on approval – post free.

*Myra's Journal of Dress and Fashion* declared on 1 March 1887 that the firm of Peter Robinson's of Regent Street was:

> a house in which we can order every detail required for mourning in a comfortable private room, free from observation or if we are unable to go to Regent Street, we can give our order to the very intelligent travelling assistants who will come to our house immediately on being summoned by letter or telegram, bringing a choice of dresses, costumes, mantles, chapeaux, petticoats, hosiery, gloves and necessary jet ornaments as brooches, earrings etc.

Peter Robinson's arch rival across the corner at the top of Regent Street was the firm of Jay's. They also boasted of their efficiently trained staff: 'It is obvious that operations so multifarious and extended, embracing as they do correspondence or personal attendance on clients in every part of the United Kingdom, cannot

110 Mourning Warehouse, Paris, about 1885. The Grande
Maison de Noir, 27 & 29, Rue Faubourg St Honoré, from a
brochure on mourning etiquette written by Mme de Abijes on
behalf of the store. (*By kind permission of Professor D. C.
Coleman and Courtaulds Ltd*)

be efficiently carried out without the maintenance of a carefully
trained staff or travelling representatives.'[288]

A booklet published in the 1880s by the Grand Maison de Noir of
27 & 29, Faubourg St Honoré, Paris, listed all the intricacies of the
funeral ritual. Bereaved customers were advised to maintain a
discreet silence in the house and warned that fresh floral tributes
were more socially admired than wire or bead offerings. In an effort
to encourage wayward customers to pay for the complete all-in-one
service, the firm warned that 'neglected details can lead to unhappy
situations which can cause considerable distress.'[289] It was, of
course, more profitable for funeral emporiums if the details of
mourning, especially the degrees of mourning in dress, were
preserved. At a time of growing defiance of the tyranny of funeral

ritual, these booklets and the carefully worded advice of the travelling representatives encouraged the artificial prolongation of the wearing of mourning dress.

The Grand Maison de Noir was one of the grandest mourning warehouses in Paris, situated as it was in the Faubourg St Honoré, near to the great establishment of the couturier Charles Worth, and the best Court dressmakers and textile emporiums in the world. The Grand Maison was one of many new shops. From about 1840 large mourning warehouses catering for the new middle-class market were opening in the most elegant shopping streets of all the big cities. They often developed from large wholesale drapers' stores which supplied furnishing, dress fabrics and household linens. They flourished on mourning mania, helped both by the invention of the sewing machine and by the low wages they paid their needlewomen, dressmakers and shop assistants.

Hannington's of Brighton was such a store, starting as a drapers in 1808, and gradually developing a huge funeral department. A bill from the stores archives, dated to the 1820s, reads: 'Bought of S. Hannington Linen and Woollen Draper to His Majesty, Nos., 3 & 4, North Street . . . Crape 9s and yd Sarsenet.' As mourning etiquette faded, the connections with mourning and death were no longer considered so desirable. They were even thought to be unlucky. By the 1880s Hannington's, for one, had built an entirely separate red brick Victorian Gothick mourning establishment in nearby Hove. The Brighton premises were turned into the elegant department store of today – a development repeated by many mourning warehouses.

In London, Regent Street contained the most famous mourning warehouses. The House of Jay opened in 1841, occupying three large houses. It was followed by Pugh's Mourning Warehouse, which opened in 1849 at 173, Regent Street, Peter Robinson's, the Argyll General and Mantle Warehouse in 1854 and the West General Mourning Warehouse, of High Holborn. Henry Mayhew wrote in 1865 of memories of a visit he paid to Jay's, as a child: 'We noted the quietness, the harmonious so to speak hush of the whole place and were impressed with the total "unshoppy" character of the establishment.' Mayhew, with his sharp eye for social pretension, caught the flavour perfectly. 'Unshoppy' is a very revealing word. It would not have done for a 'trade' atmosphere to have prevailed. Instead, Mayhew described a room with 'tall gothic windows; it was

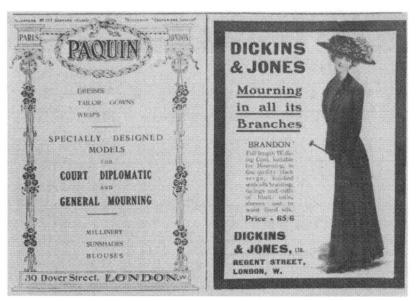

111   Advertisements for General mourning after the death of
King Edward VII, from *Black and White* magazine, London,
14 May 1910.
   *Left:* The London branch of the French haute couture house of
Mme Paquin advertises 'specially designed models for Court,
Diplomatic and General Mourning.'
   *Right:* Dickins & Jones – showing pictures of a 'Full length
Walking Coat, suitable for Mourning, in fine quality black serge,'
of high-class, ready-to-wear standard.

softly carpeted, so that you scarcely heard your own footsteps as
you trod along . . . On either side of the doorway are massive
mahogany tables, by the side of which we can take our seat and call
for any possible kind of mourning one may require.'[290]

Speed was the all important factor when ordering mourning wear.
The bereaved had to be fitted out with their mourning dresses as
soon as possible, made to measure. Before the opening of the
mourning warehouses full mourning was not put on until eight days
after the bereavement,[291] because the clothes could not be made up
in time. By the 1860s, however, the outfit was available in a day,
measured, made up and delivered. Barkers of Kensington advised its
customers in 1900 to save time by sending 'a cash deposit of about
half the value of the goods, to save the three days bank clearance
necessary otherwise.'[292] Mourning wear may have been responsible
for some of the first attempts at selling clothes by hire purchase.

The invention of the sewing machine in 1846 undoubtedly helped
the quick provision of mourning dress, though a great deal of the
sewing and trimming was done by hand right into the present

century. One of the techniques used to speed up the process was to make up most of the dress leaving only the fitting of the bodice to be completed, suiting each individual customer's measurements. Jay's announced in 1877 that mourning orders entrusted to them would be 'completed with the utmost speed compatible with the requirements of taste and technical excellence.'[293] By 1910 the dresses were offered on sale completely finished, which speeded up the provision of mourning attire still further. Dresses could still be altered as required by the store's own fitters. Despite the haste, however, it was considered essential that no hint of slapdash workmanship could be allowed to tarnish the elegant image.

The need for speed, combined with the uniformity of mourning garments, allowed the shops to stockpile mourning wear in advance. The mourning warehouses thus encouraged the development of ready-to-wear clothes for middle and upper-class clients. This was an important advance in the fashion world – one which was to lay the foundations of today's multi-million pound fashion industry. As long as the warehouses could exploit the exclusive ingredient of royal and upper-class patrons, ready-to-wear clothes became socially acceptable. By 1910 even the *Illustrated London News* was openly recommending wholesale mourning dress. After the death of Edward VII in the spring of 1910, their fashion correspondent 'Filomena' declared:

> It is one of the changes of our time that women purchase ready-made or partly-made clothing so much more than they use to do. Time was when anybody with pretensions to be a 'lady' would have snorted with indignation if charged with the wearing of ready-made clothing. Now thousands of ladies went forth and bought their mourning in the shape of ready-made garments, especially of the coat and skirt order. They need only slight alteration to adapt them to the individual figure that all the big shops are prepared to undertake and a woman of average figure feels it neither a disadvantage nor a disgrace to don garments of good fabric and style, though made by the gross.

'Filomena' does not add that these clothes were also considerably cheaper than those produced by the private dressmakers. The warehouses and department stores were able to buy their mourning fabrics in such large quantities that they were able to charge less than the small dressmaker.

Another reason for the growth in sales of mourning wear in the

*Mourning Dress*

112  Half-mourning for King Edward VII. Gown, of plain and figured silks, from the *Ladies Field*, 21 May 1910.

nineteenth century was the improvement in transport – in particular the building of railways and steamships, which made such an important contribution to the Industrial Revolution. The mourning industry was quick to take commercial advantage of this new ease and speed of travel, sending their salesmen far and wide in search of custom. Courtaulds built up an impressive overseas market for their mourning crape and as early as the 1850s had representatives working both in the United States of America as well as in many European countries.

The mourning textile manufacturers in England and France worked hard to persuade their growing number of wealthy and socially anxious clientele in the United States of America that European fabrics were the only ones truly acceptable as mourning wear. Thus in the late nineteenth century S. S. Williams, Family Mourning Store, of 20 Winter Street, in Boston, Massachusetts announced that: 'Our stock embraces all the different grades of the best English and French manufacturers.' Courtaulds declared that their mourning crape above all was the one and only true crape and would no doubt have been delighted to see that S. S. Williams advertised 'Superior English Crape' on their sales leaflets.[294]

English mourning warehouses also sent their staff travelling far and wide to follow up orders for mourning wear. Louis Mercier, in a book published by the House of Jay, in 1877, wrote that: 'It is by no means infrequent to meet in the first class railway carriages on our great lines, on the quarter decks of steamers on the Scottish rivers and lochs – even to those of the remotest Highlands, or on a return voyage in one of the magnificent steamships of the Cunard line, the courteous and experienced employees of the House of Jay.'[295]

Snobbery is constantly revealed in mourning advertisements, though the businesses had to be careful not to frighten off their less well-to-do customers. By the 1870s, with the development of ready-to-wear mourning dress, when the use of mourning clothes had reached down to the lower-middle and even to the upper ranks of the working classes, these clients provided a large proportion of the mourning wear market and needed to be encouraged. Thus *Queen* magazine published an advertisement for Peter Robinson's Family Mourning Warehouse in 1882, offering: 'Advantages to the Nobility and Families of the Highest Rank also to those of limited means.' For their customers of 'limited means' the stores provided specially woven cheaper mourning fabrics, made up in mixtures of wool and cotton, usually excluding the more expensive element of silk. The textile manufacturers had experimented from the early years of the nineteenth century with the development of machine-woven silks and wools. They now turned their attentions to this new demand for cheap mourning fabrics and produced 'the Queen's Crape Cloth', in three varieties at 4s 6d a yard in pure wool providing 'unending wear'. 'Crepe imperial' was sold by Jay's in 1888. It was 'all wool yet it looks exactly like crape.' Peter Robinson's sold a line called 'Borada Crape Cloth' in 1887, which they made up into dresses described as 'economical', selling at £2 19s 6d each. In France servants' mourning dresses were made up from a mixture of cashmere and wool, selling at 75 to 90 francs. Combined with a 25 franc shawl and paramatta hat the whole outfit cost 131 francs. The mistress of the house ordered a dress, probably of pure cashmere and dull silk, which cost 200 francs. The Maison de Noir, where these fabrics could be purchased, also offered 'especially strong fabrics made for working mourning dresses for household servants.'[296] So many and varied were the types of mourning fabrics turned out by rival manufacturers that a list of forty fabric types can easily be drawn up (see Appendix 1).

The manufacturers and store keepers had to be careful not to offend their poorer clients by making these fabrics and garments seem less desirable than their more classy counterparts and so the fabrics were given impressive names, such as the 'Victoria' crape (a cheap cotton crape) and two others of the same type called respectively 'Albert' and 'Victoria'. *Myra's Journal of Dress and Fashion*, in March 1887, included a carefully worded advertisement from Peter Robinson's extolling the qualities of cheap mourning dress: 'These extremely cheap clothes will look and wear well, a consideration for those whose means are not unlimited.' A painted sign on the wall of a street of artisans' houses, Bute Street, in East Brighton, visible until 1978, read: CHEAPEST HOUSE/TRADE WORKMANSHIP AND ECONOMY/GO TO F. R. READING UNDERTAKERS/32, HIGH STREET/CHILD'S PAIR HORSE £1.18.6d/ADULT'S SINGLE HORSE £2.15.0d./ADULT'S PAIR HORSE £5.0.0d. MRS READING, MOURNING MILLINER. This shop, which was in business between 1890 and 1920, represents the very poorest end of the trade where social pretensions could rise no further than 'workmanship and economy'. S. S. Williams of Boston found itself in considerable difficulty when, in trying to project a grandiose image for the mourning warehouse, it frightened off its less well-off clientele. The store, in order to persuade these essential customers back through its doors, was forced to issue a leaflet stating that: 'We find that an impression has been given that our goods are sold at higher prices than elsewhere in the city. THIS IS NOT SO; and to correct the impression, we would respectfully ask all to examine both goods and prices.'[297]

Louis Mercier, writing on behalf of Jay's in 1877 summed up the whole delicate situation:

Jay's have never while purveying for the wealthier and most refined classes, ceased to bear in mind that their patrons are cosmopolitan, that they are bound to cater for many divergent grades of society . . . Strict moderation in prices is not in the slightest degree in disaccordance with excellence in material, beauty in design and skilfulness in confection.[298]

The production of these cheaper fabrics and clothes was possible because of the use of new textile technology and also because of the low wages paid to weavers, dressmakers and sales staff. Samuel Courtauld, who was the biggest producer of mourning crape, paid the women crape weavers at his Essex mills some of the lowest wages in the mechanised textile industry of that time. In 1873 they complained that 8s a week was not enough to keep themselves 'respectable'. Two years later some of them left the factories when they discovered that instead of £14 a year in Essex, they could earn £18 a year in domestic service in London.[299] The dressmaking industry was notorious for the low wages paid to the sewing women, even in the grandest couture establishments. The mourning section of the trade was no different from the rest. Working conditions were just as bad, with overcrowding and poor ventilation, exacerbated by the difficulty of sewing black fabric hour after hour. In 1842 a *Report on the Employment of Women* recorded case after case of women whose eyesight had been damaged by sewing mourning fabric for long hours in poor light. In 1862 the *Report of the Children's Commission* showed some alleviation of working conditions but revealed that dressmakers still worked long, irregular hours to finish the rushed mourning orders on time. At Kendal Milne's store in Manchester the dressmakers worked from 8 am to 9 pm, with only a few additional hours of overtime, whilst Jay's too declared virtuously that overtime 'never carries on longer than from 8.30 p.m. to 10.00 p.m.' Miss Branwell, who ran a hostel for girls in nearby Great Marlborough Street, told the 1862 inquiry, however, that, 'in a large establishment where a great deal of mourning is made, they work from 8 or 9 a.m. till 11 p.m. all the year round.' Mr Lord, the inquiry official reporter, wrote: 'Mourning orders seem to be every way especially trying; they are usually in excess of the week's work and the time allowed for their completion is too frequently very short so that an especial sort of fatigue is added to work essentially dreary and depressing in itself.'[300]

The newly mechanised textile industry took full advantage of the cult of mourning. The textile trade was the foundation stone of the Industrial Revolution. It was the first industry to be fully mechanised by power-driven machines developed from the 1770s. Spinning, carding, weaving, knitting, printing and finishing machines were all in use by the 1830s, with silk production the last to be mechanised. The expansion and success of the textile industry was based upon a huge increase in demand for dress and furnishing fabrics from the early 1800s onwards. A rise in population, the emergence of a wealthy industrial class and the cultivation of overseas outlets led to the development of profitable new markets amongst the middle classes, both in Britain and abroad. (The urban poor of the Industrial Revolution could not afford to buy new fabrics, but instead bought from rag markets and dealers in 'made-over' clothes.) Coinciding as it did with the vogue for mourning wear, it is not surprising that the fashion textiles' industry was quick to catch on to the potential profitability of machine-made mourning fabrics.

The mourning textile trade, though not in itself large, had the distinct advantage during its boom years of a certain stability of product which was denied to the rest of the textile trade. Fashion textiles have always been, and still are, commercially risky because textile designs and fashions in fabric fluctuate so much from season to season that market forecasting is always hazardous. Until the curtailing of Court mourning regulations there was the additional hazard of sudden royal deaths which would plunge society women into deep mourning. The current season's dress fabrics would lie unwanted on the drapers' shelves becoming more and more out of date. The Spitalfields silk industry was badly hit in 1765 by a series of Court mourning periods, following the deaths of royalty in England, Denmark, Spain and France. The plight of the silk weavers, which was none too good anyway, became so desperate that the fancy silk producers petitioned the Court to curtail the length of official mourning. In 1786 the *Gazette* published a notice declaring that: 'His Majesty, in compassion to such manufacturers and people in trade as by the length of Court Mournings are, in this time of general scarcity and dearness of provisions, deprived in a great measure of the means of getting bread hath been pleased to give direction for shortening all such mournings for the future.'[301]

In Lyon too, the centre of the French silk industry, the weavers of the magnificent silk brocades were thrown out of work by Court mourning. During the seventeenth to nineteenth centuries La Grande Fabrique gave employment to almost the whole town. The weavers were totally dependent on the luxury demands of the Royal Courts of France and Europe. As in Spitalfields, coronations and royal celebrations such as weddings, balls and receptions provided an upsurge in demand for the rich silks used in formal Court dress and interiors. By contrast, however, the silk industry was all too vulnerable to the effects of trade slumps, caused by economic crises, wars and trade difficulties. A shortage of raw silk from Italy or China due to a bad winter affecting the mulberry leaf harvest, or a disease amongst the silk worms could hit the town drastically, throwing thousands of weavers out of work. Court mourning regulations were an additional cause of unemployment and one the whole town complained about bitterly. By the late seventeenth century and early eighteenth century on the death of important royalty, Court mourning could last a complete year, during which time, of course, no coloured or fancy brocaded silks could be worn by anyone mixing in Court society. For 'Grand Deuil', as we have seen, wool, or plain dull black silk and wool, were the only permissible fabrics. Within days of a royal death or even the rumour of a royal illness, thousands of weavers were thrown out of work. Since they could never earn enough to have any savings put by, these highly skilled craftsmen were quickly reduced to destitution and were forced to rely on charity soup kitchens to survive.[302]

By the eighteenth century the more influential silk merchants, together with the master weavers, mounted a vociferous campaign for the shortening of Court mourning regulations, complaining bitterly that the effect of mourning etiquette was by then worse than ever because of the spreading of Court and General mourning even to what they described as people *de la plus basse extraction*. So many fashionable clients were now plunging into black Court mourning that there were no customers left to buy up the season's coloured silks. The merchants would consequently suddenly find themselves saddled for several years in succession with coloured fabrics 'causing a cancellation of new orders, lack of sales, and lack of new orders for the silk manufacturers, who in their turn were forced to discharge most of their workers'.[303]

The misery and distress that the sudden imposition of Court mourning brought to ordinary weavers in Lyon is shown in surviving archives and charity records of the silk industry and in the

weavers own protest songs, poems and petitions. An early record
dating from 1655 describes a major crisis in Lyon caused by both a
ban on all trade with England (which was then ravaged by the Great
Plague) and by Court mourning in France on the death of King
Philip IV of Spain. Two thousand livres had to be provided in
charity 'due to the abundance of sick people and children put at risk
due to the total poverty of the silk workers who make up most of the
population of this town, in which all industry has almost entirely
ceased.'[304]

In 1705 the death of the Duke of Brittany again brought troubled
times to the town.[305] In 1711 on the sudden death of Louis, the
Dauphin, when the town was yet again hit by the burden of Court
mourning, the weavers sent this protest poem to Louis XIV.

> *Au Roi*
> *Six moi de deuil pour le Roi!*
> *Dix ans si l'habit noir peut lui rendre la vie.*
> *Mais, au pieds d'Atropos, comme en ge'mit en vain*
> > *Parce-qu-il est mort de maladie*
> > *Faut-il que nous mourions de faim?*
> > *Sire, du travail ou du pain!*

> To the King
> Six months of mourning for the Dauphin!
> Ten years if black clothes could bring him back to life.
> But at the feet of Atropos as we groan in vain,
> > Because he has died of sickness
> > Must we die of hunger?
> > Sire, give us work or bread![306]

Four years later, in 1715, Louis XIV died and Court mourning for
him seems to have caused such distress that pleas and petitions from
the town resulted in the publication of a Royal Ordinance on 23
June 1716, which reduced official Court mourning by half down to
six months. This was a major concession to the silk industry but one
which still failed to satisfy the town of Lyon. Supported by the
powerful Chamber of Commerce, another petition was sent to the
authorities and on 5 October 1730 Court mourning was halved again
down to three months. The problem, however, continued to crop
up again and again. In 1733 the deaths of the Dauphin's wife and
Augustus II King of Poland, following on soon after the death of the
King of Sardinia, resulted in the closing down of many firms.[307]

In 1767 a M. Prost, writing on behalf of the Syndics, or guilds, urged a further shortening of Court mourning. He declared that:

> the sight of the tears shown on all sides as soon as the illness of a well-loved king says more than all mourning etiquette observed out of a sense of duty of show. One understands why the nation wears mourning for a prince. It is the children crying for their father. It is not clear why sovereigns wear mourning for each other, for they are not of the same family . . . It is less clear why a whole nation should be obliged to demonstrate its grief on the loss of a royal prince who may have lived 400 leagues away, who did nothing for France and was quite unknown.

M. Prost protested that etiquette required neither Court nor General mourning on the death of the Pope, the head of the church, and that Court mourning had become 'nothing but an affair of tradition and an empty ceremony.' He complained that even news of an illness of the King of England caused a stopping of work in Lyon. 'By what stroke of misfortune should it be that the death of a foreign sovereign should be a veritable calamity for us, when in his life he brought us absolutely nothing.'[308]

Even in the middle of the French Revolution, only three years before the execution of Louis XVI and Marie Antoinette, the Lyon silk industry was still in a turmoil over Court mourning etiquette. On 30 January 1790 the Lyon Philanthropic Society sent an urgent appeal to the President of the National Assembly in Paris, stating that still, on the death or even illness of a European prince, 'looms are abandoned, workers discharged and thousands of men are without bread . . . Can the memory of the great of the earth be honoured by the suffering of the people?' The Philanthropic Society urged that Court and General mourning should be further drastically curtailed and proposed a new scheme whereby coloured silks could be worn at the same time as mourning fabrics. The suggestion was that Court mourning should be suspended altogether 'on Sundays and Festival days, to be taken up the day after if necessary.'[309] This would have allowed for the wearing of, and therefore the purchasing of, fashionable coloured silks, even if only worn for one day at a time.

Such a sensible compromise was not adopted and the problem of what to do with the unwanted but all too fashionably coloured fabrics, which lay unsold on the shelves of the warehouses, was not resolved until the use of mourning fabric itself went out of style.

## Mourning Dress

After the death of Queen Caroline, the estranged wife of George IV, in 1821, J. Millard of the East India Warehouses, 16 Cheapside, was forced to sell off cheaply his brightly coloured stock of clothes. In an advertisement in *The Times* he announced that: 'In consequence of the demise of Her Majesty he has determined to sell off the whole of his present very valuable stock of white and coloured dresses, with a variety of other articles.'[310] Mr Millard had no other choice. By the time the Court came out of mourning his fashion fabrics would be outdated. The silk designers of Lyon and England would have already produced new ranges of fashion silks and he, and his fellow drapers, were left with no alternative but to sell off the out-of-date fabrics cheaply. The foreign markets, particularly Australia, were a useful dumping ground for unsaleable fashion fabrics.[311]

Queen Victoria's protracted years of deepest mourning after Albert's death in 1861, and the consequential extended years of Court mourning, 'not only cast a gloom over high society but,' in the words of Lytton Strachey 'also exercised a highly deleterious effect upon the dressmaking, millinery and hosiery trades. This latter consideration carried great weight.'[312] In 1910 the problem still remained. The *Illustrated London News* reported in May of that year that, 'The lighter tints suitable for the hot weather have appeared on the scene.' After the death of Edward VII, however, everything changed. 'This was to have been a season of much colour . . . and while to some extent the charming materials referred to will now be used, there will undoubtedly be large overstocks left on the hands of the shops in consequence of the mourning during the season.'

To the mourning fabric manufacturers, or the 'Black Branch' of the trade, Court mourning and the royal use of mourning textiles was, of course, a blessing and the best possible boost for the industry. We have seen how the Victorian mourning warehouses offered an enormously wide range of mourning dress fabrics to cater for every social class. Every possible type, weight and price of mourning fabric was manufactured, from heavy woollens to the most transparent crapes and chiffons, from heavyweight silks and expensive pure cashmeres, down to the cheapest black cottons. The most widely used Victorian mourning fabrics were bombazine, paramatta and crape. All three shared the same basic characteristic – a dull, lifeless blackness.

Bombazine was made with a silk warp, a worsted weft, and a

twilled finish. It was made up into bodices, skirts and capes with the worsted surface uppermost, making the fabric look as dull as possible when worn. It was first woven in Norwich by Dutch immigrant weavers in about 1575. In the eighteenth century it was invariably chosen for the deepest stages of Court mourning. By the 1850–1900 period it was widely sold as the basic fabric of widow's weeds, to be trimmed with varying amounts of crape. The lower-class version of this fabric, made in a plain twilled cotton and worsted mixture, was called bombazet. This was used for servants' mourning in the eighteenth and nineteenth centuries (see Appendix 1).

Paramatta was another cheaper type of bombazine, though of a higher social class than bombazet. It had a worsted weft and a cotton warp, with the same dulled finish. The fabric was invented in Bradford. It derived its name from the town of Paramatta in New South Wales, Australia, from where the wool was exported to Britain. In 1846 Hannington's sent a Mrs Stilton of Shoreham a bill for mourning fabrics, including '13 yards of paramatta at £1.6.0d.' or 2s a yard. In 1902 the Army and Navy Stores in London were still selling paramatta, at a price range of 4s 0d to 4s 6d a yard (see Appendix 1).

It is mourning crape that above all epitomises the middle-class Victorian widow. It was a lightweight, semi-transparent, black silk

113  A sample of Courtaulds' black mourning crape, 1890–1900. (*By kind permission of Professor D. C. Coleman and Courtaulds Ltd*)

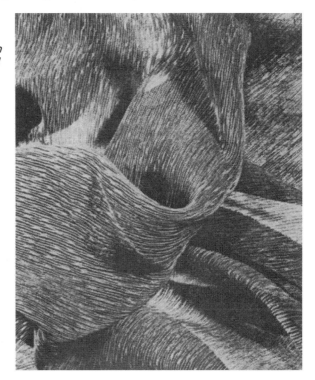

fabric, crimped into three-dimensional patterns. Every hint of the beautiful sheen and softness of silk was carefully removed by an elaborate process, giving the fabric an extraordinarily lugubrious and hard finish. Crape was used as a trimming on dresses, cloaks and bonnets worn for the first two stages of mourning. During the first period of a widow's mourning the entire bodice and skirt of her weeds were completely covered with crape. During the second period it was more sparingly applied and was often pleated, chevroned and twisted into fancy designs. For bonnets the crape was wired into buds, flowers and leaves, while for veils it was deeply hemmed. The stiff crimped finish made it difficult to sew because it would stretch and lose its shape. It also spotted in the rain and faded when packed away. Mrs Beeton offered advice on the 'Renovation of Crape' in 1869 in her book of *Household Management*. She advised steaming old crape with a kettle passing the fabric 'to and fro several times through the steam and it will be clean and look nearly new.' To restore spotted crape, spoiled by rain, she gave the following advice: 'Lay the crape – whether it be a veil or piece of trimming – on a table and place a piece of old black silk underneath the stains; then dip a soft camel-hair brush in black ink and carefully paint the stains over with it; gently wipe off with a piece of silk the superabundant ink, and the stains will disappear as the places dry.' The delicate nature of crape, though obviously a disadvantage to the customer who was not willing to spend hours with brush and ink, served the manufacturers well, ensuring repeated purchases. It was also rumoured widely (one wonders by whom) that it was unlucky to keep crape in the house after the end of mourning.

There were three firms in England who had a virtual monopoly of the production of mourning crape. These were Hinde, Hardy, Grout and Bayliss (who in 1826 were employing 3,500 people in their factories in Norwich and Saffron Walden),[313] and Samuel Courtauld's. All three were based in the traditional silk weaving areas of Norfolk and Essex, where Walloon silk weavers had settled in the middle of the sixteenth century. These three firms remained constant rivals for over a century but it was Courtaulds who finally won the upper hand.

A study of the development of mourning crape reveals clearly the social importance attached to the rituals of mourning. Britain was the last fashionable country in Europe to develop its own silk industry and for much of the seventeenth and eighteenth centuries had to rely on expensive imported Italian and French mourning silks. The use of crape in mourning dress coincided with the growth of fashionable widow's weeds from the end of the sixteenth century and English drapers had for years to import the fabric and pay heavy duties. Once the English manufacturers had mastered the techniques of mechanised crape production – a process which took one hundred and fifty years – English crape became recognised as the one superior original mourning crape and was sold worldwide.

The establishment of crape-wearing in Britain is intimately connected with the spread of silk manufacture from Italy into Europe. Until the seventeenth century silk was the exclusive prerogative of the upper ranks of society. It was prized above all other fabrics for its special qualities of lustrous beauty, strength and lightness and its ability to retain strong, clear dyes. By the eleventh and twelfth centuries weaving workshops, based on Arab and Byzantine techniques, had been set up in southern Italy. From the Middle Ages to the end of the sixteenth century Italy was the principal producer of the best woven silks, and the source of mourning crape. During the Renaissance each town had its own speciality. Genoa, for example, was renowned for its large, figured velvets, Milan for spun gold and silver thread and cloth of gold, Venice for velvets and cloth of gold and Bologna, from the Middle Ages onwards, for lightweight silk fabrics, especially crapes and gauzes.[314] The word crape is derived from the Latin *crispare*, meaning to curl. The Italian name for the fabric is *crespe*. It seems probable that Victorian mourning crape originated in the city of Bologna, which by the eighteenth century was particularly famous for its crimped crapes. The Bologna manufacturers were able to produce a delicacy of quality in their crapes that was never equalled elsewhere. The special character of the fabric lies in its crinkled finish. It was the Bologna crimp together with high-quality dyeing techniques, which enabled the town to keep ahead of all its rivals, until the middle of the eighteenth century.

Italian silks were widely exported to the rest of Europe. They were in such great demand by the wealthy, privileged circles that as early as 1377 there was a colony of Lucca silk merchants established in the great trading city of Bruges.[315] By the mid-sixteenth century Antwerp had taken over as the trading centre of Europe. In 1560 a 'Florentine Gentleman', Louis Guicciardini, drew up a list of fabrics exported from Italy to Antwerp, including all the major silk centres

NOBILE    DA LVTTO.

114  A French widow, 1596, from Cesare Vecellio's *Habiti Antichie e Moderni*.

of Naples, Milan, Florence, Genoa, Mantua, Lucca, Venice and Bologna, describing the types of fabric exported from each town. The only town exporting *crespes* was Bologna.[316]

There is evidence that Bologna silks, though not crape itself, were being imported into England by 1581. On 2 April of that year a complaint was made to Queen Elizabeth I that 'the pryces of velvets and all other sylkes are verye much enhanced w'thout any just cause.' Amongst the fabrics included in a list of fixed prices for silks sent with this letter were 'sattens blacke and colours . . . of Bologna best' and 'of Bologna seconde' (quality).[317] In 1596 Cesare Vecellio, in his book *Habiti Antichie & Moderni*, describes an aristocratic French widow as wearing *un velo bianca increspato* – a white crape veil. It seems that Bologna crape may have been known as a mourning fabric in western Europe from the second half of the sixteenth century onwards. There are, however, no clear fabric descriptions of that early date and confusion arises over the profusion of names given to crimped fabrics, be they made of silk or linen. William Beck in his *Drapers' Dictionary*, published in 1886,[318] suggested that crespe may have been a fine linen and not a silk crape. Cyprus, cypress, sipers or sypress was another mourning fabric. According to Beck this was probably a fine transparent type of cobweb lawn in black and white, used for mourning hatbands, scarves and for the draping of colours. It may also have been used for shrouds. 'In sad cypress let me lie,' declares Ophelia.[319] Norwich crape was a heavier silk and woollen fabric used in the eighteenth century for Court mourning and may well have been the type of fabric referred to in Mary Queen of Scots' inventory, taken at Holyrood Palace in 1562, as *crespe noyer* (see Chapter 3, p. 83). The term Norwich crape was used later by the firm of Grout, Bayliss and Co. of Saffron Walden, when in about 1815 they introduced a fine transparent silk cloth.[320] The names Bologna crape and crisp also appear, but whatever the name used it seems possible that from the second half of the sixteenth century mourning crape was being imported from Bologna into the Low Countries and perhaps into France and Britain, and it was in such demand that experiments were soon being made in France to imitate it.

Silk weaving had been established in France as early as the thirteenth century but it was slow to gain a hold. It was not until the late sixteenth century that the craft was successfully organised. At first imitations of Italian silks were produced but by the late seventeenth century many European fashion fabrics were either French or derivations of French designs. Amongst these fabrics were silk crapes, black, white and coloured. They were frequently referred to as Italian or Bologna style silks. One of the first records of the manufacture of crapes in France dates from 1601, when, under the patronage of Henry IV, a silk weaver named Noel Parent set up a workshop in Paris making 'Italian style crepes, satins, and damasks'. In 1665 Italian crape weavers were imported into the city of Rheims.[321]

Jacques Savary de Victor Bruslon, in his *Dictionnaire Universel de Commerce* published in Paris between 1723 and 1727 provides invaluable information on the manufacture of mourning crape or *crespe*. He describes the fabric as 'lightweight, thin gauze, made up of a warp and weft of raw silk . . . Crepes are made with a shuttle on a loom of two treadles, like gauzes, etamines and other similar fabrics, which do not have a twilled weave.' The writer then explains how the crimp is put into the fabric. 'Silk used for crimped crepes is always more highly thrown [twisted during the spinning process] than that used for soft crepes.' Both warp and weft threads were highly thrown but particularly the weft 'which produces the crimping.' Once the fabric was removed from the loom it 'is soaked in clear water and rubbed with a piece of specially made wax which gives the creped finish.' Both soft and hard-finished crapes were dyed with cold dyes and were finished with a shellacking or gumming process. Savary de Victor Bruslon states that 'both are used for mourning purposes – the soft crepes for the later stages of mourning and the crimped for deepest mourning. White crepes are used only by young people in their early years.' The dictionary continues with an account of the crape weaving industry in France. Savary de Victor Bruslon attributes the first French crape weaving to a weaver called Bourgey, in about 1667; 'though others believe it was Jacques Dupuis, who was the first to weave crepe at Lyons, under special licence granted to him by the King. Crepe is woven in various widths each one graded by twos; 2, 4, 6, 8, 10 to 36. Grade 2 is the narrowest and grade 36 the widest.' The widest, double-width crapes were used for veils, scarves, capes and head-dresses for women in deep mourning.

Savary de Victor Bruslon mentions the cities of Lyon and Avignon as centres of crape weaving but emphasises the importance of Bologna as the source of the very best quality mourning crapes. 'In Lyons a large number of crepes of all kinds, even some of very great beauty, are made. They are quite well thought of, but it must be stated that the true Bologna crapes are still preferred because of their great fineness, which the Lyonnais weavers are unable to imitate.'

The pricing of French and Italian crapes was differently arranged. In Bologna the crape was sold by weight, measured before the dyeing, bleaching, crimping and shellacking processes took place. In Lyon the fabric was sold according to its width with grade 2 at two sous an ell, grade 4 at four sous an ell up to 36. The fabric was measured after weaving but before yardage was lost in the finishing processes, particularly the crimping. According to the 'Paris measure' single crapes were woven in packets of 52 ells and double-width crapes in packets of 38 ells. 'Both widths are cut in two and sent rolled into packets of two and a half pieces folded together and wrapped in white paper on which is marked the name of the manufacturer, with his stamp, number and the yardage.'

According to Savary de Victor Bruslon, the Lyonnais crape weavers, taking advantage of the recognised superiority of Bologna crapes, used to forge the names of Bologna weavers on the outside of their own fabric packets. 'Workers at Lyons, in order to sell their crepes for more money, are in the habit of putting the names of well-known Bologna manufacturers on their packets. This should not be tolerated by honest police.' He also condemns another practice, whereby Lyon merchants bought raw, unfinished crape fabric from Bologna, 'which they dye, bleach, crimp and shellac themselves to resell the fabrics for more profit under the name of Bologna crepes, although the finishing processes are not so beautiful as those of Italy.' He comments that this is another piece of cheating that should not have been allowed. There seem to be no surviving examples of positively identified Lyon mourning crape unfortunately. The Musée Historique des Tissus in Lyon, for example, has no samples of plain silk crape amongst its enormous collection.

Many of the French silk weavers were of Protestant (Huguenot) stock. Under the Edict of Nantes of 1599 Huguenots were granted freedom of worship but when this was revoked in 1685 rigorous persecution followed. Despite the risk of the gallows, between 200,000 and 250,000 fled from France, many arriving destitute in Britain in open boats at south coast ports such as Rye and Sandwich.[322] Fifteen thousand Huguenot refugees settled in and around London.[323] They were received with kindness, given sanctuary and royal patronage, not least because amongst them were highly skilled silk weavers from famous centres such as Tours and Lyon. The potential of the weavers was soon realised, for up till then Britain had been forced to import her fashion silks from France and Italy and had paid dearly for the privilege.

England, and in particular London, already had a small silk weaving and knitting industry (incorporated into the Company of Silkemen in 1629) but it was quite overshadowed by French and Italian products. Dutch immigrant weavers in Norwich had been manufacturing a black silk and worsted bombazine for Court mourning from the late sixteenth century but England was at a considerable disadvantage because of her lack of skills in the art of dyeing – black being a particular problem. In 1553 English drapers complained that 'our Englyshmen cannot dye the Flemmysh and French blacke lyke as the Frenchmen and Flemmynges.'[324] In 1630 Charles I issued a proclamation aimed at improving silk dyeing standards in Britain by banning old-fashioned methods, such as those recommended by Rosetti's *Plictho* in 1548.[325] The use of alder, bark and iron filings was now condemned as 'deceitful' because it added false weight to the silk, thus unfairly increasing the price. New methods of dyeing in black were recommended including the use of 'Spanish black'.[326] In 1723 Jacques Savary de Victor Bruslon described this as a direct method of dyeing black, without passing through the preliminary stage of dyeing the fabric blue. Finely ground and very black burnt cork was used in this technique, which seems to have involved cold rather than heated dyes.

It is difficult to set an exact date on the first use of transparent black silk mourning crape in Britain. It may well have been in the late sixteenth century. Portraits of Mary Queen of Scots in the 1570–80 period show her wearing a transparent black widow's veil, but this may well have been of fine linen. It seems probable that it was fine black silk sarcenett that was first used for funereal trimmings, to be later replaced by the newly fashionable Italian silk 'crespe' or 'cypress'. At the funeral of James I in 1625 'Black Taffata Sarcenett' was still being used by the trumpeters, drummers and pipers,[327] but during the 1670–1700 period references to the use of mourning crape and cypress become increasingly frequent in drapers' inventories and the royal funeral accounts, suggesting a more widespread usage. The demand for mourning crape was growing, reflecting the spreading mourning etiquette to an ever-widening social circle.

In the inventory of John Davis, a draper of Bewdley, Worcester, taken in 1682, 'in the chamber over his shoppe' the following undertakers' items were listed:

54 yards of black cloth 5s. .......................... 13. 10. 00
11 yards of shrouding at 10d. per yard ................ 0. 9s. 2d.
11 pairs of holland stockings ........................ 0. 7s. 00d.
16 yards and ¼ of silk crape at 18d. per yard .......... 1. 04. 4½d.
40 yards of broad black ribbon at 12d. per yard ........ 2. 00. 0.
White sarsenett hoods at fifteen pence ................ 0. 5s. 00d.
Two dozen and a half of lustring and alamode scarfes at
    10s. a dozen ...[328]

This list does not, unfortunately, state the colour of the silk crape and shows that sarcenett was still being used for mourning hoods, together with the new lightweight mourning fabrics of silk alamode and lustring. Henry Bradford's inventory drawn up at Godalming, Surrey, in May 1685 includes 'shrouds, cuffs and mufflers for the dead' and '45 yards of white crape at 9d a yard.'[329] A similar price was charged by Thomas Colls of Crowland in Lincolnshire, who in an inventory of 1686, is shown to have owned '35 yards of black crape at 9d a yard . . . £1.06.03d.'[330]

The first mention of mourning crape in royal British funeral accounts was in 1694 at the funeral of Queen Mary II, when 'crape Scarfs for the Trumpeters and drummers, Crape colours for the first, second and third Regiments of Foot Guards' were purchased from Thomas Charret, milliner, of London.[331] At William III's funeral in 1702 the Yeomen of the Guard wore 'Black Crape Bonnet Bands', the Foot Guards wore 'Broad Black Crape' and the Coldstream Regiment was provided with 'Black Crape'.[332]

The arrival of the Huguenot weavers in 1685 was a godsend. Instead of Britain having to import luxury silks, the immigrant weavers gradually established a flourishing silk weaving industry catering for the needs of society. Mourning crape was only one of a large number of dress and furnishing silks produced by the Huguenots. The industry never managed to overcome the prestige of French brocades in the eyes of society but nevertheless produced beautiful silks of an excellent quality. Many of the Huguenot weavers settled in Spitalfields in the East End of London, where silk weaving had already been established by earlier waves of European Protestant refugees. By 1725–50 Spitalfields silk was being widely sold in Britain and also exported to Ireland, American, the West Indies, Portugal, Spain, Germany and elsewere.[333] Court demands for black silk mourning fabrics such as bombazines, lustrings, alamodes and mourning crapes provided an enthusiastic and ready-made market for the weavers and they soon started experimenting with mourning fabrics for the 'Black Branch' of the silk industry. The first patent for making black silk mourning crape in England seems to have been applied for by a weaver called Francis Pousset. It was granted for fourteen years from 1698. He had, he claimed, 'after many years of trouble and great expence found out the true art of making black silk crape and white silk crape, such as formerly were and now are used for veils, hoods, scarves and hatbands for mourning.'[334]

No specific mention is made of English mourning fabrics in the accounts of Queen Mary's funeral in 1694, four years before the patent was granted to Francis Pousset, but at the next royal funeral, that of William III in 1702, deliberate reference is made to home-produced fabrics, revealing the patronage of the Court and the influence of the silk mercers, who all wanted to encourage the fledgling industry. The Court directed that only English fabrics were to be worn for official mourning. An Order in Council published in the *London Gazette* on 9 March 1702 instructed Court mourners to wear 'black Crape . . . in consideration of the great Encouragement it will be to the English Manufacture of Lustring and Alamode.'[335] Daniel Defoe wrote in the *Weekly Review* in 1704 that the French Huguenots first produced 'our thin black crapes, a manufacture purely their own and I refer to the memory of persons conversant in trade, how universally it pleased our people.'[336]

Crape production was, therefore, attempted by Huguenot weavers working in London from the last few years of the seventeenth century onwards. It continued to be ordered for royal funerals. At the burial of Queen Anne in 1714 John, Duke of Montague, the Keeper of the Great Wardrobe, paid David Bosanquet, 'merchant' the sum of £620 16s 0d for various items of cloth purchased for the occasion, including 'purple velvet to cover the coffins . . . black crape for veils.' The account dating from 1 August to 29 September 1715 shows clearly that the wearing of crape had passed from military use into women's mourning attire.[337]

Despite the interest shown in crape fabric and the efforts made to encourage its use, progress in production seems to have been slow. The next patent for manufacturing crape was not taken out until 1730 when two more Huguenot weavers, John Gastineau and William Mons of London, took out another fourteen year patent for producing 'valle cypress or Bologna crape silk superior to that produced in the past in Italy.'[338] It seems, however, that in spite of all attempts it was still Bologna mourning crape, followed by Lyon crape, that were most widely used in Britain in the middle of the eighteenth century. Savary de Victor Bruslon made it clear in his *Dictionnaire Universel de Commerce*, of 1723–7, that Bologna crapes were thought best, though a large quantity of the fabric was being produced at Lyon. *Chamber's Encyclopaedia* of 1741 states that Lyon had by then taken over as the chief source of mourning crape: 'The invention of the stuff came originally from Bologna but the chief manufacture thereof is said to be at Lyons.'[339]

Nevertheless, the English silk weavers persisted in their experiments and the Society for the Encouragement of Arts, Manufactures and Commerce offered, in 1765, a prize for 'the greatest quantity of English crimped crape for mourning not less than an hundred yards and nearest in quality to the Italy crape.'[340] Four years later in 1769 when the London Weavers Company drew up their approved price list for 'those branches of the Weaving Manufactury called the Black Branch and the Fancy Branch', amongst the named fabrics were black silk 'alamodes, lustrings and cyprus gauzes'. This was a term sometimes used to describe silk mourning crape.[341]

The problem seemed to lie in perfecting the crimp in the crape. In 1768 James Crookshank and William Morton patented a totally useless technique for crimping which involved pouring boiling water on to woven gauze. Another effort, foreshadowing later techniques, was tried in 1772 by John Crumpler, whose method of producing Italian crape involved the use of a dressing machine with 'two large rounds, discretionally hot, which open and close, with a figure between, which engine it being properly prepared the silk has been thrown and operated on and wove, is put in such a manner as to make it pass as even as possible.' D. C. Coleman describes this machine as a 'crude anticipation of the crimping or embossing machine that came into use at a later stage.'[342]

It is interesting to note that throughout the whole of the scrapbook of fabrics put together between 1746 and 1826 by Miss Johnson (see Chapter 5) there is not one example of crimped black mourning crape included amongst the mourning fabrics. This omission can perhaps be explained by the fact that mourning crape was throughout that period still mainly used for dress accessories, such as veils and head-dresses, rather than for complete garments.

The impact of the Industrial Revolution and the resulting major technical and social changes that took place within the textile industry caused the gradual decline and downfall of the Spitalfields hand-loom weavers. Control of the craft passed out of the hands of weavers themselves and their guilds and into the hands of the silk mercers and new industrialists. Because of overmanning of the silk industry and tremendous competition from the newly fashionable fabric, cotton, wages were cut to impossibly low levels. Silk weaving, together with the new machine-powered cotton industry, moved out of the guild-controlled areas into new centres, where labour was cheap and unorganised and where water-power was available to drive the new machines. New centres grew up, particularly in the Midlands and East Anglia in the 1780–1830 period and, following the example already set by the cotton industry in the machine spinning of woven silk – a much finer fibre than cotton. First water and then steam power was tried and by 1830 the machine weaving of silk had been perfected. The effect on the Spitalfields weavers was drastic. They could more than compete in quality and always despised as inferior the machine-woven silks, but on quantity and price they were hopelessly defeated. Value was attached no longer to their highly developed skills and they were starved out of existence. In 1849 Henry Mayhew investigated the working and living conditions of the few remaining Spitalfields silk hand-loom weavers and found them living in appalling squalor and misery.

The scene in the new mechanised branches of the silk industry was different, though there too wages and working conditions were still bad. The new machine-woven silks were much in demand amongst the new middle-class customers as the circle of fashionable dressers widened, with mourning crape greatly in demand. The search for the best techniques of mass producing perfect mourning crape became more intense. The story of the eventual British break-through into successful mourning crape machine production is typical of the many enterprising business triumphs of the Victorian industrial scene. Of distinct advantage to the silk producers who attempted to manufacture machine-loomed mourning crape was the fact that 'far from needing expensive, highly taxed, high quality Italian organzine, crape was usually woven with singles, thrown from less-taxed, lower-priced, poorer quality silks in both warp and weft, though sometimes tram was used in the weft.' D. C. Coleman, in his book *Courtaulds: An Economic and Social History*, goes on to say that 'so far from needing draw-looms or jacquards and the labour of better-paid and more skilled weavers who used them, [crape] could be woven on simple looms by lower paid, semi-skilled men and women.'[343]

Because of its links with royal and aristocratic traditions which appealed so much to the snobbery of the middle-class customers, the fabric could be widely sold at expensive prices, though it did in fact cost comparatively little to produce.

Ultimate success in the production of machine-woven black silk mourning crape was finally achieved by the Huguenot family of

Courtauld. The Courtaulds first came over to England from France in the early years of the eighteenth century and worked in the wine trade and as gold and silversmiths. Their connections with the textile industry began in the 1770s when George Courtauld, with a friend called William Taylor, became apprenticed to a Spitalfields silk weaver called Peter Merzeau. In 1783 William Taylor married George's sister, Catherine, starting a family link which lasted through a hundred years of partnerships and directorships of the family textile firm. Both men were members of the dissenting church and shared fairly radical political views. Their connections with crape started in 1794 when George Courtauld was employed as a 'superior assistant' in the silk mills of Peter Nouaille at Great Ness near Sevenoaks. This mill produced various kinds of crape, though

115   Halstead Old Mill, the original throwing mill in Essex, converted by Samuel Courtauld in 1825. (*By kind permission of Professor D. C. Coleman and Courtaulds Ltd*)

probably not crimped mourning crape.[344] By 1799 George Courtauld was managing a silk throwing (spinning) mill in Debmarsh, Essex, thus starting the Courtauld links with that county. From 1809–15 he worked in partnership with Joseph Wilson in a converted flour mill at Braintree, Essex, manufacturing silk yarns and undyed crape gauzes. In 1823 Samuel Courtauld took over the family firm and began experimenting with machine production. He set up a throwing mill at Halstead, Essex, in 1825 and two years later organised his 'Steam Factory' at nearby Bocking, where he had built and installed the first of his silk-throwing, steam-driven machines. In 1827 the first attempts were made here at crape-weaving – soon to become the foundation of the family fortune.[345]

The early use of machine power brought considerable advantage

116 A Courtauld crape loom, by 'Courtauld, Taylors and Courtauld', pre-1849. (*By kind permission of Professor D. C. Coleman and Courtaulds Ltd*)

117 Courtaulds' crape throwing mills at Halstead, Essex, late nineteenth century, showing crape yarn ring spinning machinery, in wooden frames, of Courtauld's own design and manufacture. The machine operatives moved up and down the length of the machinery on trolleys running on rails. (*By kind permission of Professor D. C. Coleman and Courtaulds Ltd*)

to the firm and they were soon established as leading manufacturers of crape yarns and fabrics. Weaving, dyeing and finishing factories were set up to produce both the soft, coloured crapes and the hard-finished mourning crapes. After so many years of research Samuel Courtauld was determined that his methods of production should be denied to his rivals. Right up to the First World War all his employees had to take an oath of secrecy before a Justice of the Peace.[346]

By the end of the 1840s Courtaulds, with their factories at Bocking, Braintree and Halstead, were employing 2,000 local people and were producing mourning crape and a particularly successful, fine coloured silk called 'aerophane'. The secrets of the firm lay in their finishing factory at Bocking, described by D. C. Coleman as the 'most mysterious pillar of the enterprise'. It was here that the actual transformation of the fabric took place, from undyed silk fabric into hard black, crimped crape. The production process was organised in the following way:

1   Crape yarn was produced in the crape mill at Halstead by machines spinning highly twisted crape yarn.
2   Undyed crape fabric was woven up, first by hand-loom weavers and from 1832 by power looms at the adjacent factory at Halstead.
3   The fabric then went through a mechanical biasing or angling process, in which the crape gauze was first steamed and then drawn tight and free of wrinkles. It was then pulled sideways,

under tension, 'so as the lay of the weft threads was askew to the warp' – an important stage of Courtaulds' secret processes which helped to put the crimp into the fabric.

4 The distorted cloth was then embossed by passing the fabric through the rollers of a heated, power-driven crimping machine – another of the firm's closely guarded secrets. The upper roller was made of engraved brass. This was heated to 275°–300°F. The lower roller was made of compressed paper. The gauze was fed through this machine and emerged with the characteristic embossed or craped finish. The biasing process was vital to the success of the embossing because it gave the gauze the necessary 'give' and prevented the fine fibres from snapping or weakening under pressure.

118 Women workers from the Finishing Department of Courtaulds at Bocking, Essex. Photograph dated to 1859. At least half the women are wearing 'bretelles' (pleating from the shoulders to centre front waist) which in smart city circles were fashionable in the mid 1840s. (*By kind permission of Professor D. C. Coleman and Courtaulds Ltd*)

5  The crimping process was completed by steeping the embossed fabric in a liquid at temperatures high enough to cause the twist in the yarn to 'unwreathe', thus forcing a natural crimp into the fabric, which could contract by as much as 25 per cent in area. From 1848 valonia, a type of Mediterrean oak containing a lot of tannin, was used in this process.

6  Dyeing came next and at first vegetable dyes were used, such as copperas, logwood and valonia.

7  The final stage was the dressing of the fabric. The crape came out of the dyeing process with a soft natural sheen and this had to be removed to give the fabric a vital, hard, matt finish required for mourning. The crape was passed through various combinations of boiled up starch, glue and treacle. The final result was a triumph of engineering and technical skill – perfect, lugubrious, black silk mourning crape, the result of researches begun nearly 150 years earlier.[347]

It is not surprising to learn that their successful production of crape led the firm of Courtaulds into high profitability. From 1835 to 1885 capital rose from £40,000 to over £450,000. The boom years of 1850–85 coincided exactly with the peak of the Victorian passion for mourning etiquette. Samuel Courtauld built up a personal fortune of £70,000 and in 1850 bought himself an estate at Gosfield Hall, near his factories, with 2,000 acres of land. Because of his family traditions of Liberal-Radical dissent Samuel Courtauld was never totally accepted by the neighbouring squires.[348] In its early years the firm's owners, Samuel Courtauld and P. S. Taylor, were both involved in the Unitarian Church and with Radical-Liberal politics. Peter Taylor was an active speaker for the Anti-Corn Law League and became its chairman in 1842. His son, P. A. Taylor, was a Radical-Liberal Member of Parliament for Leicester from 1862–84. Samuel Courtauld's grandson, George Courtauld III, broke the tradition by becoming first a Liberal M.P. for Maldon, Essex (1878–85) and later both an Anglican and a Conservative.[349]

The firm of Samuel Courtauld's and Co. were known as enlightened employers, with a welfare policy for their workers. Reading rooms, libraries, schools, cottages, and coffee rooms were provided. Pensions were sometimes paid out to long-service employees and the skilled workers were paid higher wages than was usual. The unskilled labour force, however, drawn from the countryside where agricultural wages were extremely low and unemployment high, was badly paid. The factories employed a high percentage of female labour – about 70–80 per cent of the labour force towards the end of the century.

In common with other mill-owners Samuel Courtauld employed children in his factories and resented the 'legislative interference' of the 1833 Factory Act. He claimed that work for child workers in his silk mills was light and that to limit child labour to ten hours a day was unnecessary. Samuel Courtauld declared that in an area where poverty was so acute and unemployment so high, it was not the long factory hours but rather 'the want of adequate employment than its severity' that was causing distress. 'The really painful task of a master', he stated, 'is the daily necessity of refusing employment to numbers of famishing.' By the turn of the century the situation had changed. 'The labour market ceased to be a buyers' market,' explains D. C. Coleman. Throughout the history of the company in the nineteenth century, the owners remained hostile to the Trade Union Movement and Samuel Courtauld acted harshly against his workers who went out on strike.[350]

By 1886 the boom years of crape were over. Courtaulds' affairs went into a serious decline. Linked with a general crisis in trade, fabric sales slumped dramatically. From a peak of over 46,000 packets of fabric in the 1880–82 period figures dropped to 30,000 in 1892–94.[351] Between 1883 and 1894 their fabric sales figures dropped in value by 62 per cent.

The firm's owners made a concerted effort to improve their position. In 1894 they introduced new machinery for dressing and waterproofing crape.[352] It was widely advertised. The *Drapery World* pointed out on 15 May 1897 that 'hitherto one hardly dare venture out in wet weather while wearing crape for the effect of a shower was simply ruinous. But, happily, all that is done away with, owing to the general use of Courtaulds' Crape, which will withstand any amount of rain.' The company also brought out a new line of cheaper crape, manufactured by a newly developed process which enabled a cheap, unthrown Bengal silk to be used, rather than better quality yarns. The cheap silk was finished with a shellac lacquer and was purchased by the lower end of the sales market amongst working-class families where mourning traditions still survived.

Aware that mourning traditions on the Continent were still very much alive Courtaulds concentrated on boosting their overseas

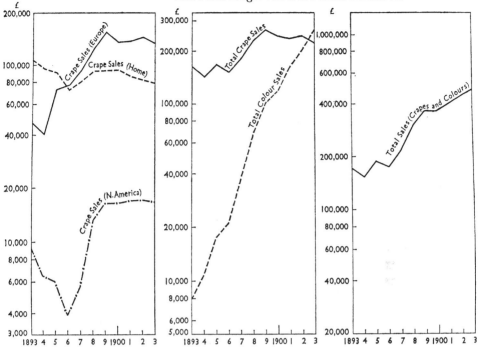

119  Courtaulds' crape sales, 1893–1903. Home and overseas
mourning and coloured crape sales figures, showing the
increase in sales of coloured crapes from 1893. From D. C.
Coleman, *Courtaulds, an Economic and Social History*, 1969. (*By
kind permission of Professor D. C. Coleman and Courtaulds Ltd*)

sales. In 1896 the new Director, H. G. Tetley, introduced a new
range of faster gas-driven machinery at their three main factories.[353]
These efforts soon paid off and in 1899 more packets of crape were
sold than ever before. In that year 65 per cent of all their crape
output was sold abroad, much of it to France, where Courtaulds'
'Crape Anglais' continued in high demand. The firm could not
possibly remain blind to the lessening use of mourning crape, but
they continued with increasing ingenuity to maintain their sales.
Following the fashion for finer, more delicate fashion fabrics, in
1896 the firm introduced new lines in both coloured silks (such as
chiffons and crepe-de-chines) and in mourning crapes.[354] In 1902
hoping against hope for a revival they introduced, for the first time,
a soft-finished mourning crape. This was a very drastic change from
the stiff Victorian product but in line with the more fluid fabrics of
the Belle Epoque period. The new line was advertised widely as a

crape which retained its characteristic appearance but was of 'a soft draping character. Such crape is being used in conjunction with the soft clinging fabrics so largely worn.'[355]

All these efforts proved to be in vain. Even some of the Royal Family, with the exception of Queen Victoria, abandoned crape: first Princess Alexandra of Wales refused to wear it at the funeral of the Duke of Clarence in 1892 and then at Queen Victoria's funeral in 1901; Princess Louise also dismayed the crape producers by wearing a black voile veil rather than one of crape. Even during the First World War the crape sales figures failed to pick up. They actually dropped slightly.[356]

Courtaulds had, however, already introduced their new lines of lightweight coloured silks and by 1903 these sales had outstripped those of mourning crape. In 1904 the company made the all important move of buying up the patents for the production of the first successful viscose process for manufacturing artificial silk – later to be called rayon.[357] Once again the firm cornered the market in a highly lucrative and experimental textile venture, which this time turned the company away from the dying mourning etiquette of Victorian Britain towards the twentieth-century international arena of synthetic fibres and fabrics.

Courtaulds' rivals, Grout and Bayliss, also remained faithful to their manufacture of mourning crape, keeping up their sales figures through their exports. In 1921 they were still selling to 'Latin countries' where crape remained in demand.[358]

Overseas sales were crucial, and had always been so. Courtaulds established agencies abroad as early as 1854, when W. G. Hitchcock of New York took on their licence. As all the sales figures dropped in 1894, H. G. Tetley travelled to Paris, Frankfurt, Cologne, Vienna, Warsaw, and Berlin to arrange for the opening or revision of his sales outlets in Austria, France, Germany, Switzerland, Italy, Belgium, Russia, Denmark, Sweden, Norway, Holland, Spain, and Portugal. South America, South Africa, and all parts of the British Empire were also markets for crape.

W. G. Hitchcock opened a Retail Mourning Establishment on the lines of Jay's in New York in February 1897, in an effort to revive the fashion for crape in the United States. It was too late, and the project failed. Nevertheless, Courtaulds continued to market crape through Briggs, Priestley and Sons, though crape sales to the U.S.A. never amounted to more than 6 per cent of Courtaulds' total sales.[359]

The firm began to spend quite large sums on well-organised advertising campaigns, always in the most select women's magazines. In America, from 1893 to 1903, they spent £1,000 a year advertising in *Queen*.[360] In France costly full-pages were taken in *Les Modes* all through the post-First World War period and on into the 1930s. These showed elegant couture widows' weeds, in 'crepe anglais Courtaulds', by designers such as Beer, Lucile, Lafontaine and Lanvin. Some success was achieved because crape sales figures to France were as high as £80,000 in 1913.[361] The firm's sales pitch was far from reticent. The Marquise de Noy wrote in *Les Modes*, in April 1914, that Courtaulds crape was 'the most distinguished, the richest . . . the most gracious, the strongest and is the only crape chosen by women of elegance and good taste.'

Courtaulds' very last attempt at renovating the design of mourning crape took place in the early 1930s when a final new line was developed at the old Bocking factory as a rival to the increasingly popular mourning fabric – black and white georgette. It was called 'Crape Myosotis' – 'forget-me-not' crape (see Chapter 11).

In 1937 Courtaulds bought both its chief rivals – Grout and Bayliss, and Hinde, Hardy – finally achieving a belated but total monopoly in crape manufacture in England. Courtaulds were thus the last company to manufacture mourning crape in Britain.[362] France was their last remaining worthwhile market and after the German occupation of Paris in June 1940 crape production in England ceased altogether. Professor D. C. Coleman confirms that the trade stopped completely and production was not resumed after the war.[363] By the 1940s society had changed beyond all recognition from the heyday of the Victorian period, when the wearing of mourning crape was a social necessity.

# CHAPTER NINE

# *Mourning Jewellery*

$A$LONG with the crape dresses, mourning parasols and black-edged handkerchiefs, specially designed mourning jewellery was required. The etiquette of wearing such jewellery was just as elaborate as that of the clothes themselves. If a shiny, faceted, black jewel was worn whilst in deepest mourning instead of one with a matt surface it could be as socially disastrous as coming out of mourning too early.

Mourning jewellery served three basic functions. First, it acted as a souvenir of the deceased, seen in some cultures as an open reassurance to the departed spirit that it had not been forgotten. Secondly, it was made as a *memento mori* – a reminder to the living of the inevitability of death. The third function, always present but subtly unstated in mourning etiquette, was that of status symbol dressing. Special jewellery and accessories became yet another expensive item to be added to the long list of requirements considered socially essential after a bereavement.

The most obvious and widely used mourning jewellery was that worn as a souvenir of the deceased. This type was made up from some object intimately connected with the dead relative. The Victorians fastened locks of hair inside lockets, rings and pendants. This hardly differed from mourning mementoes worn in pre-literate societies where bones, skulls and teeth as well as hair were favoured.

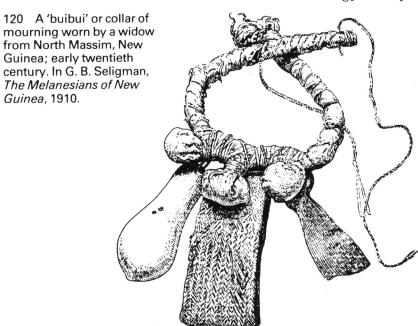

120  A 'buibui' or collar of mourning worn by a widow from North Massim, New Guinea; early twentieth century. In G. B. Seligman, *The Melanesians of New Guinea*, 1910.

In New Guinea a widow from the North Massim wore a *buibui* or mourning collar made up from the perineal band which her deceased husband had worn around his hips. This collar was wrapped round with barkcloth and hung with her husband's lime gourd, which contained a halucinatory chewing mixture of lime and betel nut. The handle of the deceased man's coconut spoon and three small, bark cloth bundles of his hair, rubbed with black mourning pigment were also hung from this collar.[364]

In Queensland, Australia, when moving from one district to another, nomadic aborigines sometimes made ornaments from the bones of their deceased relatives. The Museum of Mankind in London has just such a necklace, made from human ribs bound with string and dyed with red ochre. In New Caledonia widows carry not ribs but their deceased husbands' skulls around with them in baskets, decorated with odorous resin and scarlet seeds.[365] Victorian widows sometimes wore necklaces of their dead husbands' hair.

Teeth have been widely used as a memento mori of a deceased relative. The Maori people of Taranaki used to exhume the corpse of a dead relative three weeks after burial, knock out the molar teeth and make them into ornaments.[366] In a somewhat similar manner the Victorians also seem to have collected and worn teeth. The late Barbara Jones owned a Victorian necklace made up with skulls carved from the carefully preserved teeth of one family.[367] In Holland at the turn of the nineteenth century fashionable ladies had their pets' teeth set in silver and mounted on the knobs of elegant hat pins. Cats' and dogs' teeth were most commonly used.[368]

As a souvenir of a deceased friend or relative, a whole range of memorial jewellery was produced which often included the name or initials of the deceased and the date of death, together with the words 'In Memoriam'. The style of such jewellery changed with the fashions of the day. Throughout the eighteenth century memorial jewellery grew increasingly delicate. Mourning rings narrowed down to fine bands reflecting, from about 1770, neo-classical design. Typical mourning motifs of this period were willow trees bending over urn-tombstones, and weeping, classically draped women.

121   Mourning bracelet, about 1800, United States of America. Seed pearls strands and medallion showing two urn tombstones overhung with willows. (*By kind permission of Stanley Sax*)

Mourning jewellery of this sort was popular in the new, young republic of the United States of America in the 1780–1810 period as well as in Europe, amongst both upper and middle-class families. The exhibition, 'Mourning Becomes America', held in 1976 at the William Penn Memorial Museum, Harrisburg, included two fine mourning rings of the 1780s belonging to the Maryland Historical Society.[369] Both rings showed the willow and urn motifs. A delicate mourning bracelet of about 1800 was also exhibited. It has strands of seed pearls, set with a painted oval scene of two urn-tombstones overhung with willows.[370]

As the Victorian period progressed the design of mourning jewellery, as with almost everything else from tea services to wallpaper, grew increasingly elaborate and heavy. By the 1870s and 1880s mourning jewellery could be really huge, with great chains and enormous pendants. During the 1890s art nouveau swirls and foliage can be seen.

Memento mori jewellery is of most ancient origin. Meaning 'Remember you must die' and 'Remember Death' its function was constantly to remind the living of the ever-present possibility of death which can strike young or old, rich or poor without warning. 'Death borders upon our birth and our cradle stands in the grave,' wrote Bishop Hall, who died in 1656. Memento mori jewellery was worn not only after a bereavement but all the time, as a reminder to the living to lead good lives. Roman engraved gem stones or intaglio of this type show cupids with wings holding inverted torches – a representation of a genius of death. Others show engraved skeletons or shades or carry inscriptions such as 'Eat, drink and be merry for tomorrow we die'. One Roman memento mori theme features an elderly philosopher reading, with a skull in front of him and a butterfly nearby, symbolising the mortality of the body and the psyche of the human soul.[371]

In medieval Europe under the influence of the Catholic church, when representations of the terrors of death and hell were dwelt upon in horrific detail, death's head and skeleton motifs were frequently used on memento mori jewellery, gradually going out of use from the eighteenth century. Other favoured motifs included bones, coffins, urns, angels of death, hour-glasses, scythes, serpents, cypresses and weeping willows. Rings were the most popular type of European memento mori jewellery though watches in the shape of skulls, lockets and pendants were also made. '*Dye to Live*', and

122 Mourning jewellery.
*Left:* Brooch, jet, intertwined leaves, 1880–1900.
*Top right:* Brooch, gold and black enamel, 'IN MEMORY OF', with central oval of plaited hair.
*Lower right:* Locket, gold enamelled in black and white (for a woman) 'IN MEMORY OF' inscribed 'MARY R. TYLLE. Obt. March 28 1879. Obt. 55 years/EMMA A. L. McADAM. Obt. Jan 20. 1879 Obt. 51 years.' Two locks of hair inside. (*Worthing Museum and Art Gallery*)

'*As I am so you must be*' shown next to death's heads were commonly engraved on rings. After the death of Charles I a great number of memorial rings were worn by Royalists, some of them with the King's head, a skull and the words '*Prepared Be to Follow Me*'. This set a fashion and thereafter mourning rings were used increasingly.[372] Many of these motifs and mottoes were used in the Victorian period.

There is no doubt that the third function of mourning jewellery, that of the status symbol, added greatly to both the popularity and demand for this specialised accessory. The giving away of large numbers of rings at funerals was the mark of a wealthy family. Samuel Pepys frequently noted in his diary the receipt of rings at funerals. On 3 July 1661 he wrote: 'This day my Lady Batten and my wife were at the burial of a daughter of Sir John Cawson's and had rings for themselves and their husbands.'[373] At Pepys' own funeral the gift rings were carefully graded into three classes and bestowed according to the closeness of the friendship and the social status of the recipient.

As well as rings, there was a whole range of mourning jewellery worn only with mourning dress, and which also varied according to the depth of mourning. In deepest mourning a dulled finish was essential. Jet could easily be left unpolished, while fossilised wood and certain stones could provide naturally gloomy surfaces.

The ruling on matt finishes – both for jewellery and fabrics alike – was a survival of the most ancient superstitions concerning reflected images of the dead. The Narcissus legend of the ancient Greeks, which so fascinated Sir James Frazer, was based on the fear of looking at one's reflection in water, lest the water spirits would drag under one's reflection, or soul, and that soul-less one would die. In many cultures mirrors, portraits and photographs were (and still are) turned to the wall, or covered, after a death. Reflections had to be avoided at all costs. Thus deepest mourning jewellery had to have a matt finish.[374]

Women wore no jewellery at all during the deepest period of mourning. Court rules, which were widely copied outside Court circles, instructed men to remove all gold shoe buckles, buttons, watch chains and swords, replacing them with substitutes with a matt black finish, though in mid-eighteenth century France, bronzed buckles and swords seem to have been acceptable.[375] In the portrait of the Duchess of Bourbon, painted in deepest mourning in 1702, not one item of jewellery is shown, although Hogarth's picture of his widowed mother, Mrs Anne Hogarth, of 1735, includes only her wedding and mourning rings (see Chapter 5). By the Victorian era, as with mourning dress, the rules had become more complicated and even more of a social pitfall for the unwary. *Sylvia's Home Journal* declared in 1881 that 'no ornaments except jet' could be worn by a widow in the first year of mourning.[376] In 1884, however, Mrs Sherwood in her *Manners and Social Usages* advised that 'diamond ornaments set in black enamel are allowed even in deepest mourning and also pearls set in black.[377]

During the Second and Ordinary stages of mourning only black and white gems were permitted. In the seventeenth century aristocratic widows favoured pearls, and these can frequently be seen in portraits of the period. The portrait of Anne of Denmark, wife of James I, of 1612, now in the National Portrait Gallery, London, shows her in deepest mourning for her father, Henry IV of Denmark. She wears a mourning brooch, pinned to her bodice, and large earrings with pearl and black stone tear-drops. Large tear-drop earrings of this type and great ropes of pearls were highly fashionable. Black stones were also worn for ordinary mourning as shown in the portrait of Maria Maddalena of Austria, now in the Ranger's House, Greenwich. Painted in the 1621–30 period, the widow is shown wearing a heavy cross made up in large cut black stones. Court

123  Anne of Denmark, wife of James I, 1612, attributed to William Larkin, in mourning for her father, King Henry IV of Denmark. (*National Portrait Gallery, London*)

124  Italian widow's weeds, 1620s. Maria Maddalena, widow of Cosimo II de Medici, who died in 1621, by Justus Sustermans. (*Suffolk Collection, Ranger's House, Blackheath, GLC*)

instructions for Second mourning for George II in 1760 involved the wearing of 'white necklaces and earrings'.[378] No definition is given of the stones but probably pearls, jet and onyx were the most popular. The rules for Second Court mourning after the death of Prince Albert, which were issued on 31 December 1861, permitted the lades to wear 'black fans, feathers and ornaments'.[379]

During the third period of mourning and for half-mourning a major change took place. Ladies were allowed to wear diamonds and, in gradual stages, the men were permitted to change from black to silver buttons, buckles and swords. Thus, for the Third Court mourning period for Albert, which lasted from 17 February to 10 March 1862 ladies could wear 'pearls, diamonds or plain gold and silver ornaments'.[380] This jewellery was made up in a more ornamental manner, as can be seen in jewellery advertisements after the death of Queen Victoria in 1901. The *Ladies Field* carried a full page advertisement from the Parisian Diamond Company of New Bond

Street on 9 February 1901: 'Pearls and Diamonds for Mourning Wear'. It included hair combs, choker necklaces, bracelets and ropes of pearls, with the love knot and iris motifs that were so fashionable at that time. It would be fascinating to know if these varying jewels were worn to any large extent or whether this directive was merely wishful thinking by the Parisian Diamond Company. Only the very richest women would have been able to afford such expensive and highly specialised jewellery.

When Queen Alexandra took part in her husband's coronation in 1902 she was wearing clothes of Second mourning. She was photographed at this time wearing a Mary Stuart cap of black crape, with long falls and a dress covered entirely with crape. She wears, though, the most magnificent set of jewellery – a great stranded rope of pearls, which hangs almost to the floor, diamond bows as well as her diamond crown.

125 (*below*) Mourning jewellery for Queen Victoria, 1901. 'Pearls and Diamonds for Mourning Wear', available at the Parisian Diamond Company, 85 New Bond Street, London. From the *Ladies Field*, 9 February 1901. Hair comb and necklaces, in diamonds and pearls, – the only acceptable mourning jewellery at Court.

126 (*right*) Queen Alexandra in State robes, four months after the death of Queen Victoria. Her mourning jewellery is of diamonds and pearls. From *Black and White* magazine, 14 May 1901.

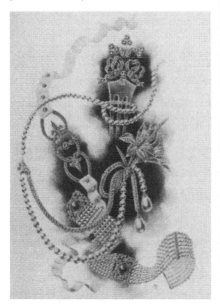

*Mourning Dress*

Middle-class women made do with much simpler and cheaper mourning ornaments. The Union des Arts du Costume in Paris has an intriguing pair of jet brooches, dating from 1890–1910. They are identically designed in the popular love-knot motif with faceted surfaces, but one has a dull, matt finish for deepest mourning, whereas the other gleams and sparkles in a style more suited to ordinary or half-mourning wear. This manufacture of the same design but with different finishes may have been quite a common practice. In the catalogues of B. Altmans of New York of 1879–80 and 1886–7 mourning jewellery was advertised with a 'dull or bright' finish. Thus a black glass bead bracelet was sold at 85c a pair with a 'cut' (or shiny) finish and 65c a pair 'dull jet'. An onyx bar pin (or brooch) could be bought for 95c 'dull or bright'.[381]

Rings were traditionally the most popular form of mourning jewellery through into the eighteenth century. It seems probable that from the original practice of bequeathing personal rings to relatives and friends, a tradition developed by the early seventeenth century whereby the deceased left money and instructions in his or her will for special mourning rings to be distributed. In 1648 Jasper Despotin M.D. ordered in his will: 'Ten rings of gold to be made of the value of twenty shillings a piece sterling, with the death's head upon them, within one month after my departure, and to be disposed of amongst my friends as my executrices shall think meet.'[382] Samuel Pepys, who died in 1703, ordered that in his memory forty-six rings at 20 shillings, sixty-two rings at 15 shillings and twenty rings at 10 shillings, be made and distributed amongst his friends.[383] When Ralph Verney's little daughter, Anna-Maria, died in the 1680s at the age of four, he gave his brother a mourning ring in her memory: 'Filled with my little girl's haire; she was fond of you and you loved her therefore I now send you this to keepe for her sake.'[384] By the eighteenth century jewellers were advertising their ability to manufacture mourning rings 'with the greatest expedition'. In the Victorian period, possibly because of the increase in the cost of making special rings, memorial rings were no longer given away at funerals, though they were still made for close members of the family.

Memorial jewellery was also made up in the shape of lockets, pendants, watches and brooches. The Greenfield Village and Henry Ford Museum at Dearborn in Michigan has a mourning locket of 1795 – very typical of its period. A painted ivory scene of a young man sitting next to an urn-topped tomb is set into a fine gold mount with the words 'WELCOME TO BLISS/SAML. BALSTUN/OB. 10 JANY/1795/AE24/HOW TRANSIENT IS HUMAN/ HAPPYNESS'.[385]

From the 1840s photographs (first daguerreotypes on glass and then paper prints) of the deceased were being mounted into lockets, pendants and mourning watches – still with mottoes such as: 'Not lost but gone before' or 'Heaven has in store what thou has lost'.

By the middle of the nineteenth century in Britain jet had become by far the most popular mourning stone. It was made up in a huge variety of objects and styles to suit every financial bracket. Jet was first used as a charm against the evil eye. It was believed to be an antidote for poison if mixed with the marrow of a stag. Pliny (AD 23–79) in his *Natural History* (XXXVII, 54) mentions the 'Antipathes' or counteracting stone – a black non-translucent stone recommended by magicians against witchcraft. It was also believed to drive away serpents. The Venerable Bede (AD 673–735) echoed this belief. He wrote that Britain 'has much excellent jet which is black and sparkling, glittering at the fire and when heated drives away serpents.'[386] Jet has two qualities to which its magical powers were attributed. First, its shiny surface was brilliant enough to attract the evil eye away from the person who was wearing it and, secondly, it was fragile enough to break quite easily taking upon itself an injury from which its bearer was therefore protected. A Spanish physician, J. L. Gutierrez, wrote in 1653 that an infant wearing a jet amulet would be protected because the jet 'would split, taking all the injury upon itself, if the wearer were exposed to the evil influence.'[387]

The use of jet has been traced back to prehistory from the finds of necklaces, rings, toggles and pendants in many parts of Europe. Jet is found in China, Asia Minor, the Swabian Alps of Germany, the Asturias region of north-west Spain and in Yorkshire in England, particularly near the town of Whitby. Jet was known to the Greeks at least two hundred years BC and was used by the Romans. Whitby jet ornaments have been found in many Romano-British sites including one pendant shaped like a bear, found on a dig at Malton.[388]

During the Middle Ages in Europe, jet not only retained its magical value but also took on a Christian significance. In Spain jet carvings were produced in large numbers at Santiago de Compostela. From the late fourteenth century until well into the present century these carvings were sold to pilgrims visiting the shrine of St James, patron saint of Spain. Figures of St James, pilgrims' badges in the shape of an oyster shell, crosses and rosaries were sold along with older and more pagan designs of lunar crescents, boars' tusks, eyes, sirens, fists and open hands. In Britain crosses, pendants and rosaries were produced from Whitby jet. One such cross, dating probably from the fourteenth century, is now in Whitby Museum. It was found fastened to the witching post of an old cottage in Egton, Yorkshire. Hugh Kendall, writing in 1936, noted that 'in the neighbourhood of Whitby up to comparatively recent times' jet was still being used as an amulet against the evil eye.[389] These beliefs still survive in parts of Spain.

Jet is made from fossilised drift-wood of monkey puzzle trees. It is a type of slate, varying in colour from dark blue to black. When scraped the surface turns brown. When polished it takes on a brilliant black sheen. The Victorians often removed the sheen for mourning purposes.

It was not until the early years of the nineteenth century, with the growing elaboration and widening use of mourning dress, that jet ornaments were produced on a large scale in England. The most important centre of production was the town of Whitby, near to the seams of jet in the surrounding hillsides and cliffs. Much of the jet was mined but some was also picked up from the seashore, either as the tide ebbed or else from cliff falls. In 1800 Captain Tremlett, a naval pensioner, persuaded two hand carvers, Robert Jefferson and John Carter, to try producing jet beads on a turning machine. By 1832 two jet shops had been established in the town employing twenty-five workers and by 1850 there were seven firms engaged in the trade.

The jet industry was organised either into workshops owned by a master who employed a foreman, workmen and apprentices or into small workshops, which were scattered all over Whitby. According to Matthew Snowden, a jet carver, these workshops were 'tenanted by men making a good living with the orders coming from the wholesale merchants regularly and their money on the spot or by return of post.'

The processes involved in the making of jet jewellery are clearly seen in a penny slot machine now in the collection at Whitby Museum. Jet workers are shown standing at treadle machines, where the jet was chopped out, cut, turned, ground, milled, brushed, polished and finished. The machines were all driven by foot treadles,

127  Penny slot machine, showing Whitby jet workers, about
1880–1900. This machine stood outside a jet shop in Whitby
until it was loaned to Whitby Museum in 1940. The heads of the
men are made from clay pipes and are said to be likenesses of
the men in the workshop. (*Whitby Literary and Philosophical
Society*)

except in the large workshop of William Wright, where they were
turned by gas engine. Each worker would specialise at one particular
design, such as foliage, fruit, cameos or engraved monograms,
working for ten hours a day in the jet dust, inhaling grit and fumes.
Matthew Snowden remembered that 'after being at work in the
grinding shops an hour or so, you would hardly be able to distinguish
one man from another, so dense was the dust.'

Whitby jet was carved into every conceivable object, each one
reflecting the passing styles of its day. Natural, rather rounded fruits
and foliage were popular in the 1850s, geometrical and Greek key
motifs became a rage in the 1860s, whilst in the 1870–90 period, jet
jewellery was made, large, heavy, and at its most lugubrious. Necklaces, bracelets, rings, pendants and earrings were made, as well as
ornaments for hats and bonnets, in the form of birds, insects,
butterflies, sprays and clasps. These were widely sold on the Con-

128 Charcoal drawing by Donald Wood, about 1910–14, of a jet worker at Whitby 'chopping out'. (*Whitby Literary and Philosophical Society*)

129 Charcoal drawing by Donald Wood, about 1910–14, of jet worker at Whitby 'cutting on lead mill'. (*Whitby Literary and Philosophical Society*)

tinent.[390] Altman's department store in New York was advertising imported 'Whitby Jet earrings', for example, in its catalogue of 1879–80.[391] Simple jet jewellery was made for day wear and for evening use highly elaborate sets of necklaces, earrings and even tiaras were produced. Some of the chain brooches and necklaces were carved from one piece of jet without a join, and these were particularly admired by the Victorians. For the hair, aigrettes in jet and mourning hat pins, made to wear with mourning bonnets, were de rigueur.

The jet carving industry of Whitby reached its peak in 1870–72, the high point of the Victorian cult of mourning. One thousand four hundred men and boys were employed in the industry at that time, but by 1884 less than three hundred men remained. In that period their piece-work rates had dropped from £3–£4 a week down to 25 shillings. By 1936 not more than five jet workers remained in business.[392]

There were several reasons for this rapid decline. First, there was a shortage of the best quality, hard, Whitby jet and the carvers were forced either to import Spanish jet or to use the inferior, soft, Whitby jet which soon lost its polished finish and broke easily. Secondly, with the great demand for mourning jewellery in the 1850–80 period a whole range of imitation jet mourning jewellery had been developed, inevitably reducing the number of real jet customers. Imitation jet was already in use for half-mourning wear in 1723, when Jacques Savary de Bruslon published his *Dictionnaire Universel de Commerce*. He wrote of 'artificial jet, cut and pierced and threaded with silk or thread', which was used for trimmings 'in half-mourning for men and women'. [393] By the second half of the nineteenth century ebonite and vulcanite, early forms of plastic, made from vulcanising rubber with an excess of sulphur, were being moulded into quite intricate mourning jewellery designs, which could be cheaply produced. Vulcanite had a shiny, very black finish. Its only drawback was that it tended to turn a brownish colour with age. Celluloid was produced from 1873, and in its turn was used for mourning jewellery. The Rhode Island School of Design, in Providence, U.S.A., has a charming mourning comb of 1880 in the shape of a butterfly, made from finely wired jet and celluloid.[394]

Dark tortoise-shell, gutta-percha and dyed and moulded horn were all used too for mourning accessories, though it was black cut glass that was the most widely used type of imitation jet. It was

130   Mourning brooch, large fret carved, Whitby jet, with fruit, leaves and two small sheep. About 1890–1900. (*Whitby Literary and Philosophical Society*)

called 'French jet', probably to give it some allure, though indeed it was made into a great variety of delicate and pretty mourning accessories, popular from the mid-nineteenth into the twentieth centuries. *The Glossary of Minerology* of 1861 noted that 'artificial jet is made of black glass, which is either cut into facets or blown into beads, and the blackness is produced by means of the black wax with which they are filled, or which fastens them to the iron backs on which they are mounted.'[395] French jet can be identified by a degree of translucence around the edges of the glass. It was made up into a huge variety of aigrettes, combs, brooches, necklaces and dress accessories. Black glass jewellery was produced in the United States of America from 1893, when the Libbey Glass Co. was founded in Ohio.[396]

The rage for French jet and other forms of imitation jet is proven by the large amounts which survive today in museums all over Britain, in private collections, in antique shops and even at jumble sales and junk shops. It could be worn beyond the period of mourning for other social occasions. Amongst less well-off families this must have made it even more desirable.

The popularity of these imitation jet ornaments, coupled with the breakdown of mourning traditions, spelled disaster for the Whitby jet industry. Unlike Courtaulds, which was able to diversify its product and produced coloured fashion fabrics as well as black crape, Whitby jet was so synonymous with mourning and death that women could not be persuaded to wear jet as a fashion jewel. The industry gradually died. Bertram Puckle, writing in 1926 when tastes had changed noted, 'the hideous lumps of crudely manufactured jet which it is still considered by some classes of society to be necessary to wear when "in mourning" . . . Whitby, which has been the seat of the jet industry, still carries on a trade on these ghoulish appendages, impervious alike to enlightenment or ridicule.'[397]

Enamel mourning jewellery was popular for as long as mourning dress traditions survived. Made up in black or white, it was used for items such as rings, pendants, brooches and pins. The Newark Museum, in New Jersey, has such an elegant mourning hat pin in its collection. It is fifteen centimetres long, with a simple black enamel flower head centred with a tiny pearl. It dates from about 1909 and is from Tiffany's, New York.[398] There is one curiously interesting type of mourning jewellery which seems unique to America and which was exported from the United States to England, France, Belgium and Austro-Hungary. It was made basically from onyx – an accepted mourning stone – but was called 'English crape stone'. The onyx was 'abraded with acids to produce a line effect, then coloured to produce a dull black finish.' Another version of this jewellery was made from black glass, moulded to the desired shapes then covered with a film of wax at certain points. The glass was then corroded in an acid bath to produce the craped finish. This type of jewellery was advertised by Altman's department store of New York in their 1886–7 catalogue where crape stone 'ball earrings, 65c pair, sleeve buttons, 85c, collar buttons, 23c, dress pins (brooches) from 1.25–85c and ear-drops, oval or square 85c' were all featured. These equate in price to the dull onyx mourning jewellery. Cut glass jewellery was cheaper – with ear-drops at 65c. This English crape stone jewellery was made by Fowler Brothers of Providence, Rhode Island, from 1874.[399] The use of the words 'English crape' is revealing. The company must have hoped this would add some sophistication and a sense of tradition to their newly invented product.

Other common and widely popular types of mourning jewellery were made from bone, carved ivory, Berlin ironwork and hair. Hair has long been used as a token of love. As hair does not decompose after death it is an obvious and tangible souvenir of a deceased friend or relative. Amongst the fashionable and elegant it was a more socially acceptable memento than bones or teeth, though the Victorians as we have seen sometimes used these too, to demonstrate their grief.

Hair (symbol of life) has associations with death and funerals in many cultures. The dishevelling or cutting of the hair was and is a common sign of grief. In the Balkans until the end of the nineteenth century women cut off their hair as a sign of mourning and hung it in great locks on the graves of deceased relatives. It was believed that through the power of sympathetic magic a person could be harmed if their hair was cut, damaged or carelessly thrown away. Hair clippings, for example, were carefully disposed of. Amongst the Hużuls in the Carpathian mountains of Romania it was believed that if mice nested in hair clippings the owner could develop headaches or even become an idiot. Similar beliefs were found in West Sussex in the late nineteenth century,[400] whilst in Mexico, Indian women kept their hair combings in a special jar which was buried with the body. It was thought that unless the body was buried whole, the soul would become exhausted searching for the missing parts and would never reach the next world.[401]

Hair has many advantages as a souvenir of the dead because it can be plaited, woven, sewn, knotted and twisted into a huge variety of shapes and designs of a remarkably fine and delicate quality. At a traditional Korean wedding, for example, the groom used to wear a special hat woven from the hair of the ancestors on his father's side of the family. At each death another lock of hair was added to the crown, woven into a fine braid or mesh. These hats were strengthened and made with high crowns and transparent turned back brims.[402] The object of this ritual was to please the departed relations by literally tying them into the surviving family.

The use of hair in European memento mori jewellery dates back to the late seventeenth century. There is sometimes a confusion between hair jewellery made as a love token, and mourning jewellery containing hair panels. Basically, the mourning ornaments were made in simpler styles and settings, whilst the love tokens were very decorated. In the 1790–1840 period a great deal of hair jewellery was

131  Bride and groom from Korea. The groom wears a crown made from his ancestors' hair. Early twentieth century. From T. A. Joyce and N. W. Thomas, *Women of All Nations*, 1908.

made up in the neo-classical and Romantic style – rather small, delicate, often bordered with seed pearls and coloured stones, and with a central glass panel containing a lock of elaborately twisted hair. These were love tokens. The mourning jewels were made in settings of black and white enamel, jet and gold, often with the words 'In Memoriam' and a panel of simply twisted hair. The differences between these two types of jewellery were sometimes confusingly blurred, especially when brilliant-cut diamonds, turquoises, corals and garnets were used in the settings. Presumably these were not worn during deepest mourning. Neither were the pretty hair bracelets and ornaments decorated with gold and stones that seem to have been quite commonly worn by middle-class women in the Victorian period.

132 A necklace made from the hair of Frederic Guillemard, who died aged 6. It was worn by his mother, Anne Pierce Guillemard, and made up by 'A. FORRER, ARTISTE EN CHEVEUX, REGENT ST' in 1847. (*By kind permission of Mr & Mrs George Guillemard*)

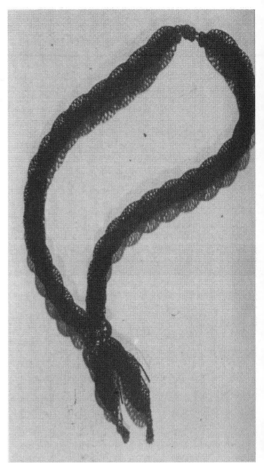

In the early 1800s French prisoners of the Napoleonic War, living in the Tunbridge Wells area of Kent, were famed for their skills at making decorative hair jewellery. The art grew into a small industry. At first the customer's own hair was made up. In the *Illustrated London News* of 11 February 1860, the firm of H. Rushton seeking the custom of 'the nobility, gentry and clergy' announced that they 'beautifully work lady's or gentlemen's own hair and elegantly mount in solid gold hair bracelets, brooches, rings, pins, studs, watchguards, Albert chains, necklaces etc. of the newest possible designs, thirty percent cheaper than any other house in the kingdom.' A book of sample specimens was sent post free to all parts of the country from the firm's manufactory in Clerkenwell, London.

Hair was, however, also made up specially for mourning purposes. The popularity of this type of jewellery was explained to American readers in *Godey's Lady's Book* of 1860:

> Hair is at once the most delicate and lasting of our materials and survives us like love. It is so light, so gentle, so escaping from the idea of death, that, with a lock of hair belonging to a child or friend, we may almost look up to Heaven and compare notes with angelic nature, may almost say: 'I have a piece of thee here, not unworthy of thy being now.[403]

Bracelets, necklaces, ear-rings and watch chains were made up from braids or beads of the dear departed's hair, and joined with catches of gold or silk thread. The hair of both men and women was made up and worn. One such necklace was made in 1847 from the hair of Frederic Guillemard, who died when he was six years old. It survives today in its original box in the safe keeping of his descendants. The box is labelled with the makers' name: 'A. FORRER, ARTISTE EN CHEVEUX, REGENT ST'. The necklace, according to a note in the box, was worn 'a great deal' by Frederic's mother. It is made of delicately plaited hair with a gold clasp, tassels and bow.

A widower might wear a watch chain consisting of a double or triple rope of his wife's hair – not very different at all in spirit from the Korean wedding crown. Just such a watch chain was shown in the 'Death, Heaven and the Victorians' exhibition at Brighton Museum in 1970. The chain, of very finely plaited black hair, belonged to an elderly local resident, Mr A. Budinger.

William Holford and Charles Young, hair jewellery manufacturers, was a firm also based at Clerkenwell, which remains today a centre for the diamond and jewellery trade. Holford and Young advertised in their 1864 *Jewellers Book of Patterns of Hair Work* symbolic mourning jewellery designs of willow trees and graveyards, urns, scythes, setting suns, anchors, hearts, padlocks and yews.[404] Mrs Guillemard's necklace from Regent Street was of a grander class than these Clerkenwell manufactories.

Women's magazines in Britain and America featured articles of instruction on the making up of hair jewellery. The *Family Friend* of 1853 published a series of these with details on the making of hair bracelets, 'nets for the hair', hair-rings and watch-guards – though not all necessarily for mourning wear. S. Mark Campbell, of New York and Chicago, issued in 1867 *The Self Instructor In the Art of*

133 (*above left*) Mourning cross of carved Whitby jet, with polished and matt surfaces and forget-me-not motif. About 1890–1900. (*Whitby Literary and Philosophical Society*)

134 (*above right*) Mourning brooch of Whitby jet carved with ferns, forget-me-nots and lilies to match a necklace. About 1870. (*Whitby Literary and Philosophical Society*)

*Hair Work.* This gave step-by-step instructions on the making up of a sixteen strand chain braid for a bracelet, with eighty hairs in each strand. The bracelet was braided on a special braiding table, which worked on the same principle as a lace-making pillow with weights instead of lace bobbins. On completion the reader was advised to boil the braid 'in water about ten minutes, and take it out and put in an oven as hot as it will bear without burning, until quite dry . . . put a little shellac on the end to keep it fast.'[405]

As the vogue for hair mourning jewellery grew, or perhaps as it slipped down the social ladder, the hair ornaments were made up out of any hair that could be purchased cheaply enough. It was no longer considered necessary for the hair to come from the deceased relative. Peter Hinks notes that in *Pringle's* magazine of 1877 hair braids used for making mourning rings were advertised at tuppence each or one and three pence a dozen.[406] It was a mixture of over-popularity and changing tastes that killed off the hair mourning jewellery market. It went out of use along with jet, paramatta and crape.

The motifs used in Victorian mourning jewellery were the same as those found on tombstones and mourning stationery of the same period. Trees recur frequently. Weeping willows became fashionable under neo-classical influence from about 1770 onwards. They were shown set against tombs and figures of weeping women in classical robes. This tree is a symbol of the resurrection and its branches were often carried at country funerals. Cypresses and yew trees denote death and immortality and are still commonly found in cemeteries. In Spain today cypresses are still grown in rows around the walls of the graveyards outside the cities and villages.

Flowers and plants were a particularly favourite motif on mourning jewellery because of their obvious aesthetic as well as symbolic appeal. Lilies were for purity, ivy for immortality and ears of corn denoted the full ear of corn reaped in maturity. Rosemary, long used at both weddings and funerals, forget-me-nots and pansies were symbols of remembrance. In France this last flower is called *pensee* – thought, and the mauvish-purple variety lent its name to a delicate mauve shade regarded as eminently suitable for half-mourning. Myrtle, bay and laurel leaves signified love and victory, whilst

135 Fashionable mourning, from Paris, for a widow. In *Les Modes*, July 1932.

136   H.M. the Queen and Queen Elizabeth the Queen Mother
arriving at Westminster Abbey for the funeral of Earl
Mountbatten, 5 September 1979. Both wear black, with pearl
and diamond jewellery. (*Keystone Press*)

passion flowers stood both for the sacrifice and suffering of Christ and also for love enduring beyond the grave. Ferns, found so often in graveyards, were commonly carved in jet and ivory.

Christian symbolism used in mourning jewellery signifies the wearer's hope to be reunited with husband, wife and children after death. Crosses, often twined with ivy, vines or liles, open books, a symbol of judgement, bibles, angels, graves and anchors all symbolised faith and hope in life after death. Love and eternity motifs were also widely used with clasped hands, knots, serpents swallowing their tails in an unending circle, padlocks and setting suns being amongst the most popular designs.

The wearing of mourning jewellery died out with the decline in the use of mourning dress. It was not a sudden demise but from the end of the First World War less and less special mourning jewellery was made. In 1926 Bertram Puckle described as 'preposterous' sets of 'half-mourning earrings and the like, in which a little silver is introduced to lighten the effect.'[407] In the mid-1930s the French fashion magazine *Les Modes* was still describing black and white jewellery made to wear with mourning outfits. In April 1952 after the death of George VI *Vogue* magazine advised its readers that silver or amethyst were suitable jewels to wear with mourning clothes for the late King. Diamonds were still de rigueur for those rich enough to afford them. These, together with pearls, are still worn today for mourning in Court society, and were recently worn by the Queen and Queen Mother in September 1979 when in mourning for Lord Mountbatten.

CHAPTER TEN

# *The Colours of Mourning*

T HE colour black is so closely associated with Victorian funerals that it is hard to imagine any other colour as an alternative. Mourning colours do vary, however, though the beliefs which motivate choice are fundamentally the same.

White was the most ancient and widespread funereal colour and is still worn in China, India, Japan and parts of Europe. It symbolises innocence, simplicity and the purity of the soul. The Chinese believe it to be an inconspicuous colour and that, when worn by mourners to a funeral, it will hide them from the unwelcome attentions of evil spirits which congregate on such occasions.[408] To the ancient Egyptians white signified purity. The priests of the great divinity Osiris wore white robes, as did the priests of Zeus, Brahma and the ancient Druidic orders.[409] The early Christians, under persecution by Emperor Trajan in the second century, wore white.[410] At about the same time Plutarch wrote: 'The body of the dead they array in white feeling that they cannot so clothe his soul and their desire therein to attend it, all bright and pure, to the grave, as one already released from the body, that has contended even to the end in the great and chequered battle of life.'[411] White was one of the five symbolic colours chosen by the levitical church in the fourth century, together with gold, purple, blue and scarlet. It had then become a festive colour. Donatus wrote, 'White is for them that rejoice.'[412] It was used in this way by the Anglo-Saxons and still in 1912 at the funeral of General Booth, the founder of the Salvation Army. Many of his followers wore white to rejoice in their belief that the General was at last joining his maker.[413]

The ancient Slavs and the Imperial Byzantine Court[414] mourned in white, a tradition which passed into European usage at the funerals of women and children, continuing to the present day. In the eighteenth century white enamel was used on mourning rings to commemorate their deaths. Yale University Art Gallery has just such a ring for 'J.N. BROVORT HICKS: OB: 23 MARCH: 1761. AE 2.Y.6.M.' This little boy was the grandson of John Brevoort and the son of Whitehead Hicks, Mayor of New York City from 1766–73.[415]

In the nineteenth and twentieth centuries white mourning was commonly used amongst the peasantry of Europe. In Hungary old women wore it even in recent years.[416] In the English countryside too, in the nineteenth century, white was worn for mourning. The village of Piddington in Oxfordshire, for example, had a set of six identical white smocks for the pall-bearers, which were kept in the church. 'On the occasion of a funeral the men could come straight from the fields and exchange them for their working smocks.'[417]

137　A funeral bearer. Oil on millboard by Robert William Buss (1804–75). About 1830–40, wearing white for the funeral of a child or woman. (*Museum of London*)

*Mourning Dress*

In France, in 1914, the fashion writer for Courtaulds, in the magazine *Les Modes*, tried to encourage French widows to add a little white crape to their black weeds. It would add a touch of lightness, she wrote, like 'a smile on a sad face'. 'In some towns,' she continued, 'London amongst others, some wear deepest mourning entirely of white. In France, we restrict this to children.'[418]

This was indeed true, for when the present Queen Mother (as Queen) paid her State visit to Paris in 1938, whilst in mourning, to see the Paris International Exhibition, her wardrobe contained many white mourning outfits. Her mother, Lady Strathmore, died just before the visit was due to take place and in three weeks Norman Hartnell adapted her wardrobe to fit in with the regulations of Court mourning. One of the garden party dresses she wore on this visit is now on show in the Fashion Gallery at Brighton Museum. In delicate white machine lace, it has short sleeves and a slightly dropped waistline. The feature of the Queen's clothes for this visit were her 'Winterhalter' skirts, and this dress, too, was designed with a full-length, tiered, floaty skirt. It was not worn over hoops but has matching petticoats in silk satin, crepe and silk net.

It is interesting to see that white is still in use as a royal colour of mourning. At the funeral of Anwar Sadat, the assassinated President of Egypt, on 10 October 1981, Prince Charles was conspicuously evident in his white naval uniform. The *Sunday Telegraph*, however, commented with disapproval on 11 October that an American woman near the delegation from the United States of America was wearing a gold belt and gold high-heeled stilettos with her white mourning trouser suit. It was not the choice of white, nor even the trousers that broke the rules. Gold, however, is still not acceptable as an accessory of mourning.

White symbolises purity and goodness, though it was also a sartorial status symbol because it was so very hard to keep clean. In Lin Taiyi's novel *War Tide*, published in 1944 and set in the Sino-Japanese War of 1937–45, a silk mercer's widow fallen on bad times, complains bitterly to her daughter who is not wearing traditional white mourning for her dead father. The girl replies, 'It is not practical to make all-white dresses and then have to wash them every day to keep clean. It is not summer and we are not ones who have so much money to spend making dresses enough to change every day.'

In parts of Africa white also symbolises purity and is connected

138 Widow covered in whitewash, part of the ceremony which ritually frees her from contact with her dead husband. Lodagaa, Ghana – about 1960. (*By kind permission of Professor Jack Goody*)

with death ceremonies. Lodagaa widows in Ghana are ritually freed from contact with their dead husbands by a whitewashing ceremony.[419] In East Nigeria some Ibo shrine carvings are painted white to show that they represent 'spirit people' or ghosts. Radcliffe Brown, the eminent anthropologist, explains that this is an instinctive use of colour, with euphoric white for light and disphoric black for darkness and that it is universal in human nature.[420]

Black for mourning was introduced by the Christian church, where it symbolised 'the spiritual darkness of the soul unillumined by the sun of righteousness.'[421] It was first used by St Benedict in the sixth century. His Benedictine monks became known as the Black Monks because of their black habits.[422] By the eleventh century black copes with cowls were commonly worn for outdoor processional garments and by Regulars in the Choir.[423] In the fourteenth century black had become generally recognised as symbolic of grief and mourning, though reds, browns and greys continued in use well into the sixteenth century.[424]

Among the European peasantry there was a great deal of confusion over the use of the colour black caused by its introduction by the church. In Denmark in the seventeenth and eighteenth centuries rich peasant women wore black for church, weddings as well as burials.[425] In Hungary it was only used in outlining embroidery motifs until the 1850–1900 period when black fabric came into use. Amongst the Matyo people, by 1910, brides, not widows, were wearing completely black wedding dresses. The Ethnographical Museum, Bucharest, has further evidence of black, this time urban black silk mourning crape, being quite wrongly used in the Hungarian villages in the late nineteenth and early twentieth centuries. They have a number of young women's 'Calvinist coifs' which were worn by young, married Protestant women, during the first twelve years of marriage. Fastened at the back of the neck were black silk ribbons and special black crape bows, imported from the towns, maybe even from England. By the 1920s these village women had abandoned their traditional white mourning and taken up black urban mourning.[426]

By the eighteenth century black mourning was totally accepted amongst all classes, in the towns of Europe, though not everyone could afford to buy it. During the Victorian period it even extended to funereal trimmings on bird cages and ladies' underwear. At Victoria's funeral in 1901, everyone watching the procession wore black. The daughter of a Nonconformist minister, who was sixteen when the Queen died, went with her family to Hyde Park.

> I had no black clothes. My mother lent me a black hat and gloves, and, of course, one had black shoes and stockings those days; but I had a rich violet costume, and as I descended the stairs the family in the Hall looked horrified. 'She will be mobbed' declared my brothers. It rather spoilt my day - I was the only bit of colour in all London.[427]

In the Victorian period, in fashionable society, shiny black fabrics were commonly used for formal visiting, evening and for servants' clothes, with dull, matt, black silk and wools reserved for mourning. Despite this widespread use there was still some controversy over its suitability. C. C. Rolfe, in his book *The Ancient Use of Liturgical Colours* (1879), declared that according to the Old Sarum usage, officiating priests at funerals should wear blue copes and white surplices. Blue symbolised 'the hue of heaven, which awaits the faithful departed.' 'What a consolation,' he continued, 'to such an one, when lying upon the bed of death to see beside him a Priest of God's church upon earth, clad in sacred vestment, like the Saints of

139 (*below left*) Mourning wedding dress of Mrs M. Gardner JP, 1874, made by 'Miss Canham, 27, Belgrave Place, Bradford', of black satin, with bustle and cuirasse bodice. It would probably have been worn with a hat, not the black veil. (*Whitby Literary and Philosophical Society*)

140 (*below right*) Detail of mourning wedding dress of Mrs M. Gardner, 1874, showing appliqué black silk cord and glass beading and black silk machine lace. (*Whitby Literary and Philosophical Society*)

old.'[428] Consolation or not, his views met with little response.

The choice of mourning colour was a continual source of anxiety to Victorian women. The wrong choice could be only too glaringly obvious – a social faux pas of the first order. One particular anguish was the question of wearing black clothes to a wedding. Black was thought an unlucky colour for such a joyful occasion but if a relative of the bride died just before the marriage, what was the bride to wear? If a widow remarried should she wear black, white or half mourning? What flowers should she carry? Should a bereaved bride wear a veil? Anxious letters poured into the women's magazines and were carefully answered by the etiquette experts. It seems that a few bereaved brides went so far as to wear black wedding dresses. Two of these survive today. The first belongs to Whitby Literary and Philosophical Society and was the wedding dress of Mrs M. Gardner, J.P., whose father died one month before her wedding in 1874. This black satin dress is cut with a fashionable 'cuirasse' bodice and

141 Wedding photograph of Miss Elspet Brown, 1888, who married Andrew Watt, a farmer from Aberdeen. Mourning wedding dress, made by 'Andrew Cameron, 19–21, Broad Street', later extensively altered. (*By kind permission of Dr Elspeth Clarkson*)

separate 'tied back' skirt with a large bustle. It was made by 'Miss Canham' of 27 Belgrave Place, Bradford, and is trimmed with black silk machine lace and appliquéd with black silk braid embroidered with black glass beads. The second dress is in a private collection in Brighton, and was worn in 1888 by Elspet Brown who married Andrew Watt, a farmer from Aberdeen. As with Mrs Gardner, the bride's father had died, this time six weeks before the wedding, in a quarry accident. This dress is in a duller black silk. The bodice fastens down the centre front with twenty-eight faceted black glass buttons, with three vertical tucks running from the shoulder line to the deep 'V' point at the centre front. Both sides of the front bodice neck and the cuffs are trimmed with heavy bands of appliquéd embroidery with black glass beading. The matching skirt is flared and slightly shaped to go over a bustle. The bodice is lined with sturdy, white-striped cotton twill, and the sleeves are edged with black machine lace. The dress was made by 'Andrew Cameron, 19–21 Broad Street, Aberdeen'. He was a draper and his shop only remained at this address from 1888 to 1889. Fortunately, a photograph survives of this occasion showing Mrs Watt wearing a posy of flowers on her left shoulder and a frill of white around her neck to relieve the gloom. It may well be that the dress was altered some time later because the existing sleeves are fuller than those in the photograph, more in the fashion of the 1895–1900 period. The skirt draping seems also to have been removed, leaving a simple flared line. This would have been quite typical within a farming family, where a best silk dress would have been made to last as long as possible. Of particular interest is the hat which Mrs Watt holds in her hand. It seems to be of shiny black straw, trimmed with black ostrich plumes and beads. It may be that Mrs Gardner too wore a hat rather than a veil with her black wedding dress.

These two dresses are not typical of the clothes of a bereaved bride. White and half-mourning colours were more usual. In 1881 the *Ladies Treasury* advised its readers that a bereaved bride should wear a white wedding gown, 'the wreath wholly white, not a tinge of colour, no green leaves. The veil white with a deep hem. The gloves white, sewed down the back with black.'[429] It was perfectly possible for a widow to remarry while still in mourning for her first husband. In France, among the aristocracy, second brides such as this were permitted to wear a long white bridal dress: 'very simple, without flowers or jewels' but with 'an immense veil of black lace

which covers her face and falls on to the train.' Middle-class widows in France were not encouraged to indulge in the use of white when remarried. Pearl grey silk was thought more suitable for their station in life, worn with a white hat trimmed with flowers such as lilacs and roses.[430]

Many grey wedding dresses can be found in museum collections, worn by both first and second brides, not always in cases of mourning. The Royal Pavilion, Art Gallery and Museums of Brighton have a grey taffeta wedding dress dating from 1877, with a 'polonaise' bustle and trimmings of Honiton lace at the neck and cuffs. It was worn by Maria Burberry of West Hoathly, and is trimmed with grey silk ribbons. Grey or half-mourning colours of heliotrope and mauve for second brides was chosen in order to strike a decorous balance between joy and regret. Second marriages could never be as socially acceptable as first ones because they involved the open recognition that a respectable woman would sleep with two men. In the eyes of many Victorian women this was beyond the bounds of decency, however legal it might be. Most of the signs of first bridal had, in consequence, to be omitted. The *Ladies Field* explained on 21 January 1899 that: 'Some recent widow-brides have chosen white but they always wear a hat or a toque, never a long veil and never orange blossoms. Of course there are no bridesmaids.' Mrs John Sherwood in *Manners and Social Usages* (1884) was more explicit. She advised such a bride to remove her first wedding ring beforehand – 'as the wearing of that cannot but be painful to the bridegroom.' She stressed the point that above all the bride 'should not indulge in any signs of the first bridal.'[431] Until the end of the nineteenth century a widow-bride, or a widower who remarried, was obliged to continue mourning for the dead spouse from the day after the second marriage.[432] This way the process was made as respectable as possible, the bride thus making a public demonstration of her continuing sorrow. She was also, for the sake of propriety, obliged to curb any feelings of enthusiasm or overt joy.

Wedding guests who were in mourning were allowed and even encouraged to dispense with black for the day and wear half-mourning colours, so as not to cast a gloom on the nuptial celebrations. This was one point of etiquette frequently defied by Queen Victoria. After her own death in 1901 when Court and General mourning regulations were being meticulously observed, shades of

143   Wedding photograph of 1909. The twin sister of the bride had just died. The bridesmaids are in black hats. (*Royal Pavilion, Art Gallery and Museum of Brighton*)

mauve, violet and grey were the only colours worn at society weddings. Many of the guests wore black and white.[433] The conflict of etiquette rules on these occasions must have caused a great deal of anxiety and worry. Brighton Museum has a wedding photograph, given by Mrs Irene Horne, taken in Hastings in 1909. Her aunt was the bride and was in her late eighties in 1974. The twin sister of the bride had died just before the wedding. The bride wore all white with a huge bouquet of white flowers, but the bridesmaids wore black hats swathed with black trimmings with their white broderie anglaise dresses and white gloves. All the women wore dark-coloured hats. One wears a white dress with dark gloves and sash and a magnificent dark hat with a bunch of white daisies resting on the front brim.

Widows attending their children's weddings were allowed the special dispensation of wearing deep red dresses instead of black or half-mourning colours. One such dress was shown at the Costume Society of Scotland's exhibition 'Costume for Birth, Marriage and Mourning' at the Cannongate Tolbooth in Edinburgh, in May–June 1974. The dress was worn in 1875 by the widowed Mrs Queenie de la Lande of Glasgow, who died in 1973 aged 93: It was made by Hunter and Roger of Glasgow in matching red silk, satin and velvet, with the bustled skirt and fitted jacket of the period. The bodice is lined in cream-coloured cotton printed with a repeat design of horse-shoes, to bring good luck to the bridal couple.

Lady Charlotte Schrieber was widowed in 1852. Four years later she described in her diary the clothes she chose for her eldest son's coming-of-age ceremony.

> I have never worn colours of any kind since I became a widow, but today, in honour of the event, I wore all white in the morning, only a simple muslin dress and mantle with a scarlet scarf over my arm to relieve the too bride-like appearance of the costume. In the evening I had red roses with white leaves on a white silk dress and wore my diamonds and rubies. Red I hold to be no colour with black and white.[434]

Mrs Sherwood would have agreed with this choice of colours. Thirty years later she wrote:

> Deep red is deemed in England a proper alternative for mourning black, if the wearer be called upon to go to a wedding during the period of the first year's mourning. At St George's, Hanover Square, therefore, one

may often see a widow assisting at the wedding of a daughter or son, and dressed in a superb red brocade or velvet, which, directly the wedding is over, she will discard for her solemn black.[435]

Red had long been used as a mourning colour. In the Christian church it represents the blood of Christ. Funeral palls, offered by friends and relatives and kept by the church afterwards as part of the mortuary gift, were usually in white, gold and red. The gold palls were made into vestments. When Bishop Kellow of Durham was laid in state, in 1316, 'laid over the body of the same, three red palls with his arms.'[436] Popes still wear red robes when taking mass and are clothed in red on their death beds. In France, judges, chancellors and members of Parliament did not wear black on the death of the king but continued to wear their red robes, representing the perpetuity of justice which overcame the mortality of the king. By a decree of 1473 any Chief Justice in private mourning was forbidden to appear in his official capacity in his mourning garments.[437] Deep red was still in use for mourning in Italy in the sixteenth century and survived in Hungarian funeral ceremonies well into this century, where laying-out sheets were stitched with red embroidery.[438]

Purple is a colour associated with royal majesty and accepted as a sign of imperial power. The emperors of Rome wore purple robes dyed by the Phoenicians with Tyrian purple taken from shellfish.[439] The colour was much more brilliant than that of other natural dyes. The Byzantine rulers also wore the same colour and the princes of the Christian church were often buried in purple robes. St Cuthbert, for example, was laid in his grave wearing a purple dalmatic.[440] Three hundred years after the death of Charlemagne in 814 AD, his body was wrapped in specially woven purple silk, brocaded with a design of royal elephants.[441] Ecclesiastically, purple and violet are symbolic of penitence and fasting and are the colours worn by the clergy on Good Friday.[442] In Europe where kings were not allowed to mourn in black, purple was worn instead. Queen Elizabeth I's inventory of 1600 included a set of mourning robes – a mantle, kirtle, surcoat and bodice of purple velvet trimmed with ermine, with details of gold.[443] Samuel Pepys 'saw the King in purple mourning' in September 1660. Charles II's brother, the Duke of Gloucester, had died of smallpox a few days earlier.[444] Purple is still used, and only used, in Britain at royal funerals, whilst softer shades of mauve were the official colour for half-mourning at Court from the eighteenth century. We have seen in Chapter 6 the consternation occasioned by the complex choice of mauve half-mourning shades in the nineteenth century. Purchasing exactly the right shade of heliotrope, pansy or scabious must, however, have been a relief after all those months in black.

In Italy today, where mourning traditions are still strongly upheld, the doorways of homes and the entrances to courtyards are hung with draperies of crushed mauve velvet, hired from the undertakers, to announce a bereavement.

Grey was the other respectable colour of Second and half-mourning, often worn with black and white. Barbara Johnson, for example, ordered eighteen yards of 'grey figured stuff' for Second

144   Detail from the Barbara Johnson album, 1746–1826. (*Victoria and Albert Museum*)

145   Detail from the Barbara Johnson album, 1746–1826. (*Victoria and Albert Museum*)

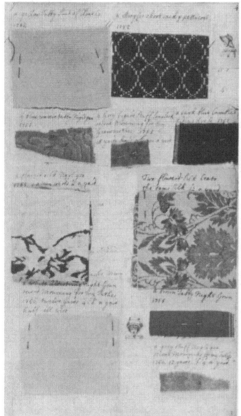
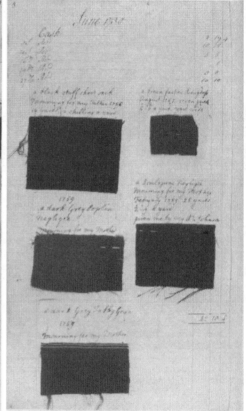

146 (*above left*) Mrs Cyrus H.
McCormick of Chicago, probably in
Second mourning for her husband, in
1884. She wears a fashionably bustled
skirt with a small amount of black crape
on her bodice and cuffs. (*Chicago
Historical Society*)
147 (*above right*) Grey half-mourning
dress designed by the House of Worth,
Paris, 1904. Made for and worn in the
photograph by the widowed Mrs Cyrus
H. McCormick of Chicago for her son's
wedding. (*Chicago Historical Society*)
148 (*right*) Half-mourning dress by
Worth, 1904, for Mrs Cyrus H.
McCormick, in heavy grey silk satin with
the hem brocaded in floral motifs in
white and mauve. (*Chicago Historical
Society*)

mourning for her grandmother in 1753 and again a 'dark grey tabby' when mourning for her mother in 1759.[445] The Chicago Historical Society owns a particularly interesting example of a grey half-mourning dress; it belonged to Mrs Cyrus Hall McCormick, of Chicago, whose husband, a millionaire agricultural machinery manufacturer, died in 1884. Following the example of Victoria, she thereafter wore only shades of half-mourning. All her hats, too, though ordered from the most elegant milliners in Paris, were styled like widows' bonnets. When her son married in Switzerland in 1904, Mrs McCormick, a well-known Presbyterian and philanthropist, ordered a silver-grey satin gown from the House of Worth. It is this dress which survives, in amazingly fresh condition. It is cut in heavy silk satin with the bodice draped in grey chiffon and trimmed with white lace, the hem and magnificent train are brocaded with a deep border of swirling art nouveau floral motifs, carefully woven, doubtless in Lyon, in half-mourning tones of white and mauve.[446] Mrs McCormick died in 1923.

Perhaps mourning colours are changing. In China, where white mourning has been worn for thousands of years, black is now seen. At the funeral of Chairman Mao in 1977, black armbands were worn and black drapery was mixed with white on the buildings of Peking. In Europe and the United States of America we will in future start to see the wearing of white for mourning as an increasingly popular choice.

CHAPTER ELEVEN

# The Breakdown of Mourning Traditions: Mourning Dress From 1910

THERE has long been a minority of people who resented
and even rejected the public display of wealth and social snobbery
attached to grand funerals. Confucius believed that, 'In funeral rites,
it is more important to have the real sentiment of sorrow than
minute attention of observances.'[447] St Swithin, Bishop of Winchester and Lord Chancellor of England, who died on 2 July 862 AD,
shared these sentiments and left instructions that his body was not to
be buried in splendour inside the Cathedral, but outside in the
churchyard amongst the poor. This was duly done, but later the
Cathedral authorities decided that his body should be moved to a
more suitable position beneath the High Altar, accompanied by a
gorgeous procession. The date was fixed for 15 July. The saint, so
the legend goes, in fury at this scant regard for his views, sent heavy
rain which lasted for forty days and washed out all the plans for
moving his corpse – hence the belief that on 15 July, St Swithin's
Day, 'if that day is fair or foul, it will be fair or foul for forty days
thereafter.'[448]

*Mourning Dress*

In the nineteenth century the stranglehold of funeral and mourning ritual caused more voices to speak out. Pleas for greater simplicity and sincerity were made, though few had the courage to break away from the etiquette demanded by respectable society. In the United States of America, in 1825, a tract was published by the New Bedford Book and Tract Association denouncing 'these trappings of grief' as 'indifferent and childish where there is real grief and where there is not they are a mockery.'[449]

Thomas Moore, the poet, took part in Lord Byron's funeral procession, which started from Westminster Abbey, on its way to Newstead, on 12 July 1824. He was horrified to find that there were 'few respectable persons amongst the crowd; and the whole ceremony . . . mixing with my recollections of him as was gone, produced a combination of disgust and sadness that was deeply painful to me.' A year later, at his own father's funeral in Dublin, the same feelings of revulsion returned. 'The scene shocked and afflicted me beyond anything,' he wrote. 'The vulgar apparatus of the ceremony seems such a profanity.'[450]

Thackeray, too, hated the hypocrisy. In a description of a country squire's funeral, in *Vanity Fair*, set in the 1820s, he wrote of

> . . . the family in black coaches, with their handkerchiefs up to their noses, ready for tears which did not come: the undertaker and his gentlemen in deep tribulation: the select tenantry mourning out of compliment to the new landlord: the neighbouring gentry's carriage at three miles an hour, empty, and in profound affliction: the parson speaking out the formula about 'our dear dear brother departed'. As long as we have a man's body, we play our Vanities upon it, surrounding it with humbug and ceremonies, laying it in State, and packing it up in gilt nails and velvet; and we finish our duty by placing over it a stone, written all over with lies.[451]

Charles Greville shared this disgust but explained the conformist attitude of most mourners. After his sister-in-law's funeral, in 1841, he was angry at the 'decking us out in the paraphernalia of woe, and then dragging us in mourning coaches through crowds of curious people, by a circuitous route, that as much of us as possible might be exhibited to vulgar curiosity. These things,' he added, 'are monstrous in themselves but to which all reconciling custom makes us submit.'[452]

Royal funerals were not free from criticism. Greville was shocked at the funeral of William IV, in 1837, by 'the host of persons of all ranks and stations . . . who loitered through the lofty halls chattering and laughing and with nothing of woe about them but their garb.' Greville decided that he 'would rather be quietly consigned to the grave by a few who cared for me (if any such there be) than be the object of all this parade and extravagance.'[453] The Duke of Sussex, the late King's brother, vowed, after attending this ceremony, that he would not be buried at Windsor, and, accordingly, in 1843, he was buried in Kensal Green, London's first metropolitan cemetery.[454]

Dickens mocked at the snobbery and ingratiating insincerity of Victorian undertakers in many of his novels. At the funeral of Pip's sister, in *Great Expectations*, Joe Gargery, surrounded by the seedy employees of Trabb and Co, the local undertakers, whispers sadly to Pip, 'I would in preference have carried her to the church myself, along with three or four friendly ones wot come to it willingly harts and arms, but it were considered wot the neighbours would look down on such and would be of opinions as it were wanting in respect.'[455]

149  William Morris's hearse – a hay-cart, painted yellow with bright red wheels and wreathed in vine, alder and bulrushes, 6 October 1896. (*William Morris Gallery, Walthamstow*)

William Morris, designer and Socialist, had no qualms about upsetting conventional attitudes. He left detailed instructions for his own funeral and when he died, in 1896, his coffin was made of unpolished oak with wrought-iron handles. It was covered with a length of his own 'Broussa' brocade and laid in a hay-cart, painted with a yellow body and bright red wheels. The wagon was wreathed in vine, alder and bulrushes, over a carpet of moss. The wreath was made from bay leaves. Morris's friend, W. R. Lethaby, Principal of the Central School of Arts and Crafts, wrote afterwards, 'It was the only funeral I have ever seen that did not make me ashamed to have to be buried.'[456]

As a Socialist, Morris's rejection of high Victorian society was total but others, whose views were much less radical, had also begun to question the merits of funeral etiquette and a gradual softening of the rules had started. The peak of elaboration was reached in the 1850–85 period when respectable families seem to have been virtually terrorised into accepting all the expense and ritual. Finally the cult overreached itself and the tide began to turn. In 1880 the Church of England Burial, Funeral and Mourning Reform Association was formed to 'encourage simplicity instead of show'.[457] The reforms were accepted slowly but eventually marked the definite downfall of the 'dismal trade'.

It was the terrible slaughter of the First World War that undoubtedly caused the major breakdown in funeral and mourning etiquette. At first the conventions were maintained, especially in France – a largely Catholic country. 'Lucile', Lady Duff Gordon, who had opened the Paris branch of her London couture business in 1911, remembered the dramatic effect of the war. In 1914 she wrote: 'In one week Paris was a changed city. The streets were full of women dressed in black; the churches were crowded all day long . . . The shops were almost deserted, everybody was too busy doing some sort of war work to want to buy clothes and for the first time in a century the Parisienne was almost indifferent as to what she wore.'[458] Edna Woolman Chase, international editor of *Vogue*, confirmed that in France 'in a country where heavy mourning had long been a tradition' mourning 'seeped like a dark tide through the towns and countryside as the casualty lists came back from the trenches and funerals were the macabre social life of the capital.'[459]

In Britain, too, mourning wear was widely worn, but it seems not so much as in France. Geoffrey Gorer writes that his mother was widowed early in the war when his father was drowned in the *Lusitania* disaster. 'In the summer of 1915 and thereafter, widows in mourning became increasingly frequent in the streets,'[460] so that his mother no longer stood out alone in her black weeds. In the summer of 1918, the private view of the Royal Academy exhibition was reported in the *Illustrated London News*.

> Over all social functions war has thrown its blight and such 'fixtures' as continue are bereft of most of the old time glory . . . This year not one solitary costume was in anyway remarkable. Where is there not a person who is not suffering family and financial losses that make display and frivolous expense seem folly . . . In the hall I met a . . . peeress – one of the richest women in England – but a bereaved mother wearing an old fashioned black satin dress made with a train to lie a few inches on the ground.

Today some women who remember this period deny that the towns were crowded with women in mourning. Mrs Marguerite John, for example, now aged 90 and living in Brighton, was a fashion model at Elspeth Phelp's (Court dressmaker, of Hanover Square) during the war. She denies vehemently that mourning was very widely worn, stating that the dressmakers continued their business as usual. The late Lady Rushbury, the widow of the painter Sir Henry Rushbury, who died in her nineties in 1981, also confirmed the lack of heavy, full mourning, although she remembered that armbands were widely worn.

As the war continued the survivors had somehow to face up to the loss of almost a whole generation of young men and the creation of a new army – this one of widows and fatherless children. Between August and November of 1917 over a quarter of a million British troops died at Passchendaele alone. Full ritual mourning dress seems not to have been worn down to the last detail. It was partly a question of morale, both for the troops on leave from the trenches and the public at large remaining at home. The sight of millions of women of all ages shrouded in crape would have been too much to bear. As made clear by Lady Duff Gordon, a great many women of every class were involved in war work and were far too busy to retire into periods of seclusion demanded by the old etiquette of mourning. As well as running charity and nursing organisations, women were taking on every kind of job left unmanned by the departing troops, from munitions work to running fire stations, ambulances and police forces. They were allowed into the Civil Service, they worked on the railways, in the mines and heaved milk churns. The fashion magazines continued to give their usual sartorial advice but they commented frequently on the changes so evident in society.

By 1916, the magazine *Modes Illustrées* commented that in Paris: 'Never has the code of mourning been less strictly applied, than in these days of anguish. Women are unable to interrupt their daily occupations in order to observe the absolute seclusion that used to be the custom, whilst in deepest mourning.' Proust, in *A la Recherche du Temps Perdu*, described in his typically detailed manner, the dress of the young and fashionable Parisiennes in 1916. He noted their long gaiters which recalled

> . . . those of our dear boys at the front; it was, so they said, because they did not forget that it was their duty to rejoice the eyes of these boys at the front, that they still decked themselves of an evening not only in flowing dresses, but in jewellery which suggested the army by its decorative themes . . . The Fashion now was for rings or bracelets made out of fragments of exploded shells or copper bands from 75 millimetre ammunition . . .

150   Afternoon dress in Courtaulds' crape, from *Les Modes*, January 1914, designed by Parents Soeurs, 9 Boulevard Malesherbes, Paris.

Proust added that women replaced cashmere (a mourning fabric) with satin and chiffon and even though in mourning kept wearing their pearls, 'while observing the fact and propriety of which there is no need to remind Frenchwomen.'

He acidly noted down the justification given by the elegantes of Paris for their lack of mourning dress. 'It was because they never stopped thinking of the dear boys, so they said, that when one of their own kin fell they scarcely wore mourning for him, on the pretext that "their grief mingled with pride", which permitted them to wear a bonnet of white English crepe (a bonnet with the most charming effect "authorising every hope" and "inspired by an invincible assurance of final victory").'[461]

This overriding wish to remain elegant and attractive was one reason for the lack of mourning wear in the war, but there was another and perhaps more seriously held view. Some women tried to find an alternative form of mourning dress, another way of showing that they mourned for their menfolk who had not died in the normal way but had died for their country. It was perhaps also an attempt to rationalise and cope with the deaths – a way of making the sacrifice and loss more bearable, and demonstrating that the deaths had not been in vain nor the lives of loved ones wasted. Geoffrey Gorer writes:

> The holocaust of young men had created such an army of widows; it was no longer socially realist for them all to act as though their emotional and sexual life were over for good, which was the underlying message of the ritual mourning. And with the underlying message, the ritual too went into discard. There was too almost certainly, a question of public morale; one should not show the face of grief to the boys home on leave from the trenches.[462]

This belief is confirmed by Parkes Weber, who noticed in 1918 that 'some English ladies who had lost sons, husbands or brothers in battle objected to the wearing of ordinary mourning but suggested the use of a purple band on the left arm as a token of the patriotic death of their relatives.'[463]

Similarly in Germany, according to a report from Berlin, in *The Times* on 30 January 1915:

> In the matter of mourning, it is agreed that the wearing of black can only tend to depress the spirits of those who have relatives at the front – so an

association has been formed which proposes to substitute for all mourning a little scarfpin, with the inscription, 'Stolz gabich ein teures Haupt furs Vaterland' (Proudly I gave a beloved one for the Fatherland).

After the war society changed so fundamentally, with women building gradually upon the freedoms won during the 1914–18 war, that there was no chance that high Victorian mourning etiquette would be revived. Such etiquette depended upon the will of women to keep it going and once that had gone it died. The total sales of Courtaulds black crape remained at around £200,000 a year from 1913 to 1918, with a slight increase in 1919 and then there was an irreversible drop.[464]

Most fashion magazines in France, where society women continued to wear mourning, still issued monthly advice on mourning dress until the advent of the next world war. Even the sophisticated *Gazette Du Bon Ton* started by Lucien Vogel in 1912, included the occasional chic black dress, which would have been suitable for mourning wear. After the death of the Duc de Soré in 1920 an article by Roger Boutet de Monvel gave details of the then socially accepted periods of mourning, with advice on dress. A widow mourned her husband for one year and six months – a whole year less than the

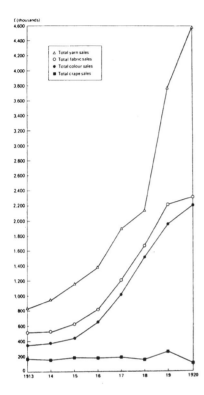

151  (*left*) Courtaulds & Co. Ltd, yarn and fabric sales, 1913–20, showing the ever-lessening importance of their sales figures for crape. (*By kind permission of Professor D. C. Coleman and Courtaulds Ltd*)

152  (*above*) 'Le Dernier Carrosse' by Roger Boutet de Monvel, from *Gazette du Bon Ton*, July 1920.

153  (*opposite and above*) French widow in various stages of fashionable mourning dress. Drawn by Roger Boutet de Monvel, in *Gazette du Bon Ton*, Paris, 1920.

## Mourning Dress

Victorian widow. 'Grand Deuil' or deepest mourning was still black wool and black crape. 'Petit Deuil' – the second stage of mourning – consisted of black silk taffeta with dull stones, whereas ordinary mourning comprised white crape with pearls or diamonds.

This article, illustrated by the fashion artist and book illustrator Bernard Boutet de Monvel, shows sketches of the various stages of widows' mourning. In 'Grand Deuil' the widow is drawn deeply veiled, in black dress and stockings sobbing into a black handkerchief. In the last sketch, at the end of her mourning, she is dressed in white, smiling broadly and nonchalantly smoking a cigarette in a long holder.

For those who could not afford to buy complete new wardrobes, the old expediency of dyeing proved economical and many black-beaded, black dresses of the 'twenties survive today as witness. On close examination of the fabric beneath the beading, where the dye

154 Fashionable French mourning in Courtaulds' crape, for a widow, from *Les Modes*, July 1932. In fine 'Myosotis' crape, with draped bodice and fashionably bias-cut skirt. For this deepest period of mourning the widow wears black stockings. Her black shoes have a touch of white and she wears a black and white necklace.

has not penetrated, shades of distinctly non-mourning colours can sometimes be found.

Courtaulds, continuing the manufacture of crape throughout the 'twenties and 'thirties, struggled in vain against the use of more fashionable black georgette and voile. The firm still made stalwart efforts to maintain their more conservative French customers by taking out regular double-page advertisements in high-class French fashion magazines, extolling the virtues of their Crepe Myosotis. In *Les Modes*, August 1932, May Maury, fashion writer for Courtaulds, warned her readers in a paid advertisement that crape georgette was not a socially acceptable mourning fabric. 'The only cloth which should be worn by elegant and conscientious women is English crape, for three or four months at least. The old style crape, which turned a woman into a scarecrow exists no more. It has been replaced by an admirable creation of Courtaulds – Crepe Myosotis – very fine and supple, with the lightness of georgette crepe.' To prove her point an accompanying photograph shows a beautiful and slender model girl in complete widow's weeds, with a voile veil edged in crape and a chic crape dress, with a draped bodice and bias cut skirt. In late April 1932 the magazine explained that veils were now worn short – by which they meant to the hip – still with a plain deep hem, but they no longer had to be worn over the face. Widows' caps were still being advertised – small and neat to fit the head, of tightly draped black crape, sometimes with a white crape chinstrap; some were still shown with a widow's peak over the forehead.

In March 1933 another advertisement advises that plain white Crepe Myosotis could be worn at home or to replace the tea-gown, whilst for evening white crape dresses, with black jewellery, could be worn in deepest mourning. Special black and white mourning jewellery was still being manufactured in France.

In Britain royal custom still demanded the upholding of the old Court mourning regulations and royal ladies wore formal mourning dress long after their subjects had abandoned it. On the death of King George V in 1936 the following orders, issued by the Duke of Norfolk, Earl Marshal of England, were published in *The Times* on 22 January:

GENERAL MOURNING – In pursuance of an order of His Majesty in Council dated January 21st 1936 – these are to give public notice that it is expected that all persons upon the present occasion of the death of his late Majesty of blessed and glorious memory do put themselves into decent mourning to begin on Wednesday, January 22nd, such mourning to continue until after his late Majesty's funeral.

COURT MOURNING – The King commands that the Court shall wear mourning for nine months from this day – for his late Majesty King George V of blessed memory. The Court to change to half mourning on Tuesday, 21st July next. And on Wednesday the 21st October next, the Court to go out of mourning.

This announcement shortened by three months the official period of mourning for the King. It had been one year, in 1910, after the death of Edward VII.

On the same day officers of the Royal Navy and Royal Marines were instructed by the Admiralty to wear black crape armbands for six months. *The Times* reported that in London, even before the official order for General mourning had been announced, 'Black neck ties and, here and there, black arm bands were worn by men. Large numbers of women were in black clothing.'

*Vogue* on 5 February 1936 published a tribute to the late King and issued their own advice to readers. 'Naturally, all people of fine feeling will follow the dictate of quiet good taste, but this no longer implies, except for those closely connected with the Royal family, an ostentatious change from ordinary activities.' Any 'ostentatious' change in dress, which before the 1914–18 war was normal practice, would, by this time, have been judged as a vulgar attempt at social climbing – unless worn by a woman who had personal connections with the Royal Family or official circles.

The death of the King coincided with the planning of the season and there was much anxiety over the propriety of continuing the round of social engagements during the official mourning period. In February 1936 *Vogue* advised that 'Ascot, being a royal enclosure, will . . . follow the rule of the Court as will the Embassies and those really closely connected with Court and official circles – All others will feel they are best helping to restore normal conditions in the interests of the thousands who depend on catering, entertainment or dress by leading a normal social life.' With consciences thus eased the season carried on, although large balls and grand functions were not de rigueur. 'Small intimate gatherings at home, at the theatre and in restaurants are indicated, with mourning wear less worn in the country for practical reasons. It is not necessary to order grey or heathery tweeds but very lucky if you happen to have them. In town there will presently be a relaxation from the smart black, grey will be

155   Mourners at a funeral in Brighton, about 1930. Men are in
black coats with black top hats. Women wear black coats, with
large roll fur collars, black hats, shoes, handbags and umbrellas.
(*By kind permission of Hannington's Ltd, Brighton*)

important and a note of lavender or mauve will be struck – one hopes
not too violently.'

The problem of the unfortunate débutantes, due to celebrate their
'coming out' that particular season was reassuringly solved with the
assurance that 'mothers can do a great deal for their debutante
daughters even though there are no Courts. They are in fact more
likely to make friends in the intimate atmosphere of summer 1936.'

The fashion magazines did not make a major feature out of
mourning dress that spring, showing the usual photographs and
drawings of the couture clothes in London and Paris, but black or
dull colours do seem to have been worn in the smart social circles of

London. On 18 March 1936 the fashion editor of *Vogue* commented: 'Up to the moment of writing, the London theatre audience is still all dressed in black and white . . . but at Schiaparelli's opening I saw they all looked with wide round eyes at the brilliantly coloured dresses. It must have been temptation in the extreme to that room full of women in black.'

Throughout the 1930s in France widows could be seen in the streets in black clothes, with flat black hats, trimmed with white crape bands.

In the United States of America the East Coast 'old guard' quietly retained the use of mourning dress in the 1920s and 30s. In areas such as Albany and Connecticut traditions survived despite the great social changes that were sweeping over America. The American costume historian, Barbara Dodd Hillerman, writes that by the 1930s 'the American upper class changed in complexion. The old guard demonstrated their superiority over the publicity seekers and the nouveau riche, with a studied disregard for display. Elaborate mourning toilettes, like dinner parties for a hundred, lost their significance.'[465]

One Connecticut family resolved the problem of finding traditional yet discreet mourning wear in a particularly interesting way, which came to light during the showing of the 'Mariano Fortuny' exhibition at Brighton Museum in 1980. The Misses Janet and Olive Boyd, spinster sisters from a highly respectable Connecticut family, were brought up by their aunt Mrs Margaret Boyd Bush, who died in 1921. The sisters mourned her in black clothes for the rest of their lives. They continued their usual social round, after a respectable interlude, but attended all evening functions wearing black gowns bought from the Fortuny shop on Madison Avenue, New York. This was opened in 1924 by Elsie McNeal, now Countess Elsie Gozzi, whom they knew personally. Miss Janet Boyd Bush wore her black Fortuny gown for evening occasions until her death in 1978. Her niece Mrs H. M. Ehrmann of Santa Barbara, California, now owns this particular robe which is one of Fortuny's famous, finely pleated 'delphos' dresses, with its own matching black braid belt. Four similar black 'delphos' robes were included in the American showing of the Fortuny exhibition at the Galleries of the Fashion Institute of Technology in New York in 1981. It is not known if any of these were ever worn for mourning.

After the Second World War, mourning dress became increasingly rare in the U.S.A. except for State and formal funerals, such as that of John F. Kennedy in 1963. The widowed Mrs Jackie Kennedy attended the funeral in a tailored black coat and pillbox hat with a shoulder-length black veil worn over her face.

In Britain by the 1950s, with attitudes to death and marriage generally undergoing radical changes, the wearing of mourning dress became much rarer, surviving longest among working-class families and royalty, with those in between paying it scant attention.

It was not only the wearing of mourning dress that survived in working-class areas, but also the whole funeral ritual including the horse-drawn hearse, the banks of flowers and the funeral meal. In many poorer districts family bonds were closely maintained and, with them, the old etiquettes. In the 1930s, before the introduction of state funeral grants, the shame associated with pauper burial by the P.A.C. (Public Assistance Committee) remained as deep as in

156  East End of London funeral in the early twentieth century, with feather-pages, the hearse with ostrich feather mounts and ostrich plumes on the horses. From Bertram Puckle, *Funeral Customs, Their Origin and Development*, 1926.

157 Funeral of Jim Lloyd, a Walworth fruiterer, East End of London, April 1949. His daughters wear deep mourning – black hats, coats, shoes and stockings. The horse-drawn hearse complete with ostrich feathers can be seen in the background. (*BBC Hulton Picture Library*)

158 Pearly funeral of Mr Henry Croft, the founder of the Pearly Kings and Queens of London; in 1930. The Pearly Kings and Queens wear black sashes. (*Pearl Binder Collection*)

Robert Tressell's day. Collections for the Friendly Societies were still made on a door to door basis. The insurance agents were 'as much part of the normal way of life in a working class street as the milkman or postman.' An average funeral then cost between £13 and £15. Middle-class funerals were more costly.[466]

*Picture Post* recorded the funeral, on 23 April 1949, of Jim Lloyd, aged sixty-four who ran a fruit and vegetable stall in Walworth in the East End of London. He was buried in traditional style. His coffin was laid in state in the front parlour of his house, and the room filled with wreaths – 'To Dad from May' – 'To Brother Jim from Duke'. On the day of the funeral the coffin was carried in an open carriage to the church. It was pulled by six black horses wearing long black canopies, their hooves blackened with a tarry substance. The coachman wore a black coat and top hat. The magazine reported that Jim Lloyd's funeral cost £30 whereas an average one in that area would cost about £18. There were, in London, in 1949 only thirty horses left which were regularly used for funerals. 'Three undertakers have the monopoly of them and they find the expense so high that they are considering selling them in the next few months.' *Picture Post* reported that many of the horses were sold off for meat, including, in 1947, the horses of the Co-operative Wholesale Society's Funeral Department. The black ostrich plumes had long since been abandoned. They had been banned in 1916 after the British Undertakers' Association had declared that the plumes caused unnecessary suffering to the horses.[467] The feathers weighed 8 lb. and even more when wet with rain, so that the horses used to shy and kick to avoid having them fixed on their heads.

The dreadful anxiety over funeral costs was somewhat alleviated by the introduction of the Death Benefit under the National Insurance Scheme, by the Labour Government of 1949, which gave every insured person, over the age of eighteen, £20 to pay for the cost of a funeral.

Traditional funerals are still favoured by the Pearly Kings and Queens of London. When Mrs Beatrice Marriott, the Festival Pearly Queen of London, died in 1976, at the age of seventy-three, she was buried in great state at the City of London Cemetery in Manor Park, London. A black limousine replaced the open carriage-hearse, but her fellow Pearly Royals walked in her procession, the men on the right-hand side and the black-sashed women on the left. Her coffin was carried from the church covered with her finest regalia coat and her large ostrich plumed hat, following the best of ancient royal tradition.

In the Sussex village of Hailsham another traditional funeral took place on 8 May 1971. The *Eastbourne Herald* described the burial of Hailsham scrap merchant Dan Townsend:

> Hundreds of people lined the High Street . . . to watch a magnificent procession of 20 black limousines headed by a horse-drawn hearse . . . The funeral, rumoured to have cost £1,000, was attended by mourners from all over the south of England. Scrap merchants from Kent, Surrey and Sussex came to pay their last tributes . . . Four black-plumed horses drew the 70-year-old pillow hearse, guided by top-hatted drivers on the box of the carriage. The hearse, believed to be the only one of its kind in Britain, was brought with the horses from Luton in Bedfordshire for the event.

Thirty-eight of Mr Townsend's grandchildren and his twelve great-grandchildren attended this ceremony – a remarkable survival of the Victorian way of death.

State funerals, as ever, maintain the old ways. At Winston Churchill's in 1965, which he had planned himself, the coffin was taken on part of its journey from London to Blenheim by river. The Thames cranes were ceremoniously inclined in respect as the funeral barge went by. London recently witnessed another state funeral – that of Earl Mountbatten, murdered by the IRA. Among the mourners at Westminster Abbey on 4 September 1979 were six kings and three queens. The troops had rehearsed their movements through the streets of London in the dead of night – just as for the great funeral of Lord Nelson in 1805.

The British royal family are still most careful to retain the correct etiquette for royal funerals. On the death of George VI in 1952, the Lord Chamberlain issued the order for Court mourning, dated 11 February: 'The Queen commands that the Court shall wear mourning until Saturday, May 31st next for his late most Gracious Majesty King George the Sixth of blessed memory, the Court to go out of mourning on Saturday, June 1st next.' No orders for General mourning were published in *The Times* and the period of Court mourning was thus reduced from six months to ten weeks.

Rumour has it that a crisis arose over the new Queen's mourning clothes. She had been on tour in Kenya when her father died so unexpectedly. She left Kenya wearing a beige dress and stepped off

159   'First picture of the new Queen', from
*The Times*, 8 February 1952. H.M. the
Queen steps out of the plane from Kenya,
wearing the mourning outfit she had taken
with her. (*Keystone Press*)

160   Queen Mary, Queen Elizabeth the
Queen Mother and Her Majesty the Queen
wearing black, with black veils, at the lying
in state of George VI, February 1952. Queen
Mary wears a Mary Stuart mourning cap.
(*Keystone Press*)

the plane at London airport in a black coat, dress and shoes with a diamond brooch on her lapel. The story goes that Norman Hartnell's staff sat up all night making up this outfit which was then rushed to the airport for the Queen to change into before she stepped off the plane. The truth of the matter, as verified to the author by Mr Hartnell before his death in 1979, is that the Queen already had the mourning outfit with her, in the usual tradition of aristocratic etiquette. At the King's lying in state all the royal ladies wore long black veils over their faces. Queen Mary, who was then eighty-five years old, wore a Mary Stuart mourning cap, with the classic deep peak over her forehead, as she had done for the funeral of her mother-in-law, Queen Alexandra, in 1925. This may well prove to be the last appearance of the Mary Stuart mourning cap. It is not favoured either by the present Queen or her mother.

As far as the general public was concerned, there was less social pressure exerted to oblige people to wear public mourning, though it was quite widely worn in establishment circles. The first edition of *Vogue* produced after the death of the King unfortunately coincided with the spring couture collections in Paris. No specific advice was given on mourning dress at all, though several of the illustrations showed black and white clothes. It was not until April that mourning dress was mentioned and then only as a series of alternatives to high fashion colour schemes. Instead of a basic navy blue dress, for example, worn with an absinthe-coloured hat and gloves, the reader was advised as 'alternatives for mourning' to wear a black dress and shoes with a white hat, gloves and silver jewellery. Other colour ranges suggested for mourning were a lilac coat, worn with a grey hat, white gloves, an amethyst scarf and black shoes and handbag, or a silver-grey coat with a smoke-grey hat, white gloves, amethyst jewellery and black shoes.

Etiquette books continue to be published, though their advice must be seriously followed by only a small minority of men and women. In one such book, called *Elegance*, written by a directrice of the couture house of Nina Ricci in 1964, a woman attending a funeral dressed in a conspicuous manner is accused of revealing

> a total lack of good taste and good manners. Even if you are not a member of the immediate family, you should dress in black, or at least in whatever you own that is most dark and neutral, and you should wear no jewellery. During the course of the year it is unfortunately likely that you will be obliged to attend a funeral ceremony, and you should

prepare for the eventuality in planning your wardrobe, just as you prepare for the luncheon and dinner invitations you receive.

Our elegante is advised to wear a black suit of wool in the winter and linen in the summer, or a grey ensemble, both with black hat, gloves, shoes and bag. For the funeral service itself 'a full black crepe veil is still worn' for a close relative and removed immediately afterwards. The only details of dress that mark out a woman in mourning from one in a smart city ensemble in black, are 'her black or dark grey stockings'.[468]

Nearly twenty years have passed since those words were written. Now, some widows still wear transparent black veils at their husbands' funerals. These are shoulder length, with deep hems and are usually sewn onto small black hats. They are worn with black suits or coats. Mrs Jacqueline Kennedy in 1963 and the widowed Lavinia, Duchess of Norfolk in 1978, both wore widows' veils of this type. Other widows, particularly at less formal funerals, make do with head scarves or black hats worn with black clothes.

It may be said that full black mourning is little seen at ordinary funerals. Mourners nowadays adapt their everyday, dull-coloured clothes by adding a black nylon armband, black tie or black head scarf. Special, usually unfashionable 'funeral hats' are kept in the back of cupboards and given a brush up when needed. Some still keep complete suits to wear to funerals and memorial services. Brighton Museum has recently been given just such a suit which was worn to funerals in the 1960s by Leila, Viscountess Hampden. In black wool and designed by the British couturier John Cavanagh in 1960, it has a smart box jacket and straight, tailored, pencil skirt.

Although some continue to wear black for months after their husbands' death, many now do not and it becomes increasingly difficult to identify widows. Central and Southern Europe provide clear exceptions to this general rule, as does the East End of London. Here some widows still wear black stockings, black coats, black skirts and often white blouses. They are ill-regarded even to this day by their neighbours if they abandon their weeds before the first year of their widowhood. However, at a time when so many marriages end in divorce, marriage is no longer seen by many as a permanent partnership and, consequently, the position of widows has altered radically. Remarriage is encouraged and seen as totally normal, though the financial worries over bringing up a family and finding

161   Suit by John Cavanagh, London, 1960, worn by Leila,
Viscountess Hampden at funerals in the 1960s; black twilled
wool, with box jacket and straight skirt; collar and cuffs of black
velvet. Hat by Jeanne Lanvin, Paris, 1960, worn by Lady Dacre;
black velvet, with deep, curled brim (with matching suit). (*Royal
Pavilion, Art Gallery and Museum of Brighton*)

suitable work still remain. Widows are joined now, in their single state, by an army of divorcees and separated wives and husbands, who share many of the same problems.

Attempts to reform funeral ritual still continue. Campaigns are waged against impersonal, conveyor-belt cremations and the ever-high cost of respectable burial. The *Guardian* of 30 June 1975 reported a proposal for 'a new form of Christian funeral co-operative, which would provide less morbid, less ostentatious and certainly less costly burials and which would seek to restore something of the believer's joy alongside the grief.' This idea was set down in a private member's motion on the agenda of the General Synod of the Church of England by a Yorkshire housewife, Mrs Dulcie Eccleston, who declared that she 'had the support of members of most denominations who would like to see funerals freed from the many commercial trappings.'

After complaints that undertakers play upon the grief of the bereaved and encourage them to pay for more elaborate funerals than they really want, a Price Commission inquiry (Report No. 22, Funeral Charges, HMSO, 1977) was set up. The commission reported that although small firms barely make a living, many of the larger undertakers' firms make profits that are 'generous or even high'. The report recommended that written estimates should always be provided, that a basic national price should be determined and that any additions should be itemised and charged as separate items. The journal *Labour Research* (Vol. 66, No. 7) noted that the price of a funeral by the London Co-operative Funeral Service had risen from £16 in 1950 to £160 by July 1977. 'The demand for a substantial increase in the death grant would not seem to be unreasonable,' the journal adds.

By 1981 prices had risen even further. In a letter to the *Sunday Times* on 15 June 1981, Mr C. J. McCashon wrote: 'I have today settled the account for my mother's funeral . . . £707.70 charged for a very simple burial.' He was charged £180 'for the re-opening of my father's grave.' Small wonder, then, at the increasing popularity of cremations. The *Brighton Evening Argus* under the heading, 'OLD FOLK FEAR PAUPER FUNERAL' reported on 15 January 1982 that 'Old Folk . . . are going without food and heating to make sure they get a decent burial.' David Smale, Brighton Council's Cemeteries Superintendent, tried to reassure the readers about the propriety of Council burials. 'Everything possible is done to make sure it is a satisfactory service and a minister is engaged even if there are no known relatives.' A local funeral director is reported as commenting that a funeral on the rates would include a simple coffin, a service, the cremation or burial, one car and the necessary bearers and that it would cost anything from £300 upwards. The death grant remains at £30. In this time of economic crisis, the anxieties among the poor and elderly over funeral arrangements remain as sharp as ever. The Price Commission of 1977 noted that as yet there is no evidence in Britain of the kind of exaggeration found in the United States of America by Jessica Mitford. Despite her merciless exposé of funeral practice in *The American Way of Death* first published in 1963, attitudes there seem unchanged. In demand now are hydrogen bomb-proof tombs, where the dead will be able to survive intact in their frilled satin sheets, while the rest of mankind is blown to ashes. The Chinese, too, are keeping their ancient traditions alive and have recently built an enormous and vastly expensive mausoleum in Peking for the remains of Chairman Mao, which was constructed by thousands of shift workers labouring for twenty-four hours a day.

Family funerals have, however, changed fundamentally over the last fifty years in many parts of Europe and certainly in Britain. They are now so discreet and private that death barely interrupts the daily routine of life. In towns where neighbours hardly know each other's names, this should not be surprising. Few even stand still out of a sense of respect to watch a funeral cavalcade drive by. In Britain today the Victorian cult of mourning, which involved not only the family but also the community, is long forgotten, except in Northern Ireland, where the tragic deaths caused by the political breakdown still unite whole communities, though not, unfortunately, the warring sides. The convoluted rules of etiquette and the inequality of the burden of ritual which was placed on the women seem almost unbelievable today. Why did women submit to it all?

It is hard now to understand how strong the conformist pressures were on women in the 1850–1900 period. Today few feel that the demands of 'society' dominate their existence. Many, without any disastrous effect on their lives, totally reject the social climbing and snobbery that drove so many respectable Victorian women to carry out the exacting rules of respectable social behaviour. It was these pressures to conform – for the sake of their families and their own social success and good name – that made women submit. They submitted, usually with enthusiasm, to the dictatorial rules, wearing depressing, dull, black clothes, sometimes for years on end.

Unlike the nineteenth century there are now no absolute norms in social behaviour and certainly not in dress. Nowadays a widow would gain no social prestige at all if she veiled herself in black and remained secluded for a year. The wearing of mourning dress is no longer a sign of social respectability or superiority. The breakdown in Christian belief, the advance towards equality by women and changing attitudes to remarriage have seen to that.

The basic system of status-symbol dressing, however, has survived absolutely intact and flourishes as strongly today as it did in 1500 when the English Queen wore a mourning tippet 'a nayle and an inch' long, whereas that of a baroness was only 'scarce a nayle'. Today's sartorial status symbols do not lie in the area of mourning dress but their functions are exactly the same – to show off wealth, position in society and social sophistication. Social ambition is as much a driving force now as ever it was, though one may be reluctant to admit it. Clothes are still the most obvious and effective way to display it.

The names or initials of expensive couturiers, shoemakers, and sportswear designers are embroidered on outside pockets, tagged onto cuffs and boots or printed onto costly silk scarves. Whatever the feelings about cruelty to animals, leopard-skin coats are still sold costing thousands of pounds. Diamonds, platinum and gold continue to be worked into vastly expensive jewellery and find the same eager market as in the past, even in these days of deep recession.

Subtle and more cunning forms of status-symbol dressing are, however, currently in vogue, such as the use of deliberately slightly crumpled, linen clothing, which started in Italy in 1979. It is still a look much favoured by expensive Italian menswear designers. To the ordinary passer-by the trousers and jackets simply look as if they need a good iron. Admiring cognoscenti, sauntering through the Galleria Vittoria Emanuele in Milan, know better. Wearing their expensively rumpled suits they can look down with confidence on their social inferiors in their well-pressed clothes, just as the correctly and expensively dressed Victorian widow looked down upon a widow in a too-bright shade of heliotrope for half-mourning. The sartorial signals send the same messages of élitism to those able to understand them. The functions of dress have changed little over the past four hundred years. *Plus ça change, plus c'est la même chose.*

# A Selection of Popular Mourning Fabrics

**Alamode**  A lightweight silk, used in black for mourning. First woven in England in the 1685–1700 period by Huguenot refugees in London. Before then alamode was imported into Britain for mourning use – as in the inventory of John Davis of Bewdley, Worcester of 1682: 'Two dozen and a halfe of lutestinge and alamode scarves at 10 shillings' (PRO Inventory 5391). The use of alamode in Britain was encouraged deliberately by the Royal Family and Court. The Lord Chamberlain issued instructions for alamode to be used for Court mourning for ladies' mourning hoods and men's scarves etc. as for the funeral of William III, in 1702, when hatbands of 'black English alamode covered with black crape' were ordered (*London Gazette* 9–12 March 1702). This fabric seems to have gone out of use by the nineteenth century, replaced by machine-made mourning crape.

**Albert crape**  A fine quality black silk mourning crape of the mid-nineteenth century (Cunnington, C. W., p. 429).

**Alpaca**  Fine soft wool, often woven with a cotton warp, dyed black for mourning; made from the wool of llamas; woven up in Britain from the 1830s (Beck, p. 3). A bill in the archives collection of Hannington's of Brighton for mourning fabrics, made out on 5 February 1846 reads: 'To Mrs. Brook of Bexhill – 44 yds alpaca at

2/- a yard=8/-.' In 1902 the Army and Navy Stores in London were selling mourning alpaca at prices from 8d to 3s 11d a yard.

**Anserine**   A mixture of silk and wool, similar to bombazine; worn at the funeral of Prince George of Denmark in 1708, as instructed by Court mourning regulations (Cunnington, C. W. & Lucas, Catherine, p. 257).

**Armozine** or **Armozeen** or **Ermosin**   A fine black silk. Guicciardini reported that in 1560 'Ermoisins' were being exported from Genoa to Antwerp (Tawney, R. H. & Power, Eileen, pp. 163–5).

By the early eighteenth century the Dutch were weaving 'Armoisins' in Holland (Rothstein, p. 155). Huguenot refugees introduced armozine into England after 1685 where it was used for mourning hatbands and scarves (Beck, p. 8). The London Weavers Company listed 'Armozine' among fabrics woven by the 'Black Branch' of the trade in 1769. This fabric seems to have been replaced by machine-made mourning crape in the nineteenth century.

**Balmoral crape**   Sold at Harrods in 1895, 44 in. wide at 1s 6½d to 2s 6½d.

**Barathea**   A silk and worsted fabric dyed black for mourning use; popular in the 1840s (Cunnington, C. W., p. 429) when heavier fabrics were fashionable.

**Barege** or **Barrége**   A semi-transparent silk and wool fabric, with the silk thrown upon the surface, with an open weave finish, later all wool. The name is said to derive from the Barréges valley in France; popular for mourning in the early nineteenth century when lighter weight fabrics were popular (Beck, p. 13 & Cunnington, C. W., p. 429).

**Barpour**   A twilled wool and silk mixture used for trimmings on mourning dresses in the Victorian period (Cunnington, C. W., p. 149).

**Bengaline**   A mixture of silk and wool. The Army and Navy Stores, London, sold this fabric for mourning use at 5s 11d a yard in 1902. Pure silk bengaline was selling at from 2s 11d–6s 3d a yard.

**Bologna crape** and **Vallee cypress**  A lightweight silk mourning crape, probably the origin of Victorian mourning crape (see Chapter 8). Exported from Bologna to Antwerp in 1560 (Tawney, R. H. & Power, Eileen, pp. 163–5). Henri Clouzot noted that in 1666 factories were founded in Lyon, St Etienne and St Chaumond, by Antoine Bourgey to produce *crêpe dans les largeurs accoutumée de Bologna* – crape in the widths usually produced in Bologna (Clouzot, H., p. 56).

**Bombazine** or **Bombasin**  A fabric with a silk warp and worsted weft with a twilled finish, with worsted on the face side to give the fabric the dull finish required for mourning. Savary de Victor Bruslon stated in 1723 that bombasin was a silk fabric 'made in Milan from where the manufacture was introduced into some provinces of France' – and that it was also made in cotton. Bombazine was dated back to thirteenth century European sources by Beck, through Strutt (Beck, p. 26). It was first woven in England by Dutch immigrant weavers in Norwich in about 1575 (Warner, Sir Frank, p. 30). From the eighteenth century bombazine was usually ordered for deepest Court mourning, right through to the second half of the nineteenth century.

In 1756, Barbara Johnson bought 26 yards of deep black bombazine, of a heavyweight silk and wool at 2s a yard for 'a bombazine negligée, second mourning for my father.' (Barbara Johnson album). Bombazine became particularly popular for widows' deepest mourning in the high Victorian period. As the cult of mourning faded it seems to have been replaced by Venetian Crape cloth as the basis of widow's weeds.

Cheaper versions were made in the eighteenth and nineteenth centuries for less well-off mourners, called bombazet, coburg and paramatta.

**Bombazet**  A plain, twilled cotton and worsted mixture – a cheap version of bombazine – used for servants and cheap mourning clothes in the eighteenth and nineteenth centuries (Cunnington, C. W. & Lucas, Catherine, p. 244).

**Borada crape cloth**  A cheaper mourning fabric, advertised in *Myra's Journal* of 1 March 1887, by Peter Robinson's mourning warehouse in Regent Street for 'economical dresses, made entirely of this new material' which sold at £2 19s 6d each.

**Broadcloth**   A plain, heavy wool with a napped finish, dyed black for mourning use. It was used for funeral hangings as well as for mourning clothes for men and women. In the sixteenth century peeresses were each given 16 yards of broadcloth for mourning garments (see Chapter 3 & Cunnington, C. W. & Lucas, Catherine, p. 210). In the nineteenth century English broadcloth was in demand abroad for mourning. In 1629 Margareta Boiji, a Finnish widow bought '16½ ells of fine English broadcloth from a tailor in Riga' to make her weeds (see Chapter 4, p. 98).

**Byzantine**   A dull, semi-transparent silk and wool, with a close weave, dyed black and used for mourning in the early 1880s (Cunnington, C. W., p. 430).

**Cashmere** or **Cachemire**   Pure cashmere goats' wool, imported from India, often mixed with cotton or wool and dyed black for mourning use. It was woven in Paisley, Scotland from 1824 (Beck, p. 58) and was always an expensive fabric. Hannington's of Brighton billed Mrs Brook of Bexhill in 1846 for '6 yards Black cashmere at 5/6d a yard – £1 18s 0d.' On 3 May 1884 their silk buyer ordered 'Black Indian Cachemire Bayast' from silk merchants in Lyon, the silk centre of France (Archive Collection, Hannington's, Brighton). In 1902 the Army and Navy Stores, London, were selling 'French cachemire' for mourning at prices ranging from 1s 10d to 3s 9d, 'Cashmere de l'Inde' sold at 2s 9d or 3s 3d, and 'Cashmere Foule' at 1s 6½d a yard. It was made up into mourning clothes, such as the 'pretty cashmere frock for fashionable mourning' sold at William Barkers' in 1901 for 3½ guineas (*Ladies Field*, 9 Feb. 1901). Cachemire was widely used for fashionable mourning in nineteenth century France.

**Coburg**   A wool and cotton twilled fabric, used for cheaper quality mourning, introduced after the marriage of Queen Victoria to Prince Albert of Saxe-Coburg in 1840. It was popular in the 1840s as a cheap version of paramatta (Beck, p. 70 & Cunnington, C. W., p. 154).

**Courtauld crape**   Crimped, dull, black silk mourning crape made and advertised by the firm of Courtaulds and widely sold abroad as the one and only true 'crape anglais'. Harrods sold this fabric in 1895 at 2s 6d to 6s 11d a yard single width and 4s 11d to 14s 6d double width, which was nearly twice as expensive as other mourning silk fabrics. It was last made in 1940 (see Chapter 8).

**Crape**   (See Chapter 8 & Beck, p. 90.) A transparent crimped, dull silk gauze, imported into Britain before about 1690, thereafter introduced by Huguenot refugees. Popularised by the firm of Courtaulds in the nineteenth century, it was sold at the Army and Navy Stores in 1902 at 28 in. wide – 3s 9d to 5s a yard, 42 in. wide at 5s 9d to 9s 6d a yard, which is about twice the price of other listed mourning silks.

**Crepe anglais**   The French name for English silk black and white mourning crape, usually Courtaulds' crape because this firm monopolised the crape export market from the mid-nineteenth century until crape production ceased in 1940 (see Chapter 8). The fashion magazine *Les Modes* declared in April 1914 that the only elegant mourning crape was *le crêpe anglais Courtauld* for use in both First and Second mourning. It was described as 'the most serene yet most distinguished and rich' crape for mourning.

**Crepelle**   A cheaper silk and wool mourning fabric, sold at the Army and Navy Stores, London, in 1902 at 2s 3d a yard.

**Crepe Imperial**   Recommended by Jay's in an advertisement in *Myra's Journal* of 1 February 1888: 'It is all wool and yet looks exactly like crape.'

**Crepe-de-Chine** or **Crepe-de-Chene**   A lightweight silk or silk and worsted fabric, sold for mourning by the Army and Navy Stores, London, in 1902, at prices from 3s 11d to 7s 11d a yard.

**Crepe myosotis**   A crimped silk mourning crape with a soft finish, introduced by the firm of Courtaulds in the early 1930s as the stiffer ordinary mourning crape was becoming increasingly unpopular (see Chapter 11).

**Crepon**   A silk and wool mixture, heavier in weight than crepe-de-chine. It was sold, black, for mourning wear in the Army and Navy Stores, London, in 1902, at 4s 3d a yard.

**Crespe**  Italian and French name for the earliest form of mourning crape – a lightweight crimped type of gauze, which was being imported from Bologna in Italy into Antwerp by 1560 (Tawney, R. H. & Power, E., pp. 163–5). In 1590 Cesare Vecellio describes a French widow as wearing *un velo bianca increspato* – a white crape veil. Savary de Victor Bruslon in 1723 describes crespe as made from raw silk and being of the same nature and quality as crape (see Chapter 8 & Beck, p. 94). This name seems to have been replaced by crape or crepe by the mid-eighteenth century in England.

**Crisp**  Another name for crespe – taken from the Latin *crispare* to curl (see Chapter 8 & Beck, p. 92).

**Cyprus, Cypress, Sipers** or **Sypers**  A fine silk or cobweb linen lawn, in black or white for mourning, an early version of mourning crape. It was used for hatbands and the draping of colours at funerals. According to Beck (p. 92) it was introduced from Cyprus. In use for mourning from the sixteenth century. It was used in 1653 at the funeral of Oliver Cromwell, when the streets were guarded by soldiers 'with their ensignes wrapt in Cypres' (Cunnington, C. W. & Lucas, Catherine, p. 231 from *Chronicle of the Late Intestine War*, 2nd Edn. 1676). Cyprus gauze was listed among black fabrics produced in 1765 by the London Weavers Company (pp. 24–5): 'Plain yard wide Cyprus – 0/6d; if corded or striped with cotton, silk or yarn – 0/8d. Plain yard wide Cyprus Handkerchiefs, per dozen, 6/0d.' In 1881 *Sylvia's Home Journal* was still recommending the respectable widow to include in the First mourning wardrobe: 'One dress, either a costume of Cyprus crape, or an old black dress covered with Rainproof crape.' (see Chapter 6, p. 140).

**De Laine**  A fine woollen fabric dyed black for mourning, originally called mousseline-de-laine or muslins-of-wool (Beck, p. 96). The *Illustrated London News* on 17 June 1910 recommended, for General mourning for Edward VII, a half-mourning walking dress in 'black-and-grey striped de laine'.

**Etamine**  A fine, very light fabric, some all silk, or silk and wool or all wool. Savary de Victor Bruslon described silk etamines in 1723 as being like 'soft crapes'. It was made at Lyon and Avignon in the early eighteenth century, and used for mourning scarves and head-dresses. This may have been the same fabric as ermoizine.

**Foulard silk**  Thin, lightweight silk in black for mourning; fine, soft with a twilled finish (Beck, p. 131). It was popular in the Edwardian period when soft fabrics were fashionable. The Army and Navy Stores sold mourning foulard at 2s 4d in 1902.

**Georgette**  A fine chiffon-like silk fashionable from the mid-1920s to mid-1930s and used in black for smart mourning – especially in France (see Chapter 11).

**Grenadines**  Sold for mourning wear at 2s to 3s 11d a yard, 'Plain' and at 4s 11d to 7s 9d a yard, 'Silk Plain' by the Army and Navy Stores, London, 1902.

**Glacé Silk**  A lightweight plain silk finished with a crisp, shiny surface so that it rustled when worn. It was very popular in the 1900–5 period, though it would have been unsuitable for deepest mourning because of its lustrous finish. The Army and Navy Stores sold it, probably for the later stages of mourning, at a price range from 1s 11½d to 4s 7d a yard in 1902.

**Grosgrain** or **Grogorine** or **Grosgram**  A heavily corded black silk fabric, sometimes mixed with cotton, dyed black for mourning, said by Beck (p. 155) to have been imported into Europe from Turkey by the East India Company in the mid-seventeenth century. In 1902 the Army and Navy Stores sold it at prices from 3s 11d to 7s 9d a yard.

**Henrietta cloth**  Advertised in *Harper's Bazaar* as suitable for 'light-weight house dresses' whilst in mourning, on 14 February 1885.

**Holland**  A fine white linen lawn, first made in Holland and exported to the rest of Europe. It was used for mourning cuffs and head-dresses before the introduction of white mourning crape in the early nineteenth century and white cotton muslin in the late eighteenth century (Beck, p. 164). At the funeral of Mary Queen of Scots in 1587 the poor women in the procession wore 'an ell of white holland over their heads' (see Chapter 1, p. 26). In 1660 at the funeral of the Duke of Gloucester 'ffine holland' was used 'for large bands and pair of double cuffs each' and for shirts, for mourning livery for the King's footmen (PRO Audit Office. Declared Accounts Wardrobe 76/2354).

**Jeandamn** or **Jean**   A heavy twilled cotton cloth said to derive its name from the town of Jaen in Spain. In 1660 at the funeral of Henry, Duke of Gloucester, it was used to trim the mourning banners for the King's Royal 'trumpettors' (see Chapter 4, p. 100; PRO. Audit Office, Declared Accounts Wardrobe, 76/2354, and Beck).

**Looking-glass Silk**   A glacé silk with a suspicion of moiré on its shiny surface, and as such suitable only for the later stages of mourning. In use for mourning in the nineteenth century (Cunnington, C. W., p. 432).

**Lustring** or **Lutestring**   A fine silk finished with a sheen obtained by dipping the fabric in gum and stretching it as it dried. This fabric was first made in England by Huguenot refugees. In 1692 the Royal Lustring Company was granted a charter for the manufacture of both coloured lustring and black lustring which was woven specifically for mourning use (Beck, p. 209). Lustring was widely used in the eighteenth century for undress (informal dress) and the later stages of Court and private mourning. At the funeral of William III in 1702 the *London Gazette* (No. 3791 fpr. 9–12 March) published Court mourning instructions ordering the wearing of 'black crape . . . in consideration of the great Encouragement it will be to the English Manufacture of Lustring and Alamode.' In 1756 Barbara Johnson purchased 12 yards of lustring at 4s 6d a yard to make 'a white lutestring night gown, second mourning for my father.' This fabric does not seem to have been used for mourning from the Victorian period onwards.

**Mantua**   A heavier-weight silk, dyed black for mourning, and popular in the eighteenth century, deriving its name from the silk centre of Mantua in North Italy. The fabric was introduced into

England by Huguenot refugees in the late seventeenth century. Ebenezer Ibbetson and William Peckett, silk mercers of the Queen's Head, Ludgate, London, were selling 'rich black Dutch mantua' at 8s per yard (Rothstein, quoting Bill No. 12853II, Dept. of Prints and Drawings, Victoria and Albert Museum).

**Merino**   A fine quality wool fabric, in black for mourning, first produced in England by Garrett of Bradford in about 1826. At first it was sold at prices between 75s to 80s a bolt – but as the fabric grew more popular the price fell to 40s to 50s a piece (Beck, p. 220). It was sold in 1902 for mourning wear by the Army and Navy Stores at a price of 1s 4½d to 2s 3d a yard.

**Moreen** or **Moireen**   A cheap quality moiré, sold in black for mourning in the nineteenth-century (Beck, p. 227). In 1902 the Army and Navy Stores sold it at a price range of 1s 4½d to 2s 3d a yard.

**Muslin** or **Muzeline**   A finely woven, lightweight cotton fabric with a downy surface. It was first introduced into Britain from India in about 1670, by the East India Company and gradually replaced linen hollands and cambrics. By the 1780s finely spun cotton muslins were being machine-produced in Bolton, Glasgow and Paisley. The name is said by Beck (p. 231) to derive from the city of Mosul near Nineveh. White muslin was used for plain mourning cuffs and collars for men and women. In 1689 Edmund Verney wrote: 'I have made me a new Black cloth suit . . . with new muzeline bands' (see Chapter 4). In 1758 Mrs Delany in Court mourning for Princess Caroline complained about having to wear 'broad hemmed muslin or white crape that looks like old flannel, 7s. a yard and won't wash.' (Cunnington, C. W. & Lucas, Catherine, p. 259. Autobiography and Correspondence of Mrs Delany, 1861, Vol. 3, p. 475).

**Ninon**   With the fashion for softer, lighter fabrics of the pre-1914–18 war period, this lightweight soft silk was used for less formal mourning, when dyed black or in half-mourning shades. On 4 June 1910 the *Illustrated London News* featured a 'gown of black silk Ninon laid over white silk' for Ordinary General mourning for Edward VII.

**Norwich crape**   Originally a silk warp and woollen wefted fabric specifically for mourning use. It was like bombazine, but was not similar to the semi-transparent crimped silk mourning crape. It may well be the type of fabric referred to in the inventory of the clothes of Mary Queen of Scots in 1562, as a dress of 'crespe noyer' (see Chapter 3). In 1575 Dutch immigrant weavers in Norwich were manufacturing Norwich crape, in imitation of bombazine, and this trade, according to Sir Frank Warner, 'continued one of the most important manufactures of Norwich down to the commencement of the nineteenth century.' The identification of this particular fabric is further confused by the development of a transparent type of crimped crape by Grout, Baylis & Co. which they also called Norwich crape. This fabric was produced at their Saffron Walden factory between about 1815 and 1834 (Warner, p. 299).

**Norwich paramatta**   A grander version of paramatta, with a worsted weft and a silk warp, sold at Harrods in 1895 at 4s 11d to 6s 11d a yard.

**Nun's veiling**   A very fine, soft woollen veiling in black for mourning, used also as a dress fabric, that was popular once mourning crape had gone out of fashion at the end of the nineteenth century. It was sold by the Army and Navy Stores in 1902 at prices between 1s 4½d and 1s 11d a yard.

**Padusoy, Padisoy, Peau-de-Soie** or **Soie de Padoue**   A heavier-weight silk, often black, with a fine smooth texture, possibly originally from Padua in Italy and imported from Holland into England and America in the early eighteenth century. It was probably introduced into England by Huguenot refugees after 1685. An advertisement published in Boston, Massachusetts in 1728 announced: 'Dutch black padisoys for mourning sold by Jonathan Barnard.' (Rothstein, p. 153). 'Padusuoy' was among the black silk fabrics listed in the silk prices published by the London Weavers Company in 1769. In 1902 the Army and Navy Stores sold 'peau-de-soie' for mourning at prices from 3s to 5s 3d a yard.

**Paramatta**   Originally woven with worsted weft and silk warp, it became a cheaper type of bombazine with a worsted weft and cotton warp widely used for mourning in the Victorian period by families who could not afford the superior fabric of bombazine. The name, invented in Bradford, is said by Beck to derive from the town of Paramatta in New South Wales, Australia, from whence the wool was exported to Britain (Beck, p. 245). On 19 January 1846 Hannington's of Brighton billed a Mrs Stilton of Shoreham for '13 yards of paramatta=£1.6.0d' – or 2s a yard. In 1902 the Army and Navy Stores were selling paramatta at a price range of 4s to 4s 6d a yard (Cunnington, C. W., p. 434 & Archives Collection, Hannington's, Brighton).

**Poplin**   Originally a mixture of silk and wool introduced into England and Ireland by Huguenot refugees, after 1685. Dublin became a well-known poplin manufacturing centre (Beck, p. 260). A dark grey poplin dress was worn for informal mourning in 1747 (Cunnington, C. W. & Lucas, Catherine, p. 245). In March 1751 Barbara Johnson chose 'a grey poplin long sack' as mourning for the Prince of Wales, which she bought at 2s 6d a yard. Wool poplin was being sold for mourning wear by the Army and Navy Stores, London, in 1902 at prices between 2s 4d to 3s 9d a yard, whilst better quality Irish poplin sold at 5s 9d to 7s 6d a yard for mourning.

**Radzimir**   A black silk, deeper mourning than bombazine and popular in the 1840s. In 1849 a mourning evening dress was made of 'Black Spitalfields radzimir', with four graduated flounces (Cunnington, C. W., pp. 154 & 434). This name may well be a nineteenth-century version of the eighteenth-century mourning fabric 'ras de Saint Maur'.

**Ras de Saint Maur, Rasdumore** and possibly **Ras de Soye**   A black wool or silk used by the French Court for official mourning in the eighteenth century. According to Victor Savary de Bruslon it was a serge-like mourning fabric, made, in the early eighteenth century, in Paris, Lyon, and Tours, using silk yarns from Piedmont and Bologna. It was used for various stages of mourning according to the way it was made up. The silk and wool type was used by widows. The fabric derived its name 'from a large market town near Paris, called St. Maur des Fosse, where M. Marcelin Charlier, the most able manufacturer of his day established the first factory in 1677.' (Savary de Victor Bruslon, 1723). In the *Ordre Chronologique des Deuils de la Cour*, published in 1765, the fabric recommended for deepest Court mourning was 'Ras de Saint Maur de Laine' (Mercier, p. 35). Beck refers to the *British Chronicle* of February 1763, in which a silk sale at Covent Garden was advertised, which included 'black armozeens, ras du mores and mantuas' (Beck, p. 271 & 8). In the early eighteenth century amongst silks produced in Holland were 'armoisins and ras de soye' (Rothstein, p. 155). This fabric is not amongst mourning fabrics listed for sale by the Army and Navy Stores in 1902, and may possibly have become radzimir by the nineteenth century.

**Sarcenet** or **Sarsnet** or **Sarcenett**   A lightweight silk, used in both black and white for mourning purposes, probably for draping items such as trumpets and mourning hoods before crimped mourning crape was woven in England. Sarcenet was introduced into England according to Beck, in the thirteenth century, deriving its name from the Spanish Saracens (Beck, p. 280). The fabric was woven with a twilled or plain finish. At the funeral of James I in 1625, 'Black taffata sarcenett clix yards' was ordered 'for the Trompettours, drummers and phiphes at 1/- a yard' (PRO E 351/3145, m. 62d). In the 1682 inventory of John Davis of Bewdley, Worcestershire, who was probably a draper and undertaker, is listed amongst shrouding at 10d a yard, silk crape at 18d a yard, and alamode scarves at 10s a dozen: 'white sarsenett hoods at ffifteen pence'. These were worn by ladies for fashionable mourning (PRO Inventory 5391. State Papers, Domestic). In 1820 Barbara Johnson bought 12 yards of fabric for a 'black twill'd Sarsnet gown . . . mourning for the Duchess of York.' This is a very lightweight, finely ribbed silk. In 1902 the Army and Navy Stores, London, were still selling mourning 'Sarsnett' at a price range of 1s 5½d to 1s 11d a yard, which made it a comparatively cheap mourning fabric.

**Serge**   Originally a twilled worsted, later a twilled woven silk or wool fabric, with a cheaper version in cotton. It was known back to the twelfth century and in black was used for mourning (Beck, p. 295). At the funeral of the Duke of Gloucester in 1660, serge was ordered from John Albert, to cover the seats of some of the mourning coaches (PRO Audit Office, Declared Accounts, Wardrobe 76/2354). On 14 February 1885 *Harpers Bazaar* recommended: 'Serge Tailor Suits for mourning . . . worn in the mornings, for shopping and for travelling.' In 1902 the Army and Navy Stores were selling mourning serge at a price range of 1s 3d to 4s 9d a yard.

**Silverets**  An English fabric of silk and wool made in the mid-eighteenth century as a cheaper version of Norwich crape (Cunnington, C. W. & Lucas, Catherine, p. 149).

**Tabby** or **Tabi**  A fine silk, rather like a taffeta, with a watered finish, possibly of Indian or Persian origin, introduced into England by Huguenot refugees after 1685 (Beck, p. 334). The fabric was popular for mourning in the eighteenth and early nineteenth centuries, particularly for Court mourning. In 1747 Mrs Delany makes a careful reference to the use of unwatered tabby for mourning – this would have been considered plainer and therefore more suitable. She was in mourning for her sister's husband's brother: 'Abroad, undrest casual, a dark grey unwatered tabby.' (Cunnington, C. W. & Lucas, Catherine, p. 245 – Autobiography and Correspondence of Mrs Delany 1861). This fabric would have been too shiny for deepest mourning.

**Taffeta** or **Taffaty**  A fine twilled silk, usually lustred, dyed black when used for mourning and used for dresses and head-dresses. It was introduced into England, according to Beck, in the fourteenth century (Beck). At the funeral of Mary Queen of Scots, in 1587, Court ladies wore head-dresses, of 'black taffaty and white lawn' (see Chapter 4). It was widely imported from Italy into France in the sixteenth century (Gaston, R., p. 57). In January 1799 Barbara Johnson spent 3 guineas on nine yards of black taffeta for 'a black taffety gown, mourning for my dear brother Robert.' This is a crisp black silk with a fine rib. It was still being worn for mourning in 1902, when the Army and Navy Stores sold 'taffeta broche' at 2s 9d to 4s 6d a yard. In 1920 the *Gazette du Bon Ton* recommended black silk taffeta with dull stones for 'petit deuil' or the second stage of widows' mourning (see Chapter 11, p. 272).

**Vallee Cypress** – (see Bologna crape.)

**Venetian crape cloth**  Probably a dull, heavy mixture of silk and wool. This seems to have replaced bombazine and paramatta as the basic fabric of widow's weeds by the end of the nineteenth century.

In 1901 William Barker's advertised a widow's skirt 'in newest shape for coming season, made in either Priestley's Venetian Crape cloth, cashmere or dull Mourning Cloth, trimmed with plain band of Courtauld's Crape . . . Price including material for Bodice 49/6d.' (*The Lady*, 4 Oct. 1900). In 1902 the Army and Navy Stores were selling shrunk 'Venetian Coating' for mourning at 3s 6d to 4s 11d a yard, which was probably an all wool fabric.

**Victoria crepe**   A cheap cotton version of crimped silk mourning crape, popular in the second half of the nineteenth century (Cunnington, C. W., p. 436).

**Voile**   A very fine silk and wool, or wool or all cotton veiling, used in black to replace mourning crape on women's deep mourning hats. It was first worn by royalty in this way by Princess Alexandra of Wales at the funeral of the Duke of Clarence in 1892, and again by Princess Louise at the funeral of Queen Victoria in 1901. The Army and Navy Stores were selling two styles of voile in 1902 – plain black voile at 1s 8d to 3s 3d a yard, and fancy striped voile at 3s 1d to 3s 6d a yard. The French fashion magazine *Les Modes* was still recommending voile mourning veils for widows in the 1930s (see Chapter 11).

**Zibelline**   A cross between a barége and a paramatta fabric, used for cheaper mourning clothes in the 1850s (Cunnington, C. W., p. 436).

NOTE: The books referred to in Appendix 1 are included in the Select Bibliography.

# APPENDIX 2

# *Periods of Mourning*

A: Table of Court Mourning Regulations in France 1765 taken from *Ordre Chronologique des Deuils de la Court*

| | First Mourning 'Wool' | Second Mourning 'Silk' | Ordinary Mourning | Half-Mourning |
|---|---|---|---|---|
| For Parents Total: 6 months | | 3 months in wool with white accessories | 6 weeks in black silk, trimmings of fringed linen | 6 weeks in black and white with diamonds |
| For Grandparents Total: 4 months | Same but spread over four months of mourning | | | |
| For Brother and Sister Total: 6 weeks and a day | 3 weeks in black wool | 15 days in black silk | | 8 days in black and white with diamonds |
| For Aunts and Uncles Total: 3 weeks and a day | None | 3 weeks in black silk | 15 days with fringed linen | 7 days in black or white with blonde trimmings |
| For First Cousin | None | None | 8 days in black silk with fringed linen | 5 days in white |
| For Second Cousin Total: 8 days | None | None | 5 days in black | 3 days in white |

| | First Mourning 'Wool' | Second Mourning 'Silk' | Ordinary Mourning | Half-Mourning |
|---|---|---|---|---|
| For Husband Total: 1 year and 6 weeks | 6 months in wool, trained robe with white trimmings, bronzed buckles | 6 months in black silk with white crape trimmings and black stones | | 6 weeks in black and white with accessories all black or all white |
| For Wife Total: 6 months | Black wool suit and black wool stockings for 6 weeks, first 3 with deep weepers on cuffs | Black suit with silk stockings and fringed linen | | 6 weeks in black suit with silver buckles and sword |

From MERCIER, Louis, *Le Deuil, sons Observation dans tous les temps et dans tous les pays comparée a son observation de nos jours*, P. Douvet, London, 1877, p. 35.

B: Recommended lengths of Family Mourning 1876–97 taken from Contemporary Sources. (See Chapter 6)

| | First Mourning | Second Mourning | Ordinary Mourning | Half-Mourning | Total |
|---|---|---|---|---|---|
| Widow for Husband | 1 year 1 day in bombazine and heavy plain crape | 9 months with less crape | 3 months in black silk with ribbon and jet | 6 months min. in half-mourning colours | 2½ years |
| Widower for Wife | 3 months in black suit, with chain, buttons and tie | | black watch | None | 3 months |
| Mother for Child | 6 months in bombazine and crape | | 3 months in black silk | 3 months in half-mourning colours | 1 year |
| Child for Parent | Black or white crape for 6 months | | 3 months | 3 months | 1 year |
| Wife for her Parents | 18 months mantle in paramatta and crape | | 3 months | 3 months | 2 years |
| Wife for Mother-in-Law | 18 months mantle in paramatta and crape | | 3 months | 3 months | 2 years |
| For Brother and Sister | 3 months in crape | | 2 months | 1 month | 6 months |
| Niece for Aunt or Uncle | None | | 3 to 6 months depending on how remote the relationship | | Usually 3 months in half-mourning |
| First Cousin | None | | 3 weeks or stretching to 3 months | 3 weeks | 6 weeks to 3 months |

*Mourning Dress*

| | First Mourning | Second Mourning | Ordinary Mourning | Half-Mourning | Total |
|---|---|---|---|---|---|
| Grand-daughter for Grandparents | 6 months in crape | | 2 to 3 months | 1 to 3 months | 6 to 9 months |
| Mothers for Parents-in-Law of their married children | None | | 6 weeks black without crape | | 6 weeks |
| Second Wife for Husband's first Wife's Parents | | | 3 months | | 3 months |
| Servants mourning | Same as their employers but in cheap, tougher fabrics, and black and white only for half-mourning | | | | |

## C: Comparison of lengths of Mourning

| | 1765 Court Mourning in France | 1876–1897 Family Mourning in Britain |
|---|---|---|
| For Parents | 6 months | 2 years |
| For Grandparents | 4 months | 6 to 9 months |
| For Brother and Sister | 6 weeks and a day | 6 months |
| For Aunts and Uncles | 3 weeks and a day | 3 months |
| For First Cousin | 15 days | 6 weeks to 3 months |
| For Husband | 1 year and six weeks | 2½ years |
| For Wife | 6 months | 3 months |

## D: 'Court Mourning Regulated by Former Precedents' from the *Hon. Mrs Fenella Fitzhardinge Armystage, London, 1883*

| | First Mourning | Second Mourning | Third Mourning | Half-Mourning | Total |
|---|---|---|---|---|---|
| King or Queen | 8 weeks | 2 weeks | 2 weeks | 12 weeks |
| Son or Daughter of Sovereign | 4 weeks | 1 week | 1 week | 6 weeks |
| Brother or Sister of Sovereign | 2 weeks | 4 days | 3 days | 3 weeks |
| Nephew or Niece of Sovereign | None | 1 week | 1 week | 2 weeks |
| Uncle or Aunt of Sovereign | None | 1 week | 1 week | 2 weeks |
| Cousin Germain | None | 7 days | 3 days | 10 days |
| More distant Royal Cousin | None | 4 days | 3 days | 7 days |

# NOTES

## CHAPTER ONE

1 Giesey, Ralf E., *The Royal Funeral Ceremony in Renaissance France*, Libraire E. Drox, Geneva, 1960, pp. 41 & 177.
2 *Ibid.*, p. 177.
3 *Ibid.*, p. 33.
4 *Ibid.*, p. 33.
5 *Ibid.*, pp. 9, 33.
6 *Ibid.*, p. 7.
7 Cunnington, Phillis & Lucas, Catherine, *Costumes for Births, Marriages and Deaths*, A. & C. Black, London, 1972, pp. 226, 234 & 237.
8 Abijes, Mme de, *Deuil, Ceremonial, Usages, Toilettes*, published by the Grand Maison de Noir, 27–29 Faubourg St Honoré, Paris, undated *c*. 1885. In the Archive Collection, Courtaulds Ltd.
9 Giesey, *op. cit.*, p. 11.
10 Arber, Edward, *An English Garner*, Constable, London, 1897, Vol. 8, quoting a tract by Abel Jeffes, *The Scottish Queen's Burial at Peterborough*, 1589.
11 Stone, Laurence, *The Crisis of the Aristocracy 1558–1641*, Clarendon Press, Oxford, 1965, p. 576.
12 *Ibid.*, p. 575.
13 *Ibid.*, pp. 578.
14 Cunnington & Lucas, *op. cit.*, p. 228.
15 Ridder, A de, *Prerogatives Nobilaires et Ambitions Bourgeoises*, Vol. III, *Deuil, Funerailles et Tombes*, La Noblesse Belge Year Book 1929–30, Brussels, 1932, p. 192.
16 Cunnington & Lucas, *op. cit.*, p. 229.
17 Briggs, Asa, *How they Lived*, Basil Blackwell, Oxford, 1969, Vol. III, pp. 9, 10, quoting Fitton R. S. & Wadsworth A. D., *The Strutts and Arkwrights*, 1958, pp. 129–30.
18 Chapman-Huston, D. (ed.), *The Private Diaries of Princess Daisy of Pless 1873–1914*, John Murray, London, 1950, p. 173.
19 Bessborough, Earl of (ed.), *Lady Charlotte Schrieber's Journal 1853–1891*, John Murray, London, 1952, pp. 5, 34.
20 Bloom, Ursula, *Victorian Vinaigrette*, Hutchinson, London, 1956, p. 200.
21 Rhys, Ernest (ed.), *The Diary of Samuel Pepys*, Everyman, Dent, London, 1943, Vol. I, p. 441.
22 Morley, John, *Death, Heaven and the Victorians*, Studio Vista, London, 1971, p. 202.
23 Stone, *op. cit.*, p. 575.
24 Rhys, *op. cit.*, p. 466.
25 Bloom, *op. cit.*, p. 202.
26 Verney, Margaret M., *Memoirs of the Verney Family 1642–1696*, Longman Green, London, 1899, Vol. IV, p. 327.
27 Woodforde, James (ed. John Beresford), *The Diary of a Country Parson*, Oxford University Press, 1949, p. 75.

28  *Ibid.*, p. 562.
29  Cunnington & Lucas, *op. cit.*, p. 198.
30  Rothstein, Natalie, *Dutch Silks – An Important but Forgotten Industry of the 18th Century or a Hypothesis*, OUD Holland, J. H. de Bussy, Amsterdam, 1964, Vol. LXXIX, p. 153.
31  Pike, Martha V. & Armstrong, Janice Gray, *A Time To Mourn – Expressions of Grief in Nineteenth Century America*. Exhibition Catalogue. The Museums of Stony Brook, Stony Brook, New York, 1980, p. 16.
32  Swenson, Evelyn, *Victoriana Americana*, Great Lakes Living Press, Matteson, Illinois, 1976, p. 96.
33  Pike & Armstrong, *op. cit.*, pp. 107–9. P. G. Buckley, *Truly We Live In a Dying World – Mourning on Long Island*, quoting Gabriel Furman, *Antiquities of Long Island*, New York, 1875, p. 161.
34  *Ibid.*, P. G. Buckley, p. 116.
35  Toynbee, J. M. C., *Death and Burial in the Roman World*, Thames & Hudson, London, 1971, p. 55.
36  Gosden, P. H. J. H., *Self-Help Voluntary Associations in Nineteenth Century Britain*, Batsford, London, 1973, pp. 26–7.
37  Consitt, Frances, *The London Weavers Company*, Clarendon Press, Oxford, 1932. Plummer, Alfred, *The London Weavers Company*, Routledge & Kegan Paul, London, 1972, pp. 252–9.
38  Foster-Brown, R. S., *An Introduction to the Worshipful Company of Armourers and Braziers*, Privately Printed for the Company, 1965, p. 19.
39  Gosden, *op. cit.*, pp. 4, 6, 7.
40  *Ibid.*, p. 9, 16, 60–1, 116.
41  *Ibid.*, p. 120.
42  Tressell, Robert, *The Ragged Trousered Philanthropists*, Panther, London, 1975, p. 510.
43  Morley, *op. cit.*, pp. 22, 26.
44  Tressell, *op. cit.*, p. 523.
45  Booth, Charles, *The Life and Labour of the People In London*, Macmillan, London, 1902, Third Series, Vol. 1, p. 248.
46  Binder, Pearl, *The Pearlies – A Social Record*, Jupiter Books, London, 1975, pp. 42–3.
47  Booth, *op. cit.*, p. 248.
48  *Ibid.*, p. 248.
49  Tressell, *op. cit.*, p. 524.
50  Lindley, Kenneth, *Of Graves and Epitaphs*, Hutchinson, London, 1965, p. 143.
51  Booth, *op. cit.*, Vol. 2, p. 245.
52  Lloyd, A. L., *Folk Song In England*, Panther, London, 1969, pp. 336–8.
53  Lindley, *op. cit.*, pp. 114–17.
54  Morley, *op. cit.*, p. 23.
55  Yeo, Eileen & Thompson, E. P., *The Other Mayhew*, Pantheon Books, New York, 1971, p. 114.

# CHAPTER TWO

56  Petrie, W. M. Flinders, *Tombs of the Courtiers and Oxyrhynkhos*, British School of Archaeology in Egypt, Bernard Quaritch, London, 1925, p. 14.

57 Grinsell, Leslie V., *Barrow, Pyramid and Tomb*, Thames & Hudson, London, 1975, p. 41, quoting Gwyn Jones, *A History of the Vikings*, London, 1968.
58 Petrie, *op. cit.*, p. 14.
59 Johnson, Rev. Samuel, *The History of the Yorubas*, Christian Missionary Society, Lagos, 1951, pp. 54–6.
60 Hentze, C., *Chinese Tomb Figures*, Edward Goldstein, London, 1928, p. 12.
61 Bendann, Effie, *Death Customs*, Dawsons, London, repr. 1969, p. 252.
62 Puckle, Bertram, *Funeral Customs, Their Origins and Development*, T. Werner Laurie, London, 1926, p. 56.
63 Fenton, Monica, *A Child Widow's Story*, Gollancz, London, 1966, p. 152.
64 Eden, Emily, *Up the Country*, Oxford University Press, 1930.
65 Seton, Grace Thompson, *Yes, Lady Saheb*, Hodder & Stoughton, London, 1925, p. 326.
66 Johnson, *op. cit.*, pp. 54–6.
67 Joyce, T. A. & Thomas, N. W., *Women of All Nations*, Cassell, London, 1908, Vol. I, p. 106.
68 *Ibid.*, p. 326.
69 *Ibid.*, p. 22.
70 *Ibid.*, p. 22.
71 *Ibid.*, p. 108.
72 Burton, Richard, *Abeokuta and the Cameroon Mountains*, Tinsley, London, 1863, Vol. I, appendix 2.
73 Seligman, G. B., *The Melanesians of British New Guinea*, Cambridge University Press, 1910, p. 620.
74 Mercier, Louis, *Le Deuil – son observation dans tous les temps et dans tous les pays, comparée à son observation de nos jours*, P. Douvet, London, 1877, p. 29.
75 *Ibid.*, p. 31.
76 Zee, Henri & Barbara, van der, *William and Mary*, Macmillan, London, History Book Club edition, 1973, p. 1.
77 Verney, Peter, *The Standard Bearer*, Hutchinson, London, 1963, p. 36.
78 *Ibid.*, p. 36.
79 *Ibid.*, p. 37.
80 Chapman-Huston, D. (ed.), *The Private Diaries of Daisy, Princess of Pless, 1873–1914*, John Murray, London, 1950, p. 172.
81 Mead, S. M., *Traditional Maori Clothing – a study of Technological and Functional Change*, A. H. & A. W. Read, Wellington, New Zealand, 1969, p. 176.
82 Dick, Oliver Lawson (ed.), *Aubrey's Brief Lives*, Penguin, London, 1967, p. 7.
83 Goody, Jack, *Death, Property and the Ancestors*, Tavistock Publications, London, 1962, p. 194.
84 Burton, Elizabeth, *The Early Victorians at Home*, Victorians and Modern History Club, Newton Abbot, 1973, pp. 42, 116.
85 Radcliffe-Brown, A. R. & Forde, Daryll, *African Systems of Kinship and Marriage*, Oxford University Press, 1956, p. 64.
86 Warner, Marina, *The Dragon Empress*, Weidenfeld & Nicolson, London, 1972, p. 30.
87 Fenton, *op. cit.*, p. 37.
88 *Ibid.*, pp. 69, 152.
89 *Ibid.*, p. 175.
90 Trappes-Lomax, Richard (ed.), *The English Franciscan Nuns 1619–1812*, Catholic Record Society, Vol. XXIV, London, 1922.

*Mourning Dress*

91 Schooneheek, Adrien, *Histoires des Ordres Religieux*, Amsterdam, 1695.
92 Sumner, William Graham, *Folkways*, Ginn, USA, 1940, reprint Mentor Books, 1960, p. 409.
93 Burton, *op. cit.*, p. 301, quoting Sir T. Martin, *Life of H.R.H. The Prince Consort*, Vol. V.
94 Rhys, Ernest (ed.), *Extracts from the Diary of Samuel Pepys*, Everyman, Dent, 1943, Vol. 4, p. 443.
95 Bloom, Ursula, *Victorian Vinaigrette*, Hutchinson, London, 1956, p. 206.
96 Ramelson, Marian, *The Petticoat Rebellion*, Lawrence & Wishart, London, 1972, p. 48.
97 Bessborough, Earl of, *Lady Charlotte Schrieber – Extracts from her Journal 1853–1891*, John Murray, London, 1952, p. 63.
98 Yeo, Eileen & Thompson, E. P., *The Other Mayhew*, Pantheon Books, New York, 1971, pp. 156–7.
99 *Ibid.*, pp. 121, 148–9, 172–3.

# CHAPTER THREE

100 Schooneheek, Adrien, *Histoire des Ordres Religieux*, Amsterdam, 1695.
101 Duchenne, Irene V., 'The Development of the Religious Habit of the Faithful Companions of Jesus' in *Costume*, the Journal of the Costume Society, Victoria and Albert Museum, London, 1972, Vol. 6, p. 87.
102 Longworth, Philip, *The Rise and Fall of Venice*, Constable, London, 1974, p. 104.
103 Strutt, Joseph, *A Complete View of the Dress and Habits of the People of England*, edited by J. R. Planché, 1842, repr. Tabard Press, London 1970, Vol. 4, p. 63.
104 Cunnington, C. W. & Cunnington, Phillis, *Handbook of English Mediaeval Costume*, Faber, London, 1952, p. 131.
105 Clayton, Muriel, *Catalogue of Rubbings of Brasses and Incised Slabs*, Victoria and Albert Museum, HMSO, London, 1968, pl. 49.
106 Cunnington, Phillis & Lucas, Catherine, *Costumes for Births, Marriages and Deaths*, A. & C. Black, London, 1972, pp. 146, 183, 241.
107 Niccolini, Geneva di Camugliano, *The Chronicles of a Florentine Family 1200–1470*, Jonathan Cape, London, 1933, p. 55.
108 Longworth, *op. cit.*, p. 124.
109 Blum, André, *The Last Valois*, Costume of the Western World Series, Harrap, London, 1951, p. 6.
110 Giesey, Ralf E., *The Royal Funeral Ceremony in Renaissance France*, Libraire E. Drox, Geneva, 1960, p. 7.
111 *Ibid.*, p. 7.
112 Brighton Art Gallery and Museum. Catalogue to the Exhibition 'Death, Heaven and the Victorians', 6 May – 3 August 1970, p. 6.
113 Cunnington & Lucas, *op. cit.*, pl. 57a.
114 *Ibid.*, pp. 208–10 quoting College of Arms MS 1.3.f52 and BM MS Harl. 1776.

308

115   Overloop, Eugene van, *L'inventaire Sforza 1493*, priv. print, Gembloux, 1934, pp. 62–3.

116   Goldsheider, Ludwig, *Unknown Renaissance Portraits*, Phaidon, London, 1952, pl. 45.

117   Pasolini, P. D. d'All'onda, *Catherine Sforza*, Ermanno Loescher, Rome, 1893, Vol. II, p. 52.

118   Ozzola, Leandro, *Il Vestario Italiano dal 1500 al 1550*, Institute of Archaeology and History of Art, University of Rome, 1940, Fig. 17.

119   Niccolini, *op. cit.*, pp. 135–40.

120   Cunnington & Lucas, *op. cit.*, p. 146.

121   *Ibid.*, p. 283, Appendix 4 'Allowances of Mourning at State Funerals', a collation of four MSS Bodleian MS Ashmole 837 (ed. F. Furnival); Harl. 1354 (ed. J. Strutt) BM MSS Egerton 2642 and Harl. 1440.

122   Boase, T. S. K., *Death in the Middle Ages*, Thames & Hudson, London, 1972, pl. 99, from Chroniques de Charles VII MS FR. 2691 f11 Bibliotheque Nationale, Paris.

123   Alexander, J. J. G., *The Master of Burgundy – A Book of Hours for Englebert of Nassau*, Phaidon, London, 1970.

124   Niccolini, *op. cit.*, p. 306.

125   Cunnington, C. W. & Cunnington, Phillis, *Handbook of English Costume in the Sixteenth Century*, Faber, London, 1954, p. 48.

126   Nicolescu, Corina, *Istoria Costumului de Curte In Tarile Romane*, Editura Stiintifica, Bucharest, 1970, pl. 73, also in exhibition catalogue 'Costume of the Rumanian Court 14th to 18th centuries', Museum of Art, Bucharest, 1970, pl. 36, fig. 54.

127   British Museum MS Ii 5–151, Y 1–40 and Y 1–41.

128   Cunnington & Lucas, *op. cit.*, p. 211 quoting BM MS Harl. 1354 f. 12 and p. 218 a collation of 4 contemporary accounts.

129   Fraser, Antonia, *Mary, Queen of Scots*, Weidenfeld & Nicolson, London, 1969, Panther edition, 1970, p. 119.

130   Dalhousie, the Marquess of, *Catalogue of the Jewels, Dresses, Furniture, Books and Paintings of Mary, Queen of Scots, 1556–1569*, The Bannatyne Club, Edinburgh, 1863, pp. 21–7.

131   *Ibid.*, p. 140.

132   Cunnington & Lucas, *op. cit.*, fig. 78 from BM MS Harl. 6064 f. 91.

133   *Ibid.*, pl. 49 from BM MS Add. 35324 f. 21.

134   Fraser, *op. cit.*, p. 531.

135   Vocino, Michele, *Storia del Costume*, Instituto Poligrafico dello Stuto, Rome, 1952, p. 193.

136   Cunnington & Lucas, *op. cit.*, p. 207.

137   *Ibid.*, p. 185.

138   Stone, Lawrence, *The Crisis of the Aristocracy 1558–1641*, Clarendon Press, Oxford, 1965, p. 572, quoting Collins, A., *The Peerage of England*, 1779, pp. 55–62.

139   Cunnington & Lucas, *op. cit.*, p. 190.

140   *Ibid.*, p. 188.

141   Victoria and Albert Museum, Department of Prints and Drawings, E. 533/1918.

142   Laing, W. & Laing, D., *Funerals of the Scottish Queen – Collections Relative to the Funerals of Mary Queen of Scots*, Edinburgh, 1822, quoting Harl. MS 1354 f. 45.

# CHAPTER FOUR

143 Ridder, A. de, *Prerogatives Nobilaires et Ambitions Bourgeoises,* Vol. III, *Deuil, Funerailles et Tombes,* La Noblesse Belge Year Book 1929–30, Brussels, 1932, p. 158.

144 *Ibid.,* p. 194.

145 Earle, Alice Morse, *Costume of Colonial Times,* Macmillan, 1903, reprint Charles E. Tuttle, Rutland, Vermont, 1971, Vol. 1.

146 Cunnington, Phillis & Lucas, Catherine, *Costumes for Births, Marriages and Deaths,* A. & C. Black, London, 1972, pls. 49–51 (BM MS Harl. Add. 353224).

147 *Ibid.,* pl. 78 (BM MS Harl. 6064, f.91).

148 *Ibid.,* pl. 30b, unknown artist, private collection.

149 Fox, George, *Gospel – truth Demonstrated, in a collection of doctrinal books,* London, 1706, p. 807, from 'An encouragement for all to trust in the Lord; who hath the breath of all mankind, and their souls in his hand. And how that not a sparrow shall fall to the ground without the will of the father. 1682.'

150 Pylkkanen, Riitta, *Baroque Costume in Finland, 1620–1721,* Helsinki, 1976, pp. 270–2.

151 Cunnington & Lucas, *op. cit.,* p. 229.

152 *Ibid.,* Fig. 91, a, b, c, and p. 231.

153 Dick, Oliver Lawson (ed.), *Aubrey's Brief Lives,* Penguin, London, 1962, p. 188.

154 Engraving, published in 1662. Victoria and Albert Museum Library.

155 Public Records Office, Audit Office. Declared Accounts Wardrobe, 76/2354. *Funerall of his Royal Highness, Henry, Duke of Gloucester,* Sept. 1660.

156 Thompson, Gladys Scott, *Life in a Noble Household, 1641–1700,* Jonathan Cape, London, 1965.

157 Verney, Margaret, *Memoirs of the Verney Family,* Longman Green, London, 1899, Vol. IV, p. 442.

158 Thompson, *op. cit.,* p. 32.

159 Verney, *op. cit.,* pp. 366–7.

160 *Ibid.,* pp. 318–19.

161 Rhys, Ernest (ed.), *Diary of Samuel Pepys,* Dent, 1943, Vol. I, pp. 186, 203, 441.

162 Verney, *op. cit.,* pp. 451–2.

163 *Ibid.,* pp. 374–6, 384.

164 Rhys, *op. cit.,* Vol. 1, p. 203; Vol. 2, p. 402.

165 Verney, *op. cit.,* pp. 384, 408.

166 *Ibid.,* p. 437.

167 Rhys, *op. cit.,* Vol. 2, p. 206.

168 Verney, *op. cit.,* p. 420.

169 Cunnington, Phillis, *Domestic Uniforms,* A. & C. Black, London, 1974, p. 40. From the Accounts of the Families of Lennard and Barnet, 1585–1691, Holly Trees Museum, priv. print, Colchester, 1908.

170 Pylkkanen, *op. cit.,* pp. 270–2.

171 Rhys, *op. cit.,* Vol. 2, p. 29.

172 *Ibid.,* Vol. 2, p. 11.

# CHAPTER FIVE

173 Rhys, Ernest (ed.), *The Diary of Samuel Pepys*, Dent, London, 1943, Vol. 2, p. 55.

174 Thornton, Peter, *Baroque and Rococo Silks*, Faber, London, 1965, p. 80.

175 Clabburn, Pamela, *Notes and Queries, Costume*, Journal of the Costume Society, Victoria and Albert Museum, London, 1972, No. 6, quoting the 'Court and Private Life In the Time of Queen Charlotte: being the Journal of Mrs Papendiek, Assistant Keeper of the Wardrobe and Reader to her Majesty.'

176 Mercier, Louis, *Le Deuil – son observation dans tous les temps et dans tous les pays comparée à son observation de nos jours*, Paul Douvet, London, 1877, pp. 65–6.

177 Armystage, Fenella Fitzhardinge, *Old Court Customs and Modern Court Rule*, Richard Bentley, London, 1883.

178 Mercier, *op. cit.*, p. 47.

179 *Ibid.*, pp. 35–7.

180 Cunnington, Phillis & Lucas, Catherine, *Costumes for Births, Marriages and Deaths*, A. & C. Black, London, 1972, p. 256, quoting the Lord Chamberlain's Instructions after the death of George II, 1760.

181 Cunnington, C. W. & Cunnington, Phillis, *Handbook of English Costume in the Eighteenth Century*, Faber, London, 1954, p. 318, quoting from the *Salisbury Journal*, Feb. 1752.

182 *Ibid.*, p. 218, quoting the *Gentleman's Magazine*, 1751.

183 Woodforde, James (ed. John Beresford), *The Diary of a Country Parson*, Oxford University Press, 1949, p. 6.

184 Cunnington & Lucas, *op. cit.*, p. 259.

185 Mansfield, Alan, 'Dyeing and Cleaning Clothes in the Late Eighteenth and Early Nineteenth Centuries' in *Costume*, Journal of the Costume Society, Victoria and Albert Museum, London, 1968, No. 2. p. 26.

186 Fitton, R. S. & Wadsworth, A. P., *The Strutts and the Arkwrights, 1758–1830*, Manchester University Press, 1973, p. 131.

187 Williams, C. N., *Life In Georgian England*, Batsford, London, 1963, p. 114.

188 Cunnington, C. W. & Cunnington, Phillis, *op. cit.*, p. 319.

189 Beresford, *op. cit.*, p. 75.

190 Buck, Anne, 'The Dress of Domestic Servants in the Eighteenth Century', in *Proceedings of the Costume Society Conference: Strata of Society*, Norwich, 1973, Victoria and Albert Museum, London, quoting from Fitton R. S. & Wadsworth, A. P., *The Strutts and the Arkwrights, 1758–1830*, p. 149.

191 Richardson, Samuel, *Pamela*, first published in 1740, Dent, London, 1962, Vol. 1, pp. 1, 2.

192 Ridder, A. de, *Prerogatives Nobilaires et Ambitions Bourgeoises*, Vol. III, *Deuil, Funerailles et Tombes*, La Noblesse Belge Year Book 1929–30, Brussels, 1932, p. 158.

193 Cunnington, C. W. & Cunnington, Phillis, *op. cit.*, p. 318, quoting the Bedfordshire Historical Society Record, Williamson Letters, 1954.

194 Mercier, *op. cit.*, p. 35.

195 Cunnington & Lucas, *op. cit.*, p. 247.

196 Woodforde, *op. cit.*, pp. 36, 75, 103.

197 Strachan, Hew, *British Military Uniforms, 1768–1796*, Arms & Armour Press, London, 1975.

198 Ridder, *op. cit.*, p. 188.


# CHAPTER SIX


199 Duff Gordon, Lady, *Discretions and Indiscretions*, Jarrold, London, 1932, p. 60.

200 *Ibid.*, p. 60.

201 *Ladies' Realm, A selection from the monthly issues Nov 1904–April 1905*, Arrow Books, London, 1972, p. 12.

202 Cunnington, Phillis & Lucas, Catherine, *Costumes for Births, Marriages and Deaths*, A. & C. Black, London, 1972, p. 250, quoting R. Brimley Johnson, *The Letters of Jane Austen*, 1926, pp. 73–4.

203 Thackeray, William M., *Vanity Fair*, Bradbury & Evans, London, 1849, p. 366.

204 Holland, Sir Eardley, 'The Princess Charlotte of Wales – a Triple Obstetric Tragedy' in *Journal of Obstetrics and Gynaecology of the British Empire*, Dec. 1951, repr. Heinemann Medical Books, London, 1952.

205 Collier, Francis, *The Family Economy of the Working Classes in the Cotton Industry 1784–1833*, Manchester University Press, London, 1964, p. 20.

206 Armystage, Fenella Fitzhardinge, *Old Court Customs and Modern Court Rule*, Richard Bentley, London, 1883.

207 Cunnington & Lucas, *op. cit.*, p. 265, quoting *The Memoirs of Susan Sibbald 1783–1812*, edited by Francis P. Hett.

208 Langley-Moore, Doris, *Fashion Through Fashion Plates 1771–1970*, Ward Lock, London, 1971, p. 68.

209 Eden, Emily, *Up the Country*, first published 1866, repr. Oxford University Press, 1930.

210 Pike, Martha V. & Armstrong, Janice Gray, *A Time to Mourn – Expressions of Grief in Nineteenth Century America*, The Museums at Stony Brook, Stony Brook, New York, 1980, catalogue no. 195, p. 178.

211 *Ibid.*, catalogue no. 194, p. 178.

212 Buck, Anne, 'The Trap Re-Baited – Mourning Dress 1860–1890', in *Proceedings of the Costume Society*, Spring Conference, 1968, Costume Society, Victoria and Albert Museum, p. 33.

213 Abijes, Mme de, *Deuil, Ceremonial, Usages, Toilettes*, Grand Maison de Noir, 27–29 Faubourg St Honoré, Paris, *c.* 1885. Archive Collection, Courtaulds Ltd.

214 *Ibid.*

215 Adburgham, Alison, *Shops and Shopping 1800–1914*, Allen & Unwin, London, 1967, repr. 1981, p. 64.

216 Buck, *op. cit.*, p. 32.

217 Swenson, Evelyn, *Victoriana Americana*, Great Lakes Living Press, Matteson, Illinois, 1976, pp. 96–7.

218 Abijes, *op. cit.*

219 Adburgham, *op. cit.*, p. 66, quoting Henry Mayhew, *The Shops and Companies of London*, 1865.

220 Kuniov, Robert, *Mr Godey's Ladies*, Bonanza Books, New York, 1971, p. 107.

221 Shonfield, Zuzanna, 'Miss Marshall and the Cimabue Browns' in *Costume*, Journal of the Costume Society, no. 13, 1979, pp. 67, 69.

222 Puckle, Bertram, *Funeral Customs, Their Origin and Development*, T. Werner Laurie, London, 1926, p. 97.

223 Jasper, A. S., *A Hoxton Childhood*, Centerprise Books, London, 1974, p. 121.

224 Abijes, *op. cit.*

225 *The Woman at Home*, edited by Annie Swan, Hodder & Stoughton, London, Vol. V, Oct. 1895–Sept. 1896, p. 483.

226 Lockheed, Marion, *The Victorian Household*, John Murray, London, 1964.

227 Benson, Viscount A. C. E. (ed.), *The Letters of Queen Victoria 1837–1861*, John Murray, London, 1908, p. 478.

228 *The Woman at Home*, *op. cit.*, March 1896, p. 483.

229 Cunnington & Lucas, *op. cit.*, p. 248, quoting R. Fulford, *Dearest Mama, Letters between Queen Victoria and the Crown Princess of Prussia 1861–64*, 1968.

230 *The Woman at Home*, *op. cit.*, p. 489.

231 Lansdell, Avril, *The Clothes of the Cut*, British Waterways Board, London, 1975, p. 25.

232 Information from Gordon Caseley, Public Relations Officer, The Greater Glasgow Passenger Transport Executive, 1975.

# CHAPTER SEVEN

233 Bedarida, François, transl. Forster, A. S., *A Social History of England, 1851–1975*, Methuen, London, 1976, p. 151, quoting the 74th Annual Report of the Registrar General, 1911.

234 Temple, Nigel, *Seen and Not Heard*, Hutchinson, London, 1970, p. 218.

235 *The English Woman's Domestic Magazine*, London, August 1863. Poem by Agnes Strickland.

236 Lindley, Kenneth, *Of Graves and Epitaphs*, Hutchinson, London, 1965, pp. 154, 157.

237 Temple, *op. cit.*, p. 213.

238 Puckle, Bertram S., *Funeral Customs, Their Origin and Development*, T. Werner Laurie, London, 1926, p. 40.

239 Vaclavik, Antonin & Jaroslav, Orel, *Textile Folk Art*, Artia, Prague, 1956, p. 40.

240 Viski, Karely, *Hungarian Peasant Costumes*, Vajna, Budapest, 1932, p. 14.

241 Johnson, Rev. Samuel, *The History of the Yorubas*, Christian Missionary Society, Lagos, 1921, reprint 1957, p. 137.

242 Goody, Jack, *Death, Property and the Ancestors*, Tavistock Publications, London, 1962, p. 149.

243 Johnson, *op. cit.*, p. 83.

244 Creighton, Ellen (ed.), *Ellen Buxton's Journal 1860–64*, Geoffrey Bliss, London, 1967, p. 86.

245 Woodforde, James (ed. John Beresford), *The Diary of a Country Parson*, Oxford University Press, 1949.

*Mourning Dress*

246 Yeo, Eileen & Thompson, E. P., *The Unknown Mayhew*, Pantheon Books, New York, 1971, pp. 171–6.
247 Lloyd, A. L., *Folk Song in England*, Panther, London, 1969, p. 328.
248 Pember-Reeves, Maud, *Roundabout a Pound a Week*, Virago Press, London, 1979, p. 68.
249 *Ibid.*, p. 71.
250 *Ibid.*
251 Cunnington, Phillis & Lucas, Catherine, *Costumes for Births, Marriages and Deaths*, A. & C. Black, London, 1972, plate 64.
252 Creighton, *op. cit.*, p. 21.
253 Cunnington, C. W., *English Women's Clothing in the Nineteenth Century*, Faber, London, 1937, p. 255.
254 Cunnington, Phillis & Buck, Anne, *Children's Costume in England*, A. & C. Black, London, 1965, p. 45, quoting 'The will of Sir David Owen', *Sussex Arch. Colln*, Vol. 8.
255 Cunnington & Lucas, *op. cit.*, p. 273, quoting the MSS of the Duke of Rutland, Vol. 1, p. 243.
256 *Funeral Obsequies of George II, Landgrave of Hesse*, Folio, Darm Stadii, 1662. Library, Victoria and Albert Museum, London.
257 Verney, Margaret M., *Memoirs of the Verney Family*, Longman Green, London, 1899, Vol. IV, p. 420.
258 *Ibid.*, p. 443.
259 Gernsheim, Alison, *Fashion and Reality*, Faber, London, 1963, plate 129.
260 Cunnington & Buck, *op. cit.*, p. 212, quoting Sellars, E., *Edinburgh's Child*, 1961.
261 Burnett, Frances Hodgson, *The Secret Garden*, Penguin, 1975, p. 17.
262 Verney, *op. cit.*, p. 460.
263 Lloyd, A. L. & Vaughan, R. V., *The Penguin Book of English Folk Songs*, Penguin, London, 1968, p. 31.
264 Cunnington & Lucas, *op. cit.*, p. 275, quoting Mrs John Sherwood, *The Life of Mrs Sherwood*, 1854, p. 328.
265 *Ibid.*, pp. 288–9, quoting R. Fulford, *Dearest Child, Letters between Queen Victoria and the Princess Royal 1858–1861*.
266 *Ibid.*, p. 289.
267 Creighton, *op. cit.*, p. 86.
268 Buck, Anne, 'The Trap Re-Baited – Mourning Dress 1860–1890' in *Proceedings of the Costume Society*, Spring Conference, March 1968, Victoria and Albert Museum, London, 1969, p. 35.
269 Kurtz, Donna C. & Boardman, John, *Greek Burial Customs*, Cornell University Press, New York, 1971, p. 152.
270 Cunnington & Lucas, *op. cit.*, p. 138, quoting Calendar of State Pater, Domestic. Jas. I, Vol. 3. Letter of William Woad, 1603.
271 *Ibid.*, p. 140.
272 Baker, Margaret, *Folklore and Customs of Rural England*, David & Charles, Newton Abbot, 1974, pp. 153–4.
273 Booth, Charles, *Life and Labour of the People of London*, Macmillan, London, 1902, Series 3, Vol. 2, p. 246.
274 Cunnington & Lucas, *op. cit.*, p. 141, quoting *Church Folklore*, 1894, p. 127.
275 *The Suffragette*, published by the Women's Social and Political Union, Vol. 1, no. 35, 13 June 1913, repr. Peter Way, London, no. 28, 1974.
276 A. L. Lloyd quoted Fochi Adrian, *Miorita*, Editura Acadamiei, Bucarest, 1964, quoting from a magazine *Liberalul*, No. 2, Moldavia, 1881.

277  Covarrubias, Miguel, *Mexico South*, Alfred Knof, New York, 1946, p. 391.

278  Viski, Karely, *Hungarian Peasant Costume*, Vajna, Budapest, 1932, pp. 175, 181.

279  Domotor, Tekla, *Hungarian Folk Customs*, Corvinna Press, Budapest, 1972, p. 70.

280  Information on death-weddings kindly given to the author by the late A. L. Lloyd. He quoted A. van Gennep, *Le Folklore du Dauphine*, Vol. I, 1932; *Le Folklore de la Flande et du Hainault Français*, pp. 122–8; *Manuel de Folklore Français Contemporaire*, 1946, p. 781.

281  Banateanu, Tancred, 'Le Marriage des Morts et ses Reflects dans le Folklore Européen' in *Revue des Etudes Indo-Européenes*, Libraria Academica, Bucharest, 1947, Vol. IV, pp. 170–207.

282  Habenstein, Robert W. & Lamers, William M., *Funeral Customs the World Over*, The National Funeral Directors Association of the USA, 1960.

283  Rodgers, Frederick, *Labour, Life, Literature*, London, 1913, repr. ed. D. Rubinstein, Harvester Press, Brighton, 1973, pp. 3–4.

284  Freedley, George & Reeves, John A., *A History of the Theatre*, Crown, New York, 1958, p. 212.

285  Goudeket, Maurice, *The Delights of Growing Old*, Michael Joseph, London, 1967, pp. 131, 138.

# CHAPTER EIGHT

286  *Illustrated London News*, 11 February 1860.

287  Advertisement for 'Priestley's Silks and Courtaulds Crapes', issued for the American market, 1897–8. Archive Collection, Courtaulds Ltd.

288  Mercier, Louis, *Le Deuil – son observation dans tous les temps et dans tous les pays*, Paul Douvet for Messrs Jay's, London, 1877, p. 80.

289  Abijes, Mme de, *Deuil, Ceremonial, Usages, Toilettes*, Grand Maison de Noir, 27–29 Faubourg St Honoré, Paris, undated c. 1885. Archive Collection, Courtaulds Ltd.

290  Adburgham, Alison, *Shops and Shopping*, Allen & Unwin, London, 1967, p. 66, quoting Mayhew, Henry, *The Shops and Companies of London*, 1865.

291  Abijes, *op. cit.*

292  *The Lady*, 4 October 1900.

293  Mercier, *op. cit.*, p. 79.

294  Pike, Martha V. & Armstrong, Janice Gray, *A Time To Mourn – Expressions of Grief In Nineteenth Century America*, The Museums at Stony Brook, Stony Brook, New York, 1980, catalogue no. 196. Leaflet from 'S.S. Williams, 20, Winter St. Boston,' from the collection at the Henry Francis du Pont Winterthur Museum Library, Delaware.

295  Mercier, *op. cit.*, p. 80.

296  Abijes, *op. cit.*

297  Pike & Armstrong, *op. cit.*, catalogue no. 196.

298  Mercier, *op. cit.*, p. 79.

299  Coleman, D. C., *Courtaulds, An Economic and Social History*, Oxford University Press, 1969, Vol. 1, p. 237, quoting Essex County Record Office. ERO. D/F. 3/3/22. pp. 82–5.

300  Buck, Anne, 'The Trap Re-Baited – Mourning Dress 1860–1890' in

*Proceedings of the Costume Society*, Spring Conference, March 1968, Victoria and Albert Museum, London, 1969, p. 35.

301 Adburgham, *op. cit.*, p. 58.

302 Godart, Justin, *L'Ouvrier En Soie*, Lyon & Paris, 1899, repr. Slatkine, Megariotis, Geneva, 1976, p. 238.

303 *Ibid.*, p. 214.

304 *Ibid.*, pp. 229, 497.

305 *Ibid.*, p. 497 quoting the 1705 Register of the proceedings of the Lyon Chamber of Commerce, in the Library of the Lyon Chamber of Commerce.

306 *Ibid.*, p. 216. Atropos was one of the three Greek goddesses of Fate and was said to cut the thread of life.

307 *Ibid*, pp. 215, 231.

308 *Ibid.*, pp. 215–16.

309 *Ibid.*, p. 217, quoting from the Town Library, Lyon, the Fonds Coste records.

310 Adburgham, *op. cit.*, p. 59.

311 Willis, Gordon & Midgeley, David, *Fashion Marketing*, Allen & Unwin, London, 1973, p. 42, quoting Bigg, Ada Heather, *The Evils of Fashion*, London, 1883.

312 Strachey, Lytton, *Queen Victoria*, Zehyr Books, Stockholm, 1943, p. 199.

313 Coleman, *op. cit.*, Vol. I, p. 63.

314 Tawney, R. H. & Power, Eileen, *Tudor Economic Documents*, Longman Green, London, 1924, Vol. III, pp. 163–5, quoting *Description de Touts les Pays-Bas, autrement appelles La Germanie Interieure ou Basse Allamagne, par Messire Louis Guicciardini*, Antwerp, 1560.

315 Palazzo Mansi, Exhibition catalogue: '*Mostra del Costume e Sete Lucchessi*', Lucca, 1967.

316 Tawney & Power, *op. cit.*

317 Warner, *op. cit.*, p. 642, quoting from the Guildhall Records, Letterbook 2, fo. 134.

318 Beck, William, *The Draper's Dictionary*, The Warehouseman and Drapers' Journal, London, 1886, p. 92.

319 William Shakespeare's *Hamlet* was written in 1599–1600.

320 Warner, *op. cit.*, p. 297.

321 Clouzot, Henri, *Le Metier de la Soie en France, 1466–1815*, Devambez, Paris, 1914, p. 45.

322 Plummer, Alfred, *The London Weavers Company, 1600–1970*, Routledge & Kegan Paul, London, 1972, p. 156.

323 Sabin, A. K., *The Silk Weavers of Spitalfields and Bethnal Green*, Board of Education, London, 1931, p. 12.

324 Tawney & Power, *op. cit.*, Vol. III, p. 135, quoting *William Cholmley's Project for Dyeing Cloth In England*, 1553.

325 Edelstein, Sidney M. & Barghetty, Hector C., Translation of *The Plictho of Gioanventura Rosetti*, Venice, 1548, MIT Press, Cambridge, Mass. 1969, p. xviii.

326 Warner, *op. cit.*, p. 628, quoting *A Dyeing Ordinance*, 1637.

327 Public Record Office, London, Pipe Office Declared Accounts, PROE 35 1/3145.

328 *Ibid.*, Inventories, 539, John Davis, Bewdley, Worcs. Draper.

329 *Ibid.*, Inventories, 17066, Henry Bradford, Godalming, Surrey.

330 *Ibid.*, Inventories, 17146, Thomas Colls, Crowland, Lincoln, Draper of Mixed Goods.

331 *Ibid.*, Pipe Office Declared Accounts, E 351/3150, Thomas Charrett, Milliner, London.
332 *Ibid.*, Pipe Office Declared Accounts, E 351/3151, Funeral of William III.
333 Thornton, Peter, *Baroque and Rococo Silks*, Faber, London, 1965, p. 58.
334 Public Record Office, London, Patent of Inventions, 1617–1852, no. 357, Sept. 1698, Francis Pousset.
335 *Ibid.*, London Gazette, no. 3791.9, 12 March 1702.
336 Beck, *op. cit.*, p. 90.
337 Public Record Office, London, Declared Accounts, Civil Wardrobe, Pipe Roll, 3140 (E 351/3140).
338 *Ibid.*, Patent of Inventions, 1617–1852, no. 520, 9 October 1730.
339 Beck, *op. cit.*, p. 90.
340 Coleman, *op. cit.*, p. 25, quoting the Royal Society of Arts Library: Guard Book, Vol. ii, Minutes of Committees, 1765–6.
341 The London Weavers Company, *List of Prices in those branches of the Weaving Manfactory called the Black Branch and the Fancy Branch*, London, 1 January 1769, original document in the Library of Goldsmith's College, University of London, photocopy in the Library at the Victoria and Albert Museum, London.
342 Coleman, *op. cit.*, p. 26, quoting BP912 (1768) and BP1013 (1772).
343 *Ibid.*, pp. 30–8.
344 *Ibid.*, pp. 34–8.
345 *Ibid.*, pp. 38, 70–2.
346 *Ibid.*, p. 84.
347 *Ibid.*, pp. 73–89.
348 *Ibid.*, pp. 127–8.
349 *Ibid.*, pp. 218–29.
350 *Ibid.*, p. 233.
351 *Ibid.*, p. 158.
352 *Ibid.*, p. 157.
353 *Ibid.*, p. 189.
354 *Ibid.*, Ch. IX.
355 Advertisement for 'Priestley's Silks and Courtaulds Crapes', *op. cit.*
356 Coleman, *op. cit.*, Vol. II, Fig. 7. Yarn and Fabric Sales, 1913–20.
357 *Ibid.*, Vol. II, p. 26.
358 Warner, *op. cit.*, p. 289.
359 Coleman, *op. cit.*, Vol. I, pp. 193–4.
360 *Ibid.*, Vol. I, p. 194.
361 *Ibid.*, Vol. II, p. 72.
362 *Ibid.*, Vol. II, p. 369.
363 Private correspondence with the author, July 1978.

# CHAPTER NINE

364 Seligman, G. B., *The Melanesians of British New Guinea*, Cambridge University Press, 1910, Fig. 12.
365 Joyce T. A. & Thomas, N. W., *Women of All Nations*, Cassell, London, 1908, Vol. 1, p. 108.

366   Heaphy, Charles, *Narrative of a Residence in various parts of New Zealand*, London, 1842.
367   Jones, Barbara, *'Design for Death'*, Andre Deutsch, London, 1967, pl. 248.
368   Scot, J. S. F. Van't, *De Hoedepen een gerdat lijk mode*, Antiek, Amsterdam, Vol. 9, March 1978, p. 801.
369   William Penn Memorial Museum, Exhibition Catalogue: *Mourning Becomes America*, Pennsylvania Historical and Museum Commission, Harrisburg, Pennsylvania, 28 March – 23 May 1976. Catalogue no. 191. Illustration 59.
370   *Ibid.*, Catalogue no. 185. Illustration 57.
371   Weber, F. Parkes, *Aspects of Death and Correlated Aspects of Life in Art, Epigram and Poetry*, Fisher Unwin, London, 1918, p. 588.
372   Kunz, G. F., *Rings for the Finger*, Dover repr. 1973, p. 42, from original of 1917.
373   Rhys, Ernest (ed.), *Diary of Samuel Pepys*, Dent, London, 1943, p. 176.
374   Frazer, James, *The Golden Bough*, Macmillan, London, 1922, Chapter XVIII.
375   Mercier, Louis, *Le Deuil, son observation dans tous les temps et dans tous les pays*, P. Douvet, London, 1877, p. 37, quoting *Ordre Chronologique des Deuils de la Cour*, 1765.
376   Adburgham, Alison, *Shops and Shopping*, Allen & Unwin, London, 1964, p. 66.
377   Cunnington, Phillis & Lucas, Catherine, *Costumes for Births, Marriages and Deaths*, A. & C. Black, London, 1972, p. 255, quoting Mrs John Sherwood, *Manners & Social Usages*, New York, 1884.
378   *Ibid.*, p. 256.
379   Mercier, *op. cit.*, edition of 1884, published by A. Christin, London, for Jay's, p. 49.
380   *Ibid.*, p. 50.
381   Swenson, Evelyn, *Victoriana Americana*, Great Lakes Living Press, Matteson, Illinois, 1976, pp. 131–3. B. Altman & Co. Catalogues 1879–80 & 1886–7 from the Baker Library, Harvard University, Cambridge, Mass.
382   Jones, William, *Finger-Ring Lore*, Chatto & Windus, London, 1898, Chap. VII.
383   Puckle, Bertram, *Funeral Customs, Their Origin and Development*, T. Werner Laurie, London, 1926, p. 268.
384   Verney, Peter, *The Standard Bearer*, Hutchinson, London, 1963, p. 113.
385   Pike, Martha V. & Armstrong, Janice Gray, *A Time to Mourn – Expressions of Grief in Nineteenth Century America*, The Museums at Stony Brook, Stony Brook, New York, 1980. Catalgue no. 19.
386   Kendal, Hugh D., *The Story of Whitby Jet*, Whitby Literary & Philosophical Society, Whitby, repr. 1977, pp. 9–10, from original of 1936.
387   Hildeburgh, W. C., 'Notes on Spanish Amulets' in *Folklore*, Dec. 1906, p. 461.
388   Kendall, *op. cit.*, p. 11.
389   *Ibid.*, p. 13.
390   *Ibid.*, pp. 10–24.
391   Swenson, *op. cit.*, p. 131.
392   Kendall, *op. cit.*, p. 24.
393   Swenson, *op. cit.*, p. 112.
394   Pike & Armstrong, *op. cit.*, Catalogue no. 221.
395   Swenson, *op. cit.*, p. 112, quoting Bristow, Henry, *A Glossary of Minerology*, Longman Green, London, 1861, p. 197.

396 *Ibid.*, p. 113.
397 Puckle, *op. cit.*, p. 271.
398 Pike & Armstrong, *op. cit.* Catalogue no. 224.
399 Swenson, *op. cit.*, pp. 131, 157.
400 Frazer, *op. cit.*, Chap. XXI.
401 Cordry, Donald & Cordry, Dorothy, *Mexican Indian Costumes*, University of Texas Press, Austin, 1968.
402 Joyce & Thomas, *op. cit.*, Vol. II, p. 521.
403 Pike & Armstrong, *op. cit.*, p. 46, quoting Taylor, Laurence, *An Anthropological View of Mourning Ritual in the 19th Century.*
404 Morley, John, *Death, Heaven and the Victorians*, Studio Vista, London, 1971, p. 67.
405 Pike & Armstrong, *op. cit.*, Catalogue no. 216, belonging to the Henry Francis du Pont Winterthur Museum Library, Delaware.
406 Hinks, Peter, *Nineteenth Century Jewellery*, Faber, London, 1975, p. 85.
407 Puckle, *op. cit.*, p. 271.

# CHAPTER TEN

408 Comber, Leon, *Chinese Ancestor Worship in Malaya*, Malayan Publishing House, Singapore, 1957, p. 15.
409 Hulme, F. Edward, *The History, Principles and Practice of Symbolism in Christian Art*, Swan Sonnenschein, London, 1897, p. 16.
410 Rolfe, C. C., *The Ancient Use of Liturgical Colours*, Parker, Oxford, 1879, p. 32.
411 Marriott, Rex Warton B., *Vestarium Christianum. The Origin and Gradual Development of the Holy Ministry in the Church*, Rivingtons, London, 1868, p. 176.
412 Marriott, *op. cit.*, p. 176.
413 *The Times* reported on 22 August 1912 that: 'At the funeral members of the Salvation Army will wear a white band round the arm on which will be a small red cross and a crown. It is not the custom of the Army to wear mourning.'
414 Vukanovic, T. P., *The Costume of the Balkan Slavs In the Middle Ages*, Bulletin of the Museum of Kosovo and Metohija, Pristina, 1956, Vol. 4, p. 199.
415 Pike, Martha V. & Armstrong, Janice Gray, *A Time to Mourn – Expressions of Grief in Nineteenth Century America*, The Museums of Stony Brook, Stony Brook, New York, 1980. Cat. no. 10, p. 133.
416 Goborjan, Alice, *Hungarian Peasant Costumes*, Corvina Press, Budapest, 1969, p. 31.
417 Hall, Maggie, *Smocks*, Shire Publications, Princes Risborough, Bucks., 1979.
418 *Les Modes*, Paris, 1914, April edition.
419 Goody, Jack, *Death, Property and the Ancestors. A Study of Mortuary Customs of the Lodagaa of West Africa*, Kegan Paul, London, 1962, pp. 57–8.
420 *Ibid.*, p. 58.
421 Hulme, *op. cit.*, p. 28.
422 Rolfe, *op. cit.*, p. 60.
423 *Ibid.*, p. 74.

424 Cunnington, C. W. & Cunnington, Phillis, *Handbook of English Mediaeval Costume*, Faber, London, 1952, p. 89.

425 Anderson, Ellen, *Danske Bonders Klae de Dragt*, Carit Anderson Forlag, Copenhagen, 1960, pp. 486–7.

426 Fel, Edit, Museum of Ethnography, Budapest. Private correspondence with the author, 1974.

427 Alden-Killen, Ellen, *Middle Age 1885–1932*, Constable, London, 1935, p. 101.

428 Rolfe, *op. cit.*, p. 226.

429 Buck, Ann, 'The Trap Re-Baited – Mourning Dress 1860–1890' in *Proceedings of the Costume Society*, Spring Conference, March 1968, Victoria and Albert Museum, London, 1969, p. 34.

430 Abijes, Mme de, *Deuil, Ceremonial, Usages, Toilettes*, Grand Maison de Noir, 27–29 Faubourg St Honoré, Paris, *c.* 1885. Archive Collection, Courtaulds Ltd.

431 Cunnington, Phillis & Lucas, Catherine, *Costumes for Births, Marriages and Deaths*, A. & C. Black, London, 1971, p. 116.

432 Abijes, *op. cit.*

433 *Ladies Field*, London, 2 March 1901, p. 459.

434 Bessborough, Earl of (ed.), *The Journal of Lady Charlotte Schrieber 1853–1891*, John Murray, London, 1952, p. 62.

435 Cunnington & Lucas, *op. cit.*, p. 116.

436 Rolfe, *op. cit.*, p. 149.

437 Giesey, Ralph, *The Royal Funeral Ceremony in Renaissance France*, Libraire E. Drox, Geneva, 1960, p. 51.

438 Fel, Edit, *Hungarian Peasant Embroidery*, Batsford, London, 1961.

439 Hulme, *op. cit.*, p. 27.

440 Rolfe, *op. cit.*, p. 74.

441 Weibal, Adele Colin, *Two Thousand Years of Textiles*, Hacker Art Books, New York, 1972, p. 41.

442 Hulme, *op. cit.*, p. 27.

443 Cunnington & Lucas, *op. cit.*, p. 147.

444 Rhys, Ernest (ed.), *The Diary of Samuel Pepys*, Dent, London, 1943, Vol. 1, pp. 94–5.

445 Textiles Department, Victoria and Albert Museum, London. The Barbara Johnson Album 1746–1820, T. 219/1973.

446 Jachimowicz, Elizabeth, *Eight Chicago Women and Their Fashions 1860–1929*, Chicago Historical Society, Chicago, 1978, pp. 9–13.

# CHAPTER ELEVEN

447 Capon, Edward & Macquity, William, *Princess of Jade*, Sphere Books, London, 1973, p. 48.

448 Campbell, Lord John, *Lives of Lord Chancellors*, Vol. I, London, 1848, p. 31.

449 Dewey, Orville, Tract published by the New Bedford Book and Tract Association. New Bedford, 1825.

450  Quennell, Peter (ed.), *The Journal of Thomas Moore 1818–1841*, Batsford, London, 1964, p. 133.
451  Thackeray, William M., *Vanity Fair*, Bradbury & Evans, London, 1849, p. 375.
452  Fulford, Roger, (ed.), *The Greville Memoirs*, Batsford, London, 1963, pp. 176–7.
453  *Ibid.*, p. 126.
454  Curl, James Stevens, *The Victorian Celebration of Death*, David & Charles, Newton Abbot, 1972, p. 70.
455  Dickens, Charles, *Great Expectations*, London, 1861.
456  Morley, John, *Death, Heaven and the Victorians*, Studio Vista, London, 1971, p. 202.
457  Cunnington, Phillis & Lucas, Catherine, *Costumes for Births, Marriages and Deaths*, A. & C. Black, London, 1973, p. 198.
458  Duff Gordon, Lady, *Discretions and Indiscretions*, Jarrolds, London, 1932.
459  Chase, Edna Woolman & Chase, Ilka, *Always in Vogue*, Gollancz, London, 1954, p. 100.
460  Gorer, Geoffrey, *Death, Grief and Mourning in Contemporary Britain*, Cresset Press, London, 1965.
461  Proust, Marcel, *Time Regained*, transl. C. K. Scott Montcrieff, Chatto and Windus, London, 1970, pp. 35–6.
462  Gorer, *op. cit.*
463  Weber, F. Parkes, *Aspects of Death and Correlated Aspects of Life in Art, Epigram and Poetry*, Fisher Unwin, London, 1918, p. 427.
464  Coleman, D. C., *Courtaulds – An Economic and Social History*, Oxford University Press, 1969, Vol. II, p. 72.
465  Pike, Martha V. & Armstrong, Janice Gray. *A Time To Mourn – Expressions of Grief in Nineteenth Century America*. Exhibition Catalogue. The Museums at Stony Brook, Stony Brook, New York, 1980. See Barbara Dodd Hillerman, *Chrysallis of Gloom: Nineteenth Century American Mourning Costume*, p. 105.
466  Branson, Noreen & Heineman, Margot, *Britain in the 1930s*, Panther, London, 1973, p. 255.
467  *Picture Post*, 23 April 1949.
468  Dariaux, Genevieve Antoine, *Elegance*, Frederick Muller, London, 1904, p. 98.

# SELECT BIBLIOGRAPHY

Abijes, Mme de, *Deuil, Ceremonial, Usages, Toilettes*, Grand Maison de Noir, 27–29 Faubourg St Honoré, Paris, c. 1885–95. Archives Collection, Courtaulds Ltd.

Adburgham, Alison, *Shops and Shopping 1800–1914*, Allen & Unwin, London, 1967, 2nd edn 1981.

Armystage, Lady Fenella Fitzhardinge, *Old Court Customs and Modern Court Rule*, Richard Bentley, London, 1883.

Beck, William, *The Draper's Dictionary*, The Warehouseman and Drapers Journal, London, 1886.

Bloom, Ursula, *Victorian Vinaigrette*, Hutchinson, London, 1956.

Boase, T. S. K., *Death in the Middle Ages*, Thames & Hudson, London, 1972.

Booth, Charles, *Life and Labour of the People in London*, Macmillan, London, 1902.

Buck, Anne, *The Trap Re-Baited – Mourning Dress 1860–1890, Proceedings of the Costume Society*, Spring Conference, 1968, Victoria and Albert Museum, London, 1969.

Clouzot, Henri, *Le Métier de la Soie en France, 1466–1815*, Devambez, Paris, 1914.

Coleman, D. C., *Courtaulds – An Economic and Social History*, Oxford University Press, 1969, Vols I & II.

Cunnington, C. W., *English Women's Clothing in the Nineteenth Century*, Faber, London, 1937.

Cunnington, Phillis & Lucas, Catherine, *Costumes for Births, Marriages and Deaths*, A. & C. Black, London, 1972.

Curl, James Stevens, *The Victorian Celebration of Death*, David & Charles, Newton Abbot, 1972.

Fenton, Monica, *A Child Widow's Story*, Gollancz, London, 1966.

Frazer, James, *The Golden Bough*, Macmillan, London, 1922.

Garden, Maurice, *Lyon et les Lyonnais au XVIII siècle*, Société d'Edition les Belles Lettres, Paris, 1970.

Gascon, Richard, *Grand Commerce et Vie Urbaine au XVI Siècle. Lyon et ses Marchands*, Mouton, Paris, 1971.

Giesey, Ralf E., *The Royal Funeral Ceremony in Renaissance France*, Libraire E. Drox, Geneva, 1960.

Goody, Jack, *Death, Property and the Ancestors. A Study of the Mortuary Customs of the Lodagaa of West Africa*, Kegan Paul, London, 1962.

Gorer, Geoffrey, *Death, Grief and Mourning in Contemporary Britain*, Cresset Press, London, 1965.

Grinsell, Leslie V., *Barrow, Pyramid and Tomb*, Thames & Hudson, London, 1968.

Harrods Catalogue, 1895, repr. in *Victorian Shopping*, David & Charles, Newton Abbot, 1972.

Jones, William, *Finger-Ring Lore*, Chatto & Windus, London, 1898.

Joyce, Thomas Athol & Thomas, N. W., *Women of all Nations*, Cassell, London, 1908.

Kendal, Hugh P., *The Story of Whitby Jet*, Whitby Literary & Philosophical Society, Whitby 1936, repr. 1977.

Lindley, Kenneth, *Of Graves and Epitaphs*, Hutchinson, London, 1965.

Lloyd, A. L., *Folk Song in England*, Panther, London, 1969.

Longbridge, R. H., *Army and Navy Stores Catalogue, 1902*, David & Charles, Newton Abbot, 1975.

Mercier, Louis, *Le Deuil – son observation dans tous les temps et dans tous les pays comparée à son observation de nos jours*, Paul Douvet, London, 1877.

Morley, John, *Death, Heaven and the Victorians*, Studio Vista, London, 1971.

Pember-Reeves, Maud, *Roundabout a Pound a Week*, Virago Press, London, 1979.

Rhys, Ernest (ed.), *The Diary of Samuel Pepys*, Dent, London, 1943.

Ridder, A de, *Prerogatives Nobilaires et Ambitions Bourgeoises*, Vol. III, *Deuil, Funerailles et Tombes*, La Noblesse Belge Year Book, 1929–30, Brussels, 1932.

Rolfe, C., *The Ancient Use of Liturgical Colours*, Parker, Oxford, 1879.

Rothstein, Natalie, *Dutch Silks – An Important but Forgotten Industry of the 18th Century or a Hypothesis*, OUD Holland, J. H. de Bussy, Amsterdam, 1964, Vol. LXXIX.

Savary de Victor Bruslon, Jacques, *Dictionnaire de Commerce*, Paris, 1723.

Stone, Laurence, *The Crisis of the Aristocracy 1558–1641*, Clarendon Press, Oxford, 1965.

Tawney, R. G. & Power, Eileen, *Tudor Economic Documents*, Longman Green, London, 1924.

Thornton, Peter, *Baroque and Rococo Silks*, Faber, London, 1965.

Toynbee, J. M. C., *Death and Burial and the Roman World*, Thames & Hudson, London, 1971.

Tressell, Robert, *The Ragged Trousered Philanthropists*, Panther, London, 1975.

Verney, Margaret, *Memoirs of the Verney Family 1642–1696*, Longman Green, London, 1899.

Verney, Peter, *The Standard Bearer*, Hutchinson, London, 1963.

Victoria & Albert Museum, Dept of Textiles, *The Barbara Johnson Album, 1746–1826*, T219/1973.

Warner, Sir Frank, *The Silk Industry of the United Kingdom*, Dranes, London, 1921.

Weavers Company, *List of the Prices in those Branches of the Weaving Manufactory called the Black Branch and the Fancy Branch*, 1 Jan. 1769. London, Goldsmiths Library, University of London; photocopy in Victoria & Albert Museum Library.

Weber, F. Parkes, *Aspects of Death and Correlated Aspects of Life in Art, Epigram and Poetry*, Fisher Unwin, London, 1918.

Yeo, Eileen & Thompson, E. P., *The Other Mayhew*, Pantheon Books, New York, 1971.

# INDEX

Printed in Great Britain
by Amazon